Kiwi
Afloat

'Navigare necesse est vivere non est necesse.'

Kiwi Afloat

Doris Coppell

Dedication

This book is dedicated to well-loved past crew
members shanghaied over the years from family and friends,
and to all the colourful characters I was fortunate enough to
meet and get to know during my exploration of the
English canals.

Special thanks to my friend John Winder for
his enthusiasm when editing and making suggestions
about Kiwi Afloat.

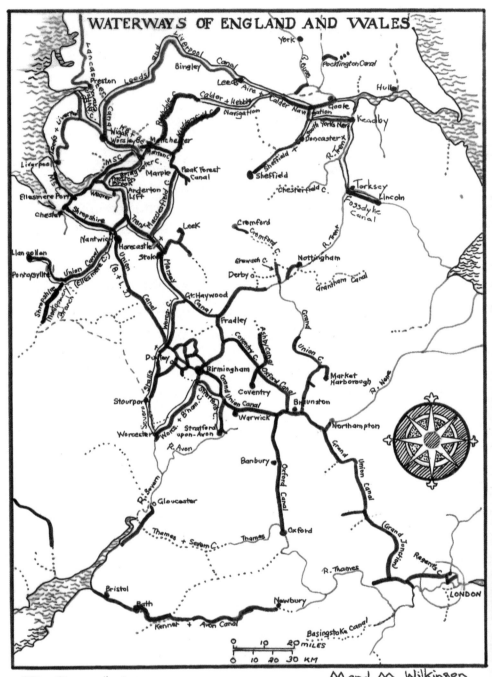

WATERWAYS OF ENGLAND AND WALES

Show author's journeys

Mand M Wilkinson

CONTENTS

Chapter One

There's something in a flying horse,
There's something in a huge balloon;
But through the clouds I'll never float
Until I have a little boat,
Shaped like a crescent-moon.

W. Wordsworth

It was a cold rain-thrashed February night in 1970 when my husband and I, enjoying a cosy conventional winter's evening by a blazing fire, somehow began discussing boats.

Ours was a fairly recent liaison. Before we married, Alec was a widower with a sixteen year old son, David; I, a widow with an eleven year old daughter, Penelope. Now, after eighteen months together, we were surprised to discover that we had a mutual feeling about boats and that both of us cherished a latent desire to be afloat.

As a young impressionable girl in New Zealand I had savoured the physical and aesthetic delights of sailing on the sparkling waters of the beautiful Waitemata Harbour — my birthplace and home being the fair city of Auckland. In those days, the Capper family went sailing with an interesting old character named Blake — at least, through youthful eyes he seemed extremely old; for Blake always carried on his salty weathered face, two or three days' growth — nice and bristly — but never any longer; I often wondered how he achieved this hedgehoggy effect.

A confirmed bachelor and something of a hermit, he lived in a wooden, two-roomed shack which was stocked with absolute basics to suit a very basic New Zealander. His friends were few and why we were so honoured I don't remember, for I was too young to bother about such relationships. When he was of a mind to work, Blake built boats and was the proud owner of a lovely thirty-foot yacht. He spent most of his days in easy solitude, pondering, sailing, chopping wood, cooking and messing about generally, (especially in boats) but not, I suspect, washing himself too often — in keeping with his shaving habits.

Every now and then, usually on a Sunday, we would pack up and go off to old Blake's. We had complete confidence in him and I was never frightened — not even when the wind freshened in the resisting canvasses above us, causing the boat (and our behinds) to lean over at steep angles as we chopped through the whipped-up waves. It was like flying on a beautiful white winged bird, exhilarating and wholly satisfying.

My lively older brother Victor once asked Mum if he could go with the boy scouts for a fortnight's holiday under a different type of canvas. Innocently she packed him off with plenty of advice, tucker and clothing and was reasonably content as to his well-being — until a few days later, that is, when she met an unsuspecting scout master to whom the news that his troop was away camping came as a complete surprise! The irrepressible Vic was, of course, thoroughly enjoying himself sailing with our equally unsuspecting 'rough diamond' friend, Blake. Needless to say, he did not enjoy his homecoming quite as much!

Where was I before I took you twelve thousand miles away into my past? Oh yes — amongst the usually pleasant mills of Huddersfield, which were now, as in 'Jerusalem', dark and satanic on a black, starless night. The conventional evening had become less so, for we were talking about boats.

'You want a boat and I want a boat, so let's have a boat,' I can remember saying.

At this time neither of us knew anything about canals nor had thought of their existence. We weren't even aware of the Calder and Hebble Navigation near to the bottom of Bradley Road where we lived — only two minutes away by car. Immediately a fusion of mutual excitement at this new idea of ours made us impatient to do something about it.

We hunted through 'ads' in the newspapers, fingered through the 'yellow pages', wondered where to look next and all without the slightest idea of what sort of boat we wanted or where we might sail it, if we actually bought one.

One day, however, an interested neighbour mentioned a boatyard near Bradford and fate took us by the hand.

On a drizzly dreary Sunday afternoon we set off, little knowing that the day was to change our leisure hours and bring a whole new dimension within our grasp. After some questionable navigation we at last read our compass aright and rattled over a swing bridge to discover the boatyard which is pleasantly sited at Apperley Bridge on the Leeds to Liverpool Canal. It gave one the pleasing impression of having been created by accident rather than design. A collection of misshapen buildings imbued with great character, greeted us. One of them, luckily for us, was containing an avidly barking dog, furious at our unseen presence and further aggrieved because he had not yet received his daily nourishment.

As we turned on our heels to return home, Mr Kippax, the elderly owner arrived most opportunely for us and for the hungry canine guard he had come to feed. When we mentioned that we were thinking of buying a boat, his eyes lit up and he conducted us, with revitalised steps, along the canal to view *Salidha* and *Vauntress*, both of which were for sale.

Mr Kippax pushed us off on a poetic voyage as he described the many and varied English canals, and we were amazed to learn that over a thousand miles of broad canals (and many more by narrow ones) awaited us. How he enthused over the beauty of the Leeds–Liverpool Canal and the Yorkshire Dales through which it winds; and what great play he made of the fact that boating was a hobby which all the family could share. He became positively lyrical about how relaxing it was, how peaceful, how rewarding and never a word escaped his lips about crises, aching limbs, flaming hard work and never ending expense! In our blissful ignorance we believed his idyllic meanderings and fell hook, line and sinker! As we harkened to his well-practised soliloquy I was already sunbathing on the spacious upper deck of *Salidha* and planning the décor of the cabin — I was afloat! Alec, always more cautious, was also impressed. However, when it came to price negotiations he, a Lancashire man was no match for a hard-headed (but fair) Yorkshireman. The Wars of the Roses had hardly begun when he capitulated and purchased the comely *Salidha*.

I suspect that, as far as Mr Kippax was concerned, he had just sold another boat, but to me she was a delightful possession. Taken from nature, fashioned, then returned to nature again, her graceful lines coolly reflecting made her part of a magic, luminiferous world of light and water, on which lived elegant, vital creatures called simply, for want of a better word — boats!

Salidha is a converted thirty-foot, clinker-built ship's lifeboat, rather grandly described on the insurance policy as a 'single screw diesel motor yacht' and the engine is a Fergusson Tractor two litre with a Perkins' marine gear-box.

One thing I have learned about diesel engines is that once they have coughed into action they seldom choose to stop; but I have also learned that, in common with most power-driven machines, they do not always start. According to the animated discussion which flies back and forth on these occasions, their immobility can be due to a variety of complicated (but simple if you know) reasons. When we had gained first-hand knowledge of all of these we forestalled many an argument with an invaluable set of jump leads.

The year was young, unpredictable and boisterous so we had to wait for time to calm its capricious nature before we dared to venture forth. We visited our beloved, though, most weekends and tended her every wish; for she was in dire need of care and attention — and we gave of our utmost. Alec's car, resigned to being neglected and grubby, soon began to get itself out of the garage and find its own regular route to that other 'thing' which never went anywhere! We cleaned, scraped, greased, rubbed, filled and painted her; then we dressed her in gay materials carefully chosen at Huddersfield's famous, colourful and bustling, Monday Market. Her personality brightened, as is usual when something is well loved, and she bobbed up and down, tickled pink with her new face-lift as people paused in their towpath perambulations to admire her attractive form. Alec probed and prodded as he sought to solve the mysteries of her inner workings, (for he desperately needed to know what made her 'tick') but she proved elusive, as females do, and he never really came close to discovering all her secrets.

A climax to all our activity was eventually reached on a Saturday morning in April when *Salidha* was in full bloom with flowering cushions and covers, bright curtains adorning sparkling windows and shining cutlery, pots and pans at the ready in the galley. Arthur, (the boatyard engineer) happily assisted by Alec had finished making last-minute adjustments and we had arranged to arrive at ten o'clock next morning for our maiden voyage.

Full of excitement and anticipation for the adventure to come we switched off *Salidha's* engine, made her secure and, taking more than one backward glance, walked with springy steps over the fresh damp grass to our still unimpressed mucky car.

Next morning I swished the sun in through the bedroom window — and — wonder of wonders, conditions were ideal for the eagerly awaited sail.

If you proceed along the canal from Apperley Bridge towards Leeds, there is a long stretch without swing bridges or locks and we were to go this way. If, on the other hand, you choose to sail in the direction of Bingley, you have to rotate a rattly swing bridge to obtain passage and then climb laboriously up Dobson's Locks just beyond.

On a traffic-free morning the drive to Apperley took us about half an hour — four bodies, atingle with expectation. The canal spangled invitingly in the sunshine as we juddered over the bridge and slewed off left into the boatyard where we could see some activity in the vicinity of our boat — 'herself' being hidden from view by some buildings. The four bodies hurried over, waving their greetings and the brains within the bodies wondered why nobody waved back.

The reason was soon horribly clear, for the lovely *Salidha*, our pride and joy, was reclining on the bottom of the canal. Our eyes were lying — we did not — we could not — believe them!

The story unfolded. Earlier, when Mr Kippax and his son had approached their boatyard, John, scanning the canal from a distance, suddenly sat bolt upright as his eyes passed by but then shot back to *Salidha*.

'What's up with *Salidha*?' queried John.

'What do you mean, what IS up with *Salidha*?' questioned his father.

'It's bloody-well sunk, that's what's up!' John exclaimed illogically.

This may not be verbatim, but Alec's unoriginal and repetitive 'Bloody Hells' when he saw her, certainly expressed HIS feelings.

Sickness, disappointment and a feeling of having been stunned by a sledge hammer were my reactions to her sunken and sodden demise. Through the windows I could see her flowery cushions floating about like wreathes for a burial at sea and I felt a sudden surge of anger against the canal for this untimely intrusion. More serious was the submersion of her engine which Arthur had tended so carefully the day before. Our friends at the boatyard commiserated with us and already a pump was appearing on the scene as willing hands stretched out to save her. The diminutive piece of sucking equipment made little or no impression on the water level and a decision was made to call out the fire brigade. A worried, unhappy Mr Kippax walked off with shoulders bowed while we stood around, dejected pieces of humanity, speculating on the reasons for the disaster.

When he returned he looked very annoyed. The fire service were sorry they could not attend because they were 'out on a BLOODY EXERCISE!' Our treasured *Salidha* lying in the depths, a real emergency on our hands and they were out on an exercise?!!

In a situation which absolutely defied credibility we waited, and after a fraught hour the fire brigade actually arrived. They quickly sized up the problem (which wasn't really difficult) and, anxious to show the increased efficiency derived from their bloody exercise, produced a whopper of a pump and connected it in double quick time so that salvage operations could commence. A young, fresh-faced fireman (obviously a new recruit) was holding the end of the hose and his task was to play the water gently back into the canal, where it undoubtedly belonged. Every man was at his allotted station and bystanders had picked their vantage points in order to obtain a clear view of the enthralling proceedings. At last the order was given to switch on and WHOOMPH! a great jet of water emerged from the nozzle. At the same time it was wrenched from the fireman's hands and flew high in the air, gyrating furiously and drenching everybody within range.

'My cap!' the fireman shouted, clutching at his naked head and quite oblivious to all the dripping bodies around him. 'Where's my cap? My cap's in the bloody canal. Somebody get my cap. It's in the bloody canal! It's in the BLOODY CANAL!'

The hose meantime, curling out of control was still doing its snake dance bit, until the fireman eventually realised that, even if he had lost his cap, it did not automatically follow that he should lose his head! At last he managed to wedge the nozzle under his arm and only then did someone of reasonable intelligence, having thought the matter through, seek to decrease the water pressure.

I was now thinking that order might be restored until I glanced at Mr Kippax's face which was fluctuating between shades of red and blue while he seemed to be on the verge of performing a Maori war dance. At last he exploded into incoherent splutterings, jumping and pulling faces with arms wildly waving in a now very realistic Haka. And no wonder; for while the fire service was kindly removing the water from *Salidha*, the capless holder-of-the-hose was merrily playing it onto another boat and filling it full of water!

Nevertheless, order ultimately prevailed, the cap was recovered dripping and shrinking from the canal, the pump began working, and the water was directed in a graceful, curving arc back into the 'cut'.

After one or two mistrustful glances, Mr Kippax (soaked right through to his Yorkshire skin) decided that he could safely return home and enjoy temporary respite from the traumatic happenings at his usually peaceful boatyard.

As the water level went down, so did Arthur — into the boat, where he found that a sea-cock had been opened accidentally the day before. As soon as we had switched off the engine and stopped the bilge pump, the canal had started oozing in. When we were sinking into a deep, contented sleep on Saturday night, *Salidha* was sinking also — onto the bottom of the canal.

The firemen worked hard to make amends and then came the heart-breaking job of removing sodden carpets, cushions and curtains to be dried off in a nearby storeroom. Of course, our trip was off because, although *Salidha* was joyfully buoyant once more, her engine would have to be stripped down and cleaned yet again. Arthur, sympathetic and concerned, sensing our apprehension, assured us that everything would be alright and everything WAS alright, but not until a fortnight later. Then, without snake dances or Maori hakas to launch us, we took a leisurely, shake-down cruise along the canal. Taking turns at the wheel we were initiated into the art of driving a boat. We all did reasonably well and felt quite pleased with ourselves at the end of a delayed maiden voyage.

Salidha had now been a member of the family for two months. Upon her adoption, six hundred pounds had departed out of our pockets into Mr Kippax's, hours and hours of labour had first of all stiffened and then developed our muscles, the garden had returned to nature, endless expenses, hitherto unthought of, cropped up regularly every week and Alec and I had nearly suffered a nervous breakdown apiece.

As a token of her gratitude, she had tried to emulate a submarine and, as a really big favour, had taken us for a short but pleasant cruise lasting two hours. In order to redress the balance a bit, we decided to take *Salidha* out again as soon as possible — but this time on our own.

Our first trip was to the historically interesting and pretty village of Rodley, covering part of the canal we'd sailed before, but going on farther. Casting off successfully proved to be quite a feat, there being four captains on board: one whose legs felt like fast-liquefying jelly, another who (despite his sex) was having kittens on the foredeck, and the other two who, because of their extreme youthfulness and total inexperience, knew better than everybody!

We moved nervously away from the shore and waved confidently to the audience at the boatyard, who were, no doubt, hoping for a side-splitting sequel to the episode enacted three weeks before. Once the ropes were aboard I suddenly felt cut off from the rest of the world and although we might have given the impression of making a smooth manoeuvre, my sweaty hands were gripping the wheel as if in a vice, while the hot flushes which enveloped me had nothing to do with my age at the time. Alec became a figurehead in the bows as he tried to peer around corners to warn any foolhardy boat owners coming the other way. We settled down, Dave and I, taking turns at the wheel.

'Don't forget to pass on the right,' cautioned an uneasy Dave, not recognising this tense, erect figure of a stepmother.

Salidha, only allowed to move slightly out of neutral, glided along at the speed of a lazy swan past an attractive Yorkshire mill, then under a large, noisy road bridge and out of sight of the boatyard where disappointed onlookers had already turned away.

The pleasant countryside, the warmth of the day, the freshening woods and all that our new environment had to offer was lost on me for a while because my apprehension had begun to mount to migraine proportions, and I was relieved, when Dave took over, to let the tensions of the occasion flow away with the glistening wake of *Salidha*.

This was better — with Dave now tense and erect in concentration, Alec still a figurehead, and Penny doing I know not what in the bowels of the cabin, I could relax and find some enjoyment in the sail. The most ordinary things took on a special interest when viewed from the canal; some bemused cows in a field were greeted in their own language and a placid sheep glanced inquiringly at Alec when he attempted a Doctor Dolittle conversation which would never have occurred by car!

As we approached Rodley we could see a line of moored boats and three captains out of four settled for tying up behind them. We put her into neutral so as to come in gently, and then wondered why we were off course and moving much, much faster than intended. The reason was an element which all boat owners know and respect ...wind!

High banks of trees had sheltered our passage for a while, but now, the landscape was much more exposed; consequently, when the engine eased, the wind took over, blowing us in sideways with a rare bump. One or two people raised their eyes but didn't seem unduly concerned at the force of our impact, whereas we, in the fluster of the moment, forgot to take a rope ashore.

When *Salidha* was safely tethered, and firm, dry land lay beneath our feet once more, we set out to enjoy Rodley. There were various shapes and sizes of craft being tended by various shapes and sizes of owners: some slapping on paint with gay abandonment, others meticulously daubing a tiny spot; men bedecked with oily rags, screwdrivers and spanners were messing about aimlessly inside engines; groups, comfortably stood at ease, were talking the afternoon away, while some, just sitting staring glassy-eyed seemed hypnotised by the play of light on the water.

The now seasoned crew of *Salidha* swaggered jauntily along the towpath appraising and comparing other boats with their own. The sense of achievement was great and we celebrated with an enormous icecream apiece.

Because we didn't relish making a spectacle of ourselves in front of the entire boating fraternity of Rodley, we decided that instead of going further on through a swing bridge, we would steer carefully along the line of boats and turn around before the bridge. So we thought!

Back once more on *Salidha*, we cast off, put her into forward and turned the wheel hard over to avoid the cruiser ahead. However, the wind, having put us ashore was reluctant to let us leave and every time we tried to move off, *Salidha* headed straight for the stern of the other boat. Needles to say they WERE watching us by now and we had visions of being stranded in Rodley until the wind dropped.

Because we were complete beginners, it took us quite a while to work out even a ridiculously simple manoeuvre — just back out, give her the gun and we were away!

Apart from this episode the sail was uneventful and we returned safe and reasonably sound to Apperley Bridge. As we made our way home we talked unceasingly and shouted 'bridge' every time one came into view. Later, as I reflected on the day, I couldn't help thinking that Mr Kippax's description of peace, tranquillity and relaxation, wasn't quite the whole story!

CHAPTER TWO

There is nothing – absolutely nothing – half so much worth doing as simply messing about in boats.

(The Wind in the Willows)
Kenneth Grahame

As soon as you own a boat you become, whether you admit it or not, boaty. You become obsessed by boats, you dream boats, you think about colours and shapes of boats, names for boats, flags for boats, covers for boats, anchors for boats and even boats for boats! You think up succulent dishes for taking on boats, wines for drinking on boats, and the rum, lacing your morning coffee, takes on a completely new meaning. All of a sudden you are buying boating magazines, visiting boat clubs and peering over bridges to discover that some navigable river or canal is flowing underneath. You discuss all kinds of nautical clothing to repel or enhance your new environment, become regular customers at the Army and Navy stores, try on sou'westers, anoraks and kagools, wear non-slip shoes to walk on non-slip paint, search for non-sweat sleeping bags and peer at clapped-out tyres with renewed interest. You experiment with ropes; thick, thin, coarse, nylon, and 'rope' ropes, and try to remember the knots you couldn't tie when you were boy-scouting or girl-guiding.

You learn an entirely new language and try desperately to remember which side is port and which starboard. As an ex-Wren, I was able to show off my knowledge of these. Then there were ground paddles, flood gates, 'Tom Puddings', swing, hump and roving bridges, leggers, buttys, (not jam or chip) narrow boats, broad boats, balance arms, pounds, lifts and 'gongoozlers', to mention but a few of the waterways expressions.

While absorbing this colourful vocabulary we also managed to bore the pants off our long-suffering friends as 'Those bloody Coppells who never talk about anything but their blasted boat!' And when we made other friends through our newly found interest, it was inconceivable that we should talk about anything BUT boats. If we decided to spend a whole day working on our boat, we had to deduct half the allotted time for chats with all the other boat owners who were spending a whole day working on their boats! 'Experts' besieged us with well-meaning advice and we found extraordinary the number of different ways of obtaining an identical result.

We were fortunate, however, to have a real expert to guide us through our first set of locks — Dobson's Locks. Graham, auburn-haired, freckled, agile when leaping on and off boats, and fancied by Penny, was employed by Mr Kippax.

I can recall as if it were yesterday the immense lock gates shutting with a clang and how *Salidha* instantly shrank into a toy boat in the bath once she was enclosed in the dank, slimy cavern. I was the only person remaining on board and my job was to fend off with the boat-hook. Graham, moving swiftly did not mess about when he 'turned on the taps'. As soon as the ground paddles were open and the resulting whirlpools surged around *Salidha*, he turned his attention to the gate paddles. Shades of the fire service! Two great jets of water were directed at the boat, both determined to push her in opposite directions. *Salidha* responded like a bucking bronco fresh out of its stall, swishing alarmingly from side to side and my boat-hook might as well have been a knitting needle for all the use it was. The surge of water was too savage and astonished faces gawped down from above at the screaming, female rough-rider, waving her boat-hook in protest at being left to cope with such uncontrollable forces!

As the ascent got under way, the tumult and the shouting died and the violent swishing became a gentle swirl. *Salidha* slowly edged her way up the side of the lock towards an unforgettable moment, for as we emerged from the depths, a whole new world was revealed.

There was a touch of magic about on that first fair spring day and the spell then woven has remained ever since. Whenever we are descending, I wait patiently for the confining gates to give, their slow movement telling of the straining unseen arms pushing them above. When lifting on the turbulent, frothy beer of a filling lock only the shifting skyscape is visible from within; but the revelation comes and is generally pleasurable and occasionally endowed with great beauty.

Another practice-run on Dobson's Locks brought the confidence we needed before inviting some apprehensive but indulgent friends, Elsie and Stan, to put their lives in our incapable hands.

Beyond these locks lies a delightful stretch of woodland and we had chosen a springy, grassy bank fanned by elegant trees as an ideal place for a picnic. It was during this expedition that a small slip of a girl leading a younger boy came strolling contentedly along the towpath. She had an appealing elfin face which fitted in with our leafy surroundings and both children waved vigorously as we approached. Then small legs worked extremely hard as they ran ahead, eager to open a bridge for *Salidha*. Afterwards, when we were moored, they hopped aboard, swapped sweets, and chatted and chewed the afternoon away. When shadows began to lengthen they decided to make for home and we gazed after them until they disappeared, hand in hand along the curve of the towpath, our brief but sweet encounter at an end. Weeks later we read in a local newspaper about a young girl who had been crushed when opening a bridge at Apperley. Serious injuries proved fatal and her brother was mentioned in the report. We felt very sad, for we were sure that the victim of this cruel accident was our delicate elf of the wood.

Except for this upsetting incident we enjoyed our time with Bradford Boat Services which, in spite of its misshapen buildings, is a neat little boatyard offering all the usual (and some unusual) services.

The original boatyard, built before the canal existed, was a barge-building yard and even today an old plaque dated 1854 hangs on the office wall. This was once the barge-builders house and Mr Kippax and his son John conducted their business from the very same spot.

Underneath one of the buildings is an old sawpit left from the days when tough, hard-drinking navvies travelled the canals sawing wood for a living. Done by hand, just one tree plank could take a day and a half to cut; consequently they would sometimes remain for a month at a boatyard before moving on. Later the business was taken over by Canal Carriers Limited who carried all kinds of cargo, including ash, manure and coal along the Leeds–Liverpool Canal. These workboats were horse-drawn and one enterprising operator moved along the canal picking up all the horse droppings left on the towpath. By the time he had journeyed one hundred and twenty-seven miles from Leeds to Liverpool in a boat increasingly emitting 'the rankest compound of villainous smell that ever offended nostril', he had a load of manure to sell. On the return journey he did exactly the same, making sure that plenty of barges had set off before him and hoping that the horses were well nourished and regular in their habits!

Some wily bargees, wanting to steal a march on their slumbering competitors, would tie sacks of straw on the horses hooves and make them wear nosebags. Then, at the first glimmer of dawn, they could lead them out of the stables without so much as a clip-clop or whinney. Once inside the locks they had achieved their objective and led all the way.

Sometimes they used teams of horses and operated fly-boats non-stop, by a rota system; one horse, or two in tandem, would pull the boat to a certain point and then another would take over; the sequence being repeated until their destination was reached. When the boat returned days later, the tethered horses were waiting where they had been left and needed no guidance along the very familiar stretch of towpath they were destined to plod, over and over again. If time was pressing, people, boats and horses became shadowy shapes in the darkness and then white-washed bridge arches marked with navigational centre stripes were invaluable guides to these intrepid boatmen of the night.

Another intrepid boatman of a different kind had already dabbled with boats on the Norfolk Broads when he took over from Canal Carriers Limited at Apperley Bridge. In 1947 barge transport had declined and pleasure craft were not yet popular, so it was a risky time to launch a new business. At the outset they specialised in repairs and later bought second-hand boats to start a hire fleet; then John went away to study boat design and from that time onwards they began to develop their own boat building, at first in wood, converting ships' lifeboats. Although they were not aware of it at the time, a significant inquiry came their way when a fishing gear merchant asked them to supply him with dories.

The dory is an interesting boat which has developed over the centuries along with the invention of the power saw — the source of power originally being water. This enabled wide timbers, which are characteristic of the dory, to be cut; for the craft is literally made of three pieces of wood, two sides plus a bottom. It is extremely seaworthy and took on the role of standard open work-boat in many lands. Portuguese fishermen chose them for line fishing on the Newfoundland Banks because they could be nested one inside the other for transporting across the Atlantic.

Many of these versatile boats were built at Bradford Boat Services and when one was exhibited at Earls Court in London, it was noticed by Captain John Ridgeway. He had a crazy idea — to row across the Atlantic! In *English Rose III*, he and Chay Blyth took ninety-two days to complete their epic voyage, and the now famous dory was designed and constructed at this enterprising boatyard.

By now *Salidha*'s crew was getting restless and felt the need to seek fresh (if not always fragrant) waters and pastures new.

Over the boaters' highly efficient canal-communication system, we had heard about two admirable boat clubs at Bingley, and it was inevitable that, one fine day, we should find ourselves setting off to reconnoitre. Seeking the top of Bingley Five Rise Locks, our poor navigation made for several halts to shanghai polite, head-scratching but badly-selected informants. By luck more than logic, we eventually found the intimate little lane which leads to this very famous part of the canal system.

I was not prepared for the aspect which greeted us. A stunningly beautiful valley opens out, rising steeply and away into the hazy distance, luxuriantly green and sometimes wooded; a graveyard shows up white against green to catch the eye and the majestic staircase of locks drops unbelievably, with the 'three-rise' just beyond, ninety feet to the canal below. Here tall, spreading trees cast their shade and admire themselves in the glassy water, while beyond the soft flexible outline of their branches, the mill chimneys stand out in sharp relief. The canal glinted in the sunshine, its surface ruffled by a gentle breeze and a feeling of immense pleasure filled me as I contemplated a moment when all seemed right with the world.

We strolled up and down the banks bordering the deep, dark wells of the locks, marvelling at the whole project; but when the thought intruded that we were actually bringing *Salidha* up this awesome flight, disturbances reminiscent of a swirling lock stirred in the depths of my stomach. The nerve-shattering experience of our first attempt was still fresh in my mind. To multiply it by five must be inviting disaster!

These locks are unusual in their formation for each voluminous chamber proceeds directly into the next, and even experienced boaters can, and do, go horribly wrong.

When we could tear ourselves away from this fascinating spectacle, we meandered along the moorings belonging to Bingley Boat Club. It was here that we engaged in the inevitable conversation with the inevitable boat owner — a member of the Airedale Boat Club whose moorings lay further along the canal.

In retrospect, I doubt whether his boating experience even matched ours, but as soon as he realised that he'd captured a couple of novices he visibly expanded and blossomed into a veritable Chay Blyth, airing his vast knowledge in a very grand manner. HE had already sailed the canal from Apperley Bridge to Bingley and although HIS boat drew only one foot six inches, it had scraped bottom several times! I thought of *Salidha*'s two foot six and hoped for a cloudburst before our attempt. As his unstoppable delivery became more verbose, I lapsed into silent uneasiness wondering if we were really cut out for this boating lark!

One good thing came out of this encounter — an application for membership of the Airedale Boat Club was surprisingly, accepted. Our mooring was duly allotted and waiting for us. All we had to do was travel about seven miles, negotiate sixteen locks, (some of these staircases of two and three) and, according to 'Chay' avoid the shallows. The crowning achievement at the finish would be our triumphant ascent up the Bingley Five Rise. Because of our rawness it seemed more like an expedition up the Amazon ending with an assault on Everest — if this could have been geographically possible!

Innumerable heated discussions ensued in preparation for this epic trip. These included great porings over locking instructions in the Leeds–Liverpool canal booklet. They read like a headache-producing algebraic problem. Things like 'Open gates (A) and enter No 1 Lock and close gates (A). See ground and gate paddles (U) are closed. Walk down to Locks 5, 4 and 3 and half open ground paddles (Z, Y and X). Proceed to Lock No 2 and open ground and gate paddles (W). Return to Lock 1 and open ground and gate paddles (V)', and so on; all this with a neat little diagram to help you on your merry way!

At last our cruise was arranged. Alec, Penny and yours truly were to be the unlikely crew of *Salidha* when she departed from Apperley Bridge. Further along we would be joined by Dave and some of his energetic school friends at the interesting village of Saltaire.

Dreamed up by Sir Titus Salt, a wealthy Victorian mill owner who was concerned about living conditions, it was a sort of mill worker's Utopia on the banks of both the River Aire and the canal. The result is a well-laid-out pleasant village boasting a charming Italian style square. Two friendly lions guard the local library. Originally commissioned to defend yet another intrepid boatman — Lord

Nelson on his column in Trafalgar Square — they were considered not to be ferocious enough.

In a spacious well-used park, a statuesque Titus admires his handiwork and a large, symmetrical mill dominates all. Alongside the canal an elegant Italianate church is unusual in a Yorkshire village and it was here that we were to rendezvous with Dave's talented mates, violinists Vaughan Kitchen and Martin Priestly and (the original) J.R.

We stowed everything away in a feverish manner; Alec and I somewhat edgy, and Penny (also anxious to meet the talent congregating at the church)!

Alec stood by to switch on and I stood by with the 'Easy Start'. In the past, this magic formula had often brought a reluctant *Salidha* to life, but on this important day she was as dead as a canal-drowned sheep — no sign of a twitch, let alone a healthy kick. On Alec's impatient command, I squirted indiscriminately and successfully removed all hope of a response. We were loath to fetch Arthur, for our goodbyes had already been said; but he came and to our relief only found some battery leads which needed cleaning. Soon *Salidha*'s pulse was throbbing normally and as we began to untie her restraining ropes, Alec consulted the instrument panel. The engine sounded marvellous — but it wasn't charging. We tied up again!

Mortification and gloom descended and there was a feeling of pre-ordination about events. My stimulated imagination warned that here was an omen to stop us going.

The floor boards (more up than down that day) were removed yet again. Alec then made his approach from under the companion-way, (taking it unawares so to speak) and its guilty secret was out — a loose fan belt was the culprit. Dare we fetch Arthur again? We had to! Quickly he tightened the belt but to no avail. We needed a new one.

A frustrated Alec went off to do the rounds of the local garages and I made some coffee and hoped for the best. The way things were shaping up we would still be at our starting place for lunch!

If you had told me that we would soon be casting off on our epic cruise, negotiating Dobson's Locks like veterans, and slipping up the canal towards our destination, I would not have believed you. It is marvellous how quickly things can change. One minute, despondency and despair, next minute a new belt arrives, is swiftly put on and 'Quick — cast off before anything else happens!'

I wonder if Mr Kippax heaved a sigh of relief when we finally departed? We certainly did.

We were now at least two hours behind schedule and worried about our meeting with Dave; but as there wasn't a faster, alternative route, we had to press on.

This stretch of canal meanders through some very attractive countryside with the River Aire keeping it company through many delightful leafy glades.

It was exhilarating and exciting to think that, if and when we reached Bingley, there were hundreds of miles opening up before us, offering voyages of discovery in a completely new environment, so different from our everyday, work-a-day world.

Where else could you wash the dishes and glance at a water vole swimming against his own little bow-wave; or marvel at the sheen of bluebells in a misty wood? Or look up again at green carpets of fields stretching away for miles and then suddenly at a group of tail-flicking, curious cows? The variety was endless and my heightened senses absorbed it all.

Alec was in his usual, figure-head position, and all at once I was reminded of another Englishman who liked being to the fore — in this instance of an English destroyer, undergoing a refit at Philomel dockyard in Devonport on Auckland's North Shore.

I had served nearly three years in the Navy when we met. Prior to joining I was employed at the Auckland Star, first of all as general dogsbody in the reporters' room. Here, my years of commercial training helped me to fetch fags for nicotine-soaked journalists, run frequent errands to Anne's Pantry (at the bottom of Shortland Street) to fetch delicious, squelchy vanilla slices, brew endless cups of strong, sweet tea and occasionally take 'copy' into the linotype room.

Later I became a more superior dogsbody in the sub-editor's room, where bullet-like projectiles rattled out of a Lansom tube and plopped into a wire basket by my desk. These contained Press Association news from all over the world — which I read and distributed to the appropriate editors. One memorable December day in 1941 I read a message which made the whole office go berserk. The Japanese had bombed Pearl Harbor!

Eventually I ended up in advertising where I served at the counter, relieved the telephone operator and took advertisements over the 'phone. These telephones had mouthpieces shaped like daffodils, stood on a stand and had elongated lily-like earpieces which hung on a hook at the side. We sat like Dickens characters at very high desks, and on similar stools which I, suffering from acute duck's disease, could not easily climb onto. If you did not answer the jangling instrument straight away, our boss Jim Brand (from Billingsgate, London) would confirm his roots with a piercing, nasal-produced, fish-seller's voice and shout 'PUT YER 'AND OUT DORIS!' And, of course, Doris did!

The War, which was only going to last six months, was well into its third year. Vic, in the army had been away most of this time and in a burst of patriotic fervour I had applied to join the Navy.

My boring occupation and thoughts of all those lovely sailors may have influenced this decision, but whatever the reason I was even more determined to join when the newspaper (without my knowledge) appealed against my going.

Next time 'Brand' bawled at me to put my 'and out — I didn't! He tried again — but no matter how red-faced he became or how loud he bellowed, I refused. Inside, of course, I was dying of fright — it was such an unheard-of thing for a woman to strike. The normally friendly attitude of my office pals changed and I was treated to furtive, unbelieving looks as if I had suddenly changed into an alien from outer space!

Summoned to the holy of holies, I quaked outside the manager's office and thought that my last moments had come. Instead, Norman Brett greeted me with an amused smile, asked about my reasons for joining up, said I could, shook my hand, wished me luck and completely took the wind out of my sails!

As a member of the Women's Royal New Zealand Navy I became number 325, was issued with heat-stroke and rash-inducing navy-blue smocks, thick, grey lisle stockings, sensible shoes and a hot, uninteresting, brimmed felt hat. Underneath we were supposed to wear long, warm, navy-blue bloomers called 'passion killers'. Later our uniforms improved and we became glamour girls all; especially when going 'ashore'. Then (against regulations) grey lisle stockings changed to sheer, black silk and 'short' hair was allowed to spill out over our shoulders.

In order to broaden our limited nautical experience, we dry-land sailors were occasionally allowed to board a visiting warship and go out into the Hauraki Gulf on sea trials. Prior to this exciting event the selected Wrens would be entertained by the ship's officers and invited to inspect the vessel. This is how I came to join an expectant flock of chattering Wrens fluttering up a gangway, saluting the quarter deck and hopping on board the English destroyer, H.M.S. *Wessex*.

Down in the wardroom G's and T's were at the ready and after some formal greetings it became obvious to us naïve New Zealand sheilas that our hosts had anticipated our arrival and were already half sloshed. One, a wild-eyed individual, kept jerking his cigarette in and out of his mouth while jumping up and down like a jack-in-a-box. When he was introduced as a ship's doctor (from another ship) I was quite shocked (and temporarily lost interest in H.M.S. *Wessex* and all who sailed in her). Needless to say, we weren't shown around the vessel, our superiors being more inclined to drinking and friendly fraternisation below decks! Later, a completely innocent Yeoman of Signals, dictating a message from *Wessex*, was left in no doubt as to my opinion of officers in general and English officers in particular. Six weeks later he and I were married! But not before I was vetted by his commanding officer and introduced to a very junior officer, Sub. Lieutenant Gherkin.

'GHERKIN?' I exclaimed rudely in a good, down-to-earth New Zealand accent.

'Yes,' he replied in a frightfully, frightful English one. 'You know — little green things in bottles!'

Whenever *Wessex* steamed out on manoeuvres, he always took up a contrived stance well forward, and being blonde and very good looking, made me think of a Greek god as he posed, displaying his handsome profile to all who (he hoped) were watching.

In August 1945, Leading Wren Capper (transformed in a flowing lace frock loaned by another Wren) married Yeoman of Signals Colin Wood Evans in Pitt Street Methodist Church and (little green things in bottles) Gherkin was best man.

After a brief honeymoon on a dairy farm at Kaihere, during which I rose at 5.30 every morning to milk cows — my friend Joan Fernyhough being unwell — *Wessex* received orders to leave. She headed out to sea, majestically elegant with her Yeoman on the bridge (frantically signalling fond 'goodbyes' to me) and Greek god Gherkin on the prow!

Now Alec has never reminded me of a God, Greek or otherwise, but his signals as we cruised along did, sometimes, put me in mind of a Greek windmill on the island of Mykonos.

At first he tried to communicate by shouting, gesticulating and pulling faces. It took quite a few trips for him to realise that, no matter how hard he hollered I, positioned directly over the engine, couldn't hear him. After I learnt that Alec was oblivious to my flippant responses, I'm afraid I went my own sweet way and ignored his desperate verbal and visual directions. Later, we reached a compromise and agreed upon some recognisable signals.

If he held his hands in an arc above his head in a ballet-like pose, it meant a hump bridge was ahead; if pressed together in prayer, another boat was coming; frantic pushing movements towards me meant, 'Go astern — at once!' Movements to port or starboard meant, 'Go left or right — at once!'

If these manoeuvres were not executed within seconds I was treated to glares and colourful expletives which I attempted to lip-read, but mercifully could not hear! These signals worked fairly well except when Alec's arms rotated erratically against a swarm of gnats or some such annoyance.

On this trip we had not yet reached our compromise and there were dodgy moments passing through swing bridges and avoiding shallows, logs, plastic bags, moored craft and so on. But we managed reasonably well until our arrival at Field Locks, a three-rise staircase. I don't know what went wrong, but by the time we had ascended the second lock, Alec was sloshing around in water on what should have been good dry land, whilst a floundering *Salidha* looked in danger of floating out of the lock onto the towpath. Oh, the peace and tranquillity of it all, just as Mr Kippax had described! Instead — chaos! People shouting, paddles opening, paddles shutting and frantic feet (in squelching pumps) running and splashing about to add to the idyllic scene. Somehow we lowered the water level and *Salidha* sank gratefully back into the lock. After what seemed an interminable delay, we continued on our now nerve-frazzled way.

By the time we reached our rendezvous at Saltaire it was three o'clock, there wasn't a sign of Dave, we hadn't had any lunch and were exhausted!

Our relief crew, fed up with waiting at the church, had optimistically walked down the towpath to meet us, but after a couple of miles (which they had to retrace) had given it up as a bad job. Then they thought — almost correctly — that we had broken down somewhere and decided to take the car and check all the bridge points in the hope that they would look over one and find us. Thinking rationally, (as Dave put it) they knew that we were on the canal somewhere between Apperley Bridge and Saltaire. However, for all their ingenuity and bridge hopping, never the twain did meet until they returned to Saltaire somewhat aggrieved to find us (having got our priorities right) sitting down to a whacking great lunch.

Garbled discussion and disjointed explanations went back and forth between mouthfuls of food and gulps of tea and after we had sorted things out we felt refreshed and ready for the second leg of our voyage.

Hurried calculations had revealed that the distance *Salidha* had covered in four and a half hours — we were due to leave at ten thirty — would have taken about ten minutes by car!

A short sail brought us to Hurst Lock where quite a few interested idlers (Gongoozlers) were watching our progress. We now had a young, agile crew anxious to demonstrate how things should be done. Everything was performed at the double with much acrobatic leaping to and from the boat and lassoing with ropes. Dave seemed to be creating an Olympic record for getting *Salidha* up and out of a lock. Whatever the motivation, it had the desired effect and before you could say 'splice the mainbrace' we were passing over Dowley Gap Aqueduct and up to the locks beyond. Here again, the same story of sickening efficiency prevailed and I began to wish that something would go wrong for a change. They, of course, were throwing out original jibes like 'Can't understand what took you so long,' and 'Nothing to it! Piece of cake! Child's play!'

A mile further on we could see 'base camp' in the shape of the three-rise locks which preceded 'Everest' and excitement bubbled at being so close. As *Salidha* rose, held steady by her ropes, I kept counting off the locks like the score at a cricket match — four to go, three to go, two, one — up the last lock and we had won. LAETI TRIUMPHANTES!

We have mounted this staircase many times since, but on that exceptional evening, although we were (some of us) the weariest, grubbiest-looking crew imaginable, the sense of personal achievement and satisfaction overruled all.

When we pulled skilfully into our very own mooring, tied up and turned off the engine, a terrific wave of relief and relaxation engulfed me — but not for long — for no matter how tired you are, left-overs have to be packed and clothes sorted out with all the other bits and pieces, before the camel-train procession up to the car takes place.

After many adjustments to her ropes we at last left *Salidha* in peace.

Was that just a creaking timber I heard, or did she (in sympathy with Mr Kippax) give a little sigh at our departure?

Thoughts about the day, its highlights, its anxieties, gave us plenty to discuss on our drive home. I slept very heavily and, in between sleeping and waking next morning, wondered for a moment if the events of the previous day had just been a dream. But sore hands and aching muscles reassured me that *Salidha* was, in fact, safely moored at Bingley, pointing her shapely bow towards the Dales and resting up for her next adventure.

Chapter Three

The canals, linked to navigable rivers, form a fascinating network of moving roads throughout the country and their engineers showed great innovative insight allied to an inspired ability to blend with and enhance the natural environment.

The delightful hump bridges for instance. Did they visualise them reflecting full circles to frame some enchanting pastoral landscape? They arch invitingly over the canals drawing us closer and closer until, charmingly seduced, we pass through to become part of the scene beyond.

Gaily painted boats add bright splashes of colour to an imaginative canvas. Romantic old barges, traditional narrow boats, slick, sophisticated cruisers and even the unusual do-it-yourself versions which are somebody's pride and joy, are symbolic of a longing for freedom.

When taking a quiet stroll on a summer's evening, your feet press into footprints from the past while ghostly images of marvellous characters and long-suffering animals flicker across the mind. The highly decorated boats were symbols of their indominitable spirits, for life was extremely tough and afforded little comfort or remuneration.

During the early days, when canal transport was in its hey-day, a boatman's family lived ashore, probably in a cottage, and they fared reasonably well until the railways took over and forced freight charges down. In the interest of balancing the family budget, whole families then took to the boats where wives and children became unpaid crew members. Long, tiring hours were their lot and it was easy, at the end of an arduous, twenty-four-hour working day, in inky darkness, for a child to fall into a lock or for a horse to stumble to disaster on an icy towpath.

Men and beasts used to haul boats from these paths. Occasionally mules and donkeys were used as well as horses, and I suppose that if a mule became mulish, or if a donkey became stubborn, the boat would keep going and the hauling positions would be reversed!

Towpaths varied of course. Some would be well-laid and perhaps, metalled but others, just a track, uneven and overgrown, would in winter produce a wet muddy quagmire, sucking at the hooves of animals and the feet of the human hauler. When the towpath changed from one side of the canal to the other, animals had to transfer and the romantic silhouette of a towing horse curving over a hump bridge must have been a common sight along the way.

On the rivers it was another story, for towing-paths were not fenced off from the adjoining land, so when horses came to a boundary they had to pass through gates which closed automatically behind them. And if a towpath did not belong to the navigation, an annual rent had to be paid for their right of way.

At one time, in the Bedford district, stiles (sometimes over two feet high) were used instead of gates, forcing the horse to jump over them. A sort of steeple-chase with boat attached!

Sometimes, if the paths changed from one side to the other and there wasn't a convenient bridge, the horse would hop onto the barge or boat he was pulling and have a ride instead!

During the second half of the eighteenth century, most of the traffic on the Upper Thames consisted of large barges carrying up to two hundred tons each. These would be hauled (against the stream) by twelve to fourteen horses or fifty to eighty men. Some could be of the worst possible character, (the men!) and I try to imagine the terror and destruction they left in their wake.

Towpaths are an integral part of the canal-system and apart from their nostalgic association with the past, they are invaluable to us boaters for access to villages, shops and pubs. As you ply from place to place, your front path goes with you, an ever-present link with civilisation. Interested passers-by peer in at your boat windows or pause to have a friendly chat and dogs, taking their owners for a walk, give you a bark or a sniff, according to their fancy. Children, wiggling on their stomachs wafting nets at sticklebacks, look up to wave while little ones have their arms flapped for them by their elders.

The locks, clearly visible as they stretch out sturdy black and white arms, remind us that life is full of ups and downs. Fishermen (and fisherwomen these days) squat for hours immobile staring, thoughtful, like figures woven in a tapestry, trying to solve their problems on some quiet restful bank; until a boat approaches to cast ripples on their serenity. We also disturb the many plants which hang thirstily down from the towpath where an infinite variety of flora creates a colourful border. I must admit that I couldn't put a name to many but I can botanise in my own quiet way, for I have eyes to appreciate the exquisiteness of a common wild flower, while my inner eye marvels at its creation.

We were fortunate to be moored facing a particularly lovely stretch of towpath and canal, along which *Salidha* would eventually carry us towards and into the Yorkshire Dales. Astern of us lay *Adagio*, a twenty-foot marine-ply cruiser and the day when we met its proud owners, Brian and Mabel Kershaw, must be recorded as a memorable one. During our first encounter we exchanged polite greetings and I tried to make conversation regarding the name *Adagio*.

'Yes,' said Brian. 'It's a musical term you know.'

As teaching music was my profession, I did know! Adagio means leisurely and anything less in keeping with the adventures of that particular boat, I have yet to hear!

Brian and Mabel had purchased *Adagio* a few weeks previously and their first long trip happened to coincide with our own departure on Spring Bank Holiday Saturday. We had on board Stan, Elsie, our two-selves and Penny, and you may recall that *Salidha* is an airy, roomy boat. On *Adagio*, twenty feet in length and very short of headroom, were Mabel, Brian, their two sons, Paul and Simon, a school friend of theirs, two big dogs, (without leads) and Alexander the parrot, on a lead! A cat came into the crew at a later date. Add to these the stores and bedding to feed and sleep the same and you will understand why Mabel had to sit on the toilet when she was cooking the dinner — the stove being, conveniently, exactly opposite.

Alexander is an exotic, blue and gold South American macaw, so I apologise for calling him a parrot, and although *Adagio* was not exactly in keeping, Brian looked every inch a Long John Silver with the tethered Alexander perched on his shoulder. Of course, Brian didn't sport a wooden leg or a patch over one eye, but one's imagination could easily complete the picture!

A joint decision to sail part of the way in company was made mainly to help them because they were even greener than we were. We undertook to open most of the swing bridges which are frequent on this length of the cut and our progress was smooth and unhurried as we enjoyed a pleasant run to Keighley where we moored stem to stern for lunch. Here the canal winds high on a hillside and panoramic views invited appreciative contemplation as we ate. Below lay the steep velvet slopes of a golf course and the day was cosily warm and relaxing — especially when we were full of lunch. Alec was employed out on deck somewhere and I below, when Brian was heard calling.

'Alex, A . . . lex!' No reply.

Again came the urgent call, 'ALEX! ALEX!'

'Why the hell don't you answer him?' I queried impatiently through the cabin window.

'It's not me he wants, it's the bloody parrot — it's got away!'

Alexander had indeed slipped his mooring and flown off over the broad fairway, squawking and exulting in his freedom, with Brian in full flight after him. Actually, if Brian could have been in full flight it would have helped, for Alexander aimed for and made 'in one' the top of a very high tree. Out of reach, he disdainfully ignored all attempts to coax him down. Everybody was rather excited by this act of mutiny except an unruffled Mabel, who was calmly getting on with the clearing up. Her life, she told me later, had been one long series of crises and she didn't take any notice of them.

For an hour the rebellious Alexander remained monarch of all he surveyed in the tree, and Brian, still on the golf course, had entered into the spirit of the game by making several attempts to score a 'birdie'. When at last he speared some best steak on a boat hook and shoved it in the parrot's direction, Alexander, unable to resist, rose (or rather fell) to the bait and fluttered down, showing both surprise and annoyance when he found himself safely tethered once more.

It was here that we parted from *Adagio* and her entourage because we wanted to proceed further and at a faster speed. Leaving Brian in command of a full ship's company again, we continued our cruise towards Gargrave.

At last, separated from mutinous birds and indignant golfers, we were able to unwind and revel in the offerings of our new environment: the bright water, the warm pulsating sun and the ever-changing pastures unfolding.

Coxswain Alec was steering and First Mate Stanley was with him in the wheelhouse. Elsie, Penny and I had picked a small area astern, away from any breeze. There we sat, legs straddled amongst the ropes, 'sun-oiled' and content. As we sailed through Silsden we passed under the shadow of a hump bridge and through half closed eyes I was aware of a swan swimming in our restless wake. I hazily admired it but was far too sleepy and limp with heat to take much notice. I raised heavy lids to glance again and was horrified to see great flapping wings striking the water as the swan took off, its stiff, aggressive neck and beak coming at us in an angry attack. We were right in the line of fire! What a melée of arms, legs and ropes as shrieking females scrambled in all directions to get out of the way! To make matters worse the wheelhouse door, which is a folding one, was only half open.

Alec was shouting 'Hit it with the boat hook! . . . It won't hurt you . . . CHRIST!' from his secure position inside. Meantime he was steering an alarming zigzag course but not, I hasten to add, with a view to any organised evasive action. Somehow we all fell into the safety of the wheelhouse, shutting the door in the nick of time as the swan hit the propellor with a mighty crack. He repeated this aggression three or four times, falling back each time to get a run at us. This, our first encounter with a swan on the canals was disconcerting but we realised, as we discussed the incident later, that he was only protecting his territorial waters. After seeing us well removed from them he calmly swam back towards the nest.

Salidha, slightly bruised, was quick to recover and settled down once more, as we did, to enjoy our cruise. What a sensuous, yielding canal this is, meandering around soft green hills, reflecting steep wooded areas, remote stone villages and nestling farm houses, while the River Aire, a shy but attentive lover, follows admiringly from afar. I was absorbed into our surroundings and hypnotised by the cool, following bank wave and *Salidha*'s turbulent wake scintillating like champagne in the sun. However, whenever one began to slip into a trance-like state, the call 'SWING BRIDGE!' soon jolted one back.

Swing bridges are generally fun, but under certain conditions can be difficult too. To be heading for a bridge being opened by one's spouse, and see it (for no obvious reason) stop opening, is not funny. He, knowing the reason, gives a stop sign which the boat (well under way) will not obey!

It is nerve-wracking to be left holding a heavy baby (Salidha) on a gravely path in a howling gale while he goes to swing a bridge which you, in your weakness, could not manage. When six tons was pulling me, gravel and wind assisting, slowly to the edge of the canal, I thanked God for the man who materialised to assist.

Having the steering cable break when plying towards an opening bridge destroys all confidence, especially if the place is crowded with 'Gongoozlers' and YOU are a woman driver!

Worse still to be closing a heavy, steel traffic bridge and have it ride over the catch to crush the fingers of your left hand.

A small scar still reminds me of this unpleasant incident.

But, looking on the lighter side — when rain, plus plodding, plopping cows have transformed an area into a quagmire — what could be nicer than squelching up to your ankles in mud and cow cacky, slipping and sliding with the rain dripping down your neck and running up your sleeves as you try to push open a stubborn bridge? Leaning forwards you slither backwards deeper into the mire which sucks off your shoes just when the bridge begins to give.

This time, however, we were not bedevilled by rain or high winds and all was well. We moored within scent and sight of Johnson's Baby Powder factory, not far from Holme Bridge Lock, the first of three which were to raise *Salidha* to the pretty Dales village of Gargrave. Then we watched the day come to a spectacular conclusion as fascinating colour patterns played from a vivid, vivacious sky onto a serene canal. I dropped asleep wondering how the crew of *Adagio* were faring and if Alexander had become acquainted with the Silsden swan.

Next day we slipped easily up the locks, filled a thirsty *Salidha* with water, visited the Waterways toilets, added to the mound of rubbish disposal and then moved along the pound to seek a mooring place. We were obliged to go almost to the next lock before we could find depth enough to keep *Salidha* afloat. On these occasions Alec is usually ashore walking slightly ahead, peering into the canal and sounding the depths with a boat-hook. I have to keep our progress to an absolute minimum and then, all of a sudden, when he discovers a desirable spot, execute an impossible sideways manoeuvre to bring the boat alongside!

Gargrave, with the River Aire flowing through its centre lies at the head of Airedale. The Yorkshire Dales National Park borders the navigation here, so there is no wonder that all manner of folk pass through, happy to lose themselves in its spectacular, as well as sweet, embracing landscape.

Boaters ascend locks, hikers scale the fells, bikers push up hills, motorists grate up slopes, caravaners surmount difficulties, children and sheep clamber over rocks and in Gargrave itself, masses of roses climb stone cottage walls. A place of great character, diverse with its busy rumbling road and quiet havens if you turn a corner; peaceful though bustling — timeless — for when the tourists have departed, it settles back into itself as easily as a grandmother sinks into her rocking chair when all the noisy family have gone.

Mind you, it is not the safest place on earth to moor. Many boats congregate there during the canal boat mating season and their crews, often lacking experience, leave gate and ground paddles open, causing grave water shortages. Having left your boat lazily floating while you seek much-needed lubrication at The Anchor, you may return to blame the effects of recent alcoholic intake for the sight of your beloved craft beached and leaning drunkenly at her mooring. Frantic 'phone calls will then ensue and late-night, sobering treks up the towpath to allow water to course through the locks above, before equilibrium is restored to her beam, and what is more important, to your bunk — into which you are thankful to crawl.

Hedley, a retired lock-keeper, lived in one of Gargrave's rose-entwined cottages close to the top lock, and although he had been advised by his doctor not to drink, we came across him in The Anchor happily consuming a frothy pint. Short, rotund, red of face, he kept his small, bright eyes on things, was helpful if you wanted your boat watched over, could conjure up bottles of milk and was more than eager to relate his prowess at cricket when young.

Later in the evening, when the bar had become a vocalising, imbibing, smoking crush of bodies, we were reunited with two more bodies — Brian and Mabel. Alexander notwithstanding, they had arrived safely at Gargrave and *Adagio* was once more nestled astern of *Salidha*.

When we were squeezed indivisible, drinks in hand, I asked Mabel if she had enjoyed her sail.

'What sail?' was her surprising reply.

Apparently she had alternated between walking and running nearly all the way to Gargrave. Brian, (being very 'new boat' conscious) having put Mabel ashore to open a swing bridge, had been extremely reluctant to come close to the towpath in case he scratched his delicate mistress's immaculate paint. Mabel, not possessing Graham's kangaroo qualities, could not summon enough courage to leap at the vital moment when he positioned *Adagio* at what he thought was a reasonable distance. Consequently, a sort of zigzagging in-and-out operation had taken place — Mabel running or walking according to the speed of *Adagio* and trying to find the nerve to take off. Before she did, another swing bridge would come into view and off she would race again. Of course, if you think about it, with Brian, three children, two dogs and a parrot on board, even if one did leap, where would one land? Poor Mabel was understandably disenchanted, not to say exhausted, while a coddled *Adagio* bobbed up and down at her mooring 'trim and prim', fresh as a daisy, with paint work unscarred.

However, Mabel is very resilient, (she has to be) and after a few reviving, event-clouding drinks she was declaring their intention to go on further next day. *Salidha's* hyper-active crew remained content to sojourn at Gargrave and then make their leisurely way back to Bingley.

While we stayed put next morning, they pushed on to Greenberfield which is the summit of the canal. From here it begins a long laborious descent towards Liverpool and, as Brian was soon to find out, the country is rugged and very exposed. As they sailed out of the top lock with the canopy up but no side screens, *Adagio*, no longer sheltered by the lock, was instantly transformed into a sailing balloon, her canopy-sail causing her to veer alarmingly in all directions. A narrow boat which was gently gliding in to moor on the towpath side, suddenly frightened by the sight of a packed *Adagio* headed by an alarmed, flapping South American macaw, had to take immediate evasive action. In the twinkling of an eye, it was colliding with the opposite bank to where it had been heading. The owner jumped off into a muddy field, released his rope in panic and his boat moved off leaving him stranded to graze with a harem of startled cows jealously guarded by a possessive bull!

As far as Mabel was concerned, their eventual landfall proved to be a mixed blessing. Not surprisingly, they ran out of bread and when one of the locals told them a short way to the village shops, Mabel (with Alexander in tow) being also a glutton for punishment, volunteered to go. The village materialised into the sizeable town of Barnoldswick and, because Mabel made a detour via a Rolls Royce factory, 'just around the corner' became an hour's trek. The shops were, of course, closed. Mabel had to retrace her steps (Alexander pecking her ears in hunger) minus the bread and without her usual good humour.

In the meantime, oblivious to the doings of *Adagio* and her disaster-prone crew, we had begun our journey back to Bingley and it was here, much later in the day, that we were reunited with Mabel and Brian.

In search of some much-needed peace and quiet they had, on their way back, pulled in at Silsden Quarries Wood, an arboreous mooring made more interesting by enormous rock sculptures pressed into a hillside which rises from shadowy hollows and grassy banks. Mabel, standing on one of these banks, was holding the boat steady and, having cautioned the children not to fall in, promptly fell in herself! Much threshing and frothing of water accompanied by cries of 'I'm drowning' followed, while Brian, always alert in a crisis, began rescue operations.

When Mabel had managed to grab hold of *Adagio*, Brian grabbed hold of Mabel and attempted to pull her out by the seat of her trews. Although he heaved with all his might, Mabel remained floundering in the canal — for, instead of getting a handful of Mabel, Brian recovered an ever-increasing quantity of stretch nylon. Then a strategically placed button came off and a desperate situation developed, for soon Brian would have the trews and no Mabel, and the canal would have Mabel with no trews! Finally, as a last resort, he suggested that she put her feet down and walk out — which is what she did! Of course, her dry clothing was in the car miles away at Bingley, so the rest of the journey had to be completed soaking wet and without the vital button. Consequently, at swing bridges, Mabel clutched at her modesty for as long as she was able, but as she pushed and the bridge slowly opened, so did the gap between her waist and the trews; and at particularly heavy bridges, they gradually folded concertina-like about her feet.

A few weeks later we learned that she had been ill after Spring Bank holiday and, unable to pinpoint her complaint, had blamed some obscure virus. However, she improved by the next weekend and they took off once again; Brian practising his sailing and Mabel keeping him company on the towpath! Come Monday, she was again laid low by the mysterious bug, but with amazing stamina recovered just in time for another weekend jaunt. When the virus struck for the third time, it at last occurred to them that two days of concentrated, strenuous exercise every week was affecting Mabel's health. When this was realised, Mabel, restored to favour, took her rightful place inside the boat again and a not-so-bright *Adagio* was allowed a few knocks and grazes in the interest of her well-being.

CHAPTER FOUR

*Into this Universe, and why not knowing
Nor Whence, like Water willy-nilly flowing;
And out of it, as Wind along the Waste,
I know not Whither, willy-nilly blowing.*

Edward Fitzgerald

In a hectic world where everyone is rushing from A to B, it is so exhilarating to move slowly.

The time factor is so interesting on the canals. We once allowed four days for a local canal jaunt, which, if we had travelled by car, would have taken less than an hour. I often recall that particular Whitsuntide cruise, in fact every facet of it remains clear in my mind, but I never think about the last time I speeded there by car. Of course, friends are amused and make disparaging remarks especially when they discover, after a long day's cruising, that they are only a few miles from their starting place.

In the days when boats were bow-hauled progress was even slower. According to Bradshaw's handbook of Inland Navigation one narrow boat loaded, hauled by one horse, averaged about two miles an hour; two narrow boats loaded, only one and a half miles an hour. Today we are limited to four knots — a knot being six thousand and eighty feet, which is a nautical mile.

He points out that it wasn't advantageous when mechanical haulage of narrow boats and barges took over from horses. 'Whatever horse power may be developed, the rate of progress is limited by the ease with which the water can get past the vessel as it travels, which is governed by the proportion of the cross section of the waterway to the immersed section of the vessel, subject to the proviso that, with a given immersed section of the vessel and a given section of the waterway, the waterway which has the most water beneath the vessel and the sides of which more closely approximate to the vertical, will give the best result. Any attempt to increase the speed beyond what the section of the waterway permits merely causes a waste of power, heaps up water in front of the vessel, creates a breaking wave highly injurious to the bank of the canal and renders the vessel more difficult to steer.'

So it would seem that, from an environmental point of view, the slower the better. Also with regards to safety; if a crisis occurs and you are heading out of control straight for another boat, four knots seems more like forty at the point of impact.

After our uneventful first trip up to Gargrave and *Adagio*'s very eventful one, *Salidha* tootled up and down this stretch of canal many times and we became quite adept at handling her. One skill, however, we found beyond us. This was a special knack of throwing a rope away from a bridge so that it curved under and appeared up the other side. Graham was an expert at this. To explain — as you approach a lock there is often a footbridge spanning the canal or lock-chamber, and when during our early days we bow-hauled *Salidha*, tensing muscles would pull her into the lock mouth, where ropes must then pass under the footbridge for her entry to be completed.

Sometimes Alec would kneel down prayerfully and swing the rope like incense towards the other side — where his fully extended fingers grasped — thin air! In the meantime, *Salidha* would be slightly under way, and if he wasn't quick, the rope would be gone altogether. So, he usually ended up flat on his face, (now red with exertion) desperately shoving the rope-end beneath the bridge from one hand to the other. This worked admirably if you possessed arms as long as a gorilla's or were capable of performing the Indian rope trick — horizontally; otherwise the extended piece of rope became impotent just when your hand reached to grasp it.

Graham, however, the envy of all, could coil his rope, throw it to the winds, and miraculously it would curve and curl under the bridge into his waiting fingers. Inexperience caused these complications and we were soon sailing nonchalantly into locks and tossing ropes about in true 'wild West' style.

The Leeds–Liverpool Canal, on which we were based, was opened in 1816, took forty-six years to build and there are ninety-one locks to be negotiated during its one hundred and twenty-seven miles course. It boasts two tunnels — Foulridge, about a mile long and Gannow, five hundred and forty-nine yards. These cold facts give some indication of the scope of this waterway and help one to visualise all the picks, shovels and aching backs that went into digging the hole. If all the ale consumed by the thirsty, sweating navvies working on the navigation had been reservoired, it would have made a useful feeder to the canal and for those unlucky (or lucky) enough to fall in!

This canal has everything. One of our favourite haunts is Banknewton, a delightful mooring-place between Gargrave and Greenberfield, where the owner of a drowsy canalside cottage helps to tend an immaculate, grassy towpath bordered by yellow and orange poppies splashed along a weathered, stone wall. Here is a very special place, slightly remote and possessing a dream-like quality of undisturbed restfulness; especially when the locks have ceased their activities and darkness folds to enshroud you within your sleeping bag — where you lie and marvel at the miracle of absolute silence. This is a place to return to over and over again, as we did for restorative weekends.

From Banknewton to Greenberfield lies a lock-free, four-mile stretch of ravishing waterway, its scenery unsurpassed, except perhaps, by the last few incredible miles of the Welsh Canal weaving its way to Llangollen. The canal is generously wide, the water clear and deep as it embraces contours of gentle hills on its winding course. Perched on top of one of these hills is a queer rocket-shaped object which looks ready to project itself to another planet. But who would want to leave such a place? When we are there, we never want to leave!

Our first Spring with *Salidha*, spent in the Dales, was full of pleasure-giving hours and special moments of observation as we plied up and down this uninterrupted pound. At Banknewton, the smooth, oily, ever-hungry ducks and their fluffy young would pay us a visit, waiting for and receiving the crumbs from our table. I remember one perfect Sunday in particular, as we wound along a blue satin ribbon of water dropped from an azure sky, watching the plump young lambs running and jumping over invisible hurdles in the field, two of them converging to feed upon their mother with such force, that she was lifted clean off her feet. She, shocked and aggrieved, admonished them in no uncertain manner. Some adventurous moorhen chicks, disturbed by our wake and paddling like fury after their parents, almost became airborne balls of thistle-down, their feet barely touching the water in their frantic efforts to rejoin the brood. We spotted parent-swans lying softly with their cygnets — two white, two brown periscopes poking above the reeds, and a young, slimy calf, groggy at the knees, making its first efforts to stand up in the world — the mother nudging it encouragingly with her nose. The trees wore fresh colours of newly-born leaves, bright, clear, unfaded and the feeling of new life stirring all around us was infectious, especially in such bewitching surroundings.

Banknewton Locks are a flight of six which raise the canal fifty feet and lingering steps accounted for many contented hours strolling this perfectly situated, well-kept and well-loved climb. It's a pleasant pastime to watch other boats locking through, their crews running, throwing, winding, pushing, revving and shouting while you lean on the great wooden arm which opens the lock, hoping to interrupt someone's activity for a leisurely chat.

Alec is a lock-addict. If there are any in the vicinity, he is irresistibly drawn to open gate and ground paddles, catch ropes, stare down at boats and push his vulnerable back against resisting lock gates. Start brewing a cuppa, and when it is ready — where is Alec? — usually half a mile away at the locks! On *Salidha* we had a particularly raucous but useful airhorn which startled many a passerby when I summoned Alec from his locking activities.

Unfortunately, at a later date, as we squeezed under some bridge scaffolding, this horn suffered an accident from which it never recovered and thereafter gave a tight-chested wheeze which wouldn't have summoned Alec from the toilet, let alone half a mile away.

On our wanderings we met many interesting boats and their equally interesting owners. These men delight to talk about their boats and discuss oils, gear boxes, hulls, rudders, props, pistons and ratios with love-light shining in their eyes. No sooner are you happily launched into a favourite story about your boat, than you find yourself listening to his! When he pauses to replenish his lungs you whip in smartly with your own experience again. So it goes on until the time comes to part company. We cannot always remember the names of these aquatic acquaintances, but we do remember their boats.

'You know,' we will say, trying to recall a certain encounter, *Pennine Wanderer* or *Gift Horse*, and the mists roll away leaving individuals clear in our minds once more.

Characters and waterways seem to go together and not always in the past. During one of our many weekends at Banknewton, we had battened down the hatches on Saturday evening, were ensconced feet up absorbing some dubious inherited literature when the movement of *Salidha* heralded an approaching boat. Not being nosey, we immediately dropped our books, took off our glasses and peered out through the gloom at a large camping barge with an imposing bearded figure leaning on the tiller.

Curiosity satisfied, we settled back to our reading. At first gently rocked by his wake, soon, all became still and we assumed that he had moored a little further on near the locks. Suddenly, our peaceful world was shattered by excited voices rising in a crescendo of anger. Instantly alert, with 'lugholes' well pinned back, we strained to hear — but failed to decipher a word. We stretched our eyes out into the darkness — but couldn't see either. Disgruntled and wondering what we were missing, we peered still unseeing into our books and returned to our former state of mute deafness as jarring voices faded into silence.

Enlightenment came later. The bearded figure, which we had seen gliding along, was an old bargeman taking a group of boys and masters belonging to an approved school, on a canalling holiday. His arrival at Skipton next morning was imperative, for another 'approved' bus-load of passengers would arrive there for the return journey. Consequently he was most anxious to proceed and when this particularly intrepid boatman was informed that he mustn't descend the flight during the hours of darkness, he grabbed a startled lock-keeper by the seat of his pants and directed him to the edge of the lock! The lock-keeper, being a man of his word, quickly inaugurated a change of plan and allowed his attacker to go down. We heard all this from an eye-witness to the affray, who wasn't popular with either the bargeman or the lock-keeper for trying to act as a conciliator between the two. A first hand account from the bargee himself, when we saw him in Skipton, happily sucking his pipe and refuelling his boat, added confirmation. Seeing his ample breadth in broad daylight made it easy to imagine his fierce aspect when roused, and I also found him, as did the lock-keeper, to be a man of few words.

Having savoured all the pictorial and sensory delights of this ideal part of the waterway, namely from Bingley to Greenberfield, we responded to a primeval urge for further exploration. After reading about the famous Foulridge Tunnel which lay some miles beyond Greenberfield, we set our sights firmly upon it.

Questions arose. How high was the tunnel? How high was *Salidha*? If rainfall unexpectedly raised the water level, could we possibly become stuck in the dark, mile-long cavern? Should we use more ballast? Were we too wide? What about a spotlight? Supposing *Salidha* broke down inside the tunnel — would we end up 'legging' through as they did in the old days? Would our legs in fact, REACH?

Endless ridiculous speculation took place and we actually took *Salidha* to test our clearance beneath a bar which crosses the entrance. Here, a notice announces that, if your boat can get under the same, you should be able to navigate the rest of the tunnel.

'Of course, if you couldn't get under the bar, you wouldn't be able to go through the tunnel anyway,' I wisely observed!

We cleared it by an inch!

'Well, we can always let some water in,' said Alec cheerfully, causing me to start in alarm as I recalled the last time water entered *Salidha*.

Having told Alec what I thought of his idea we squeezed in and out under the bar and agreed, with no confidence at all, that *Salidha* and her now highly experienced crew would be fine.

We discussed the story of a famous cow which fell into the cut near the gaping tunnel mouth. It decided to cow-paddle the whole length and arrived one thousand six hundred and forty yards later, a wiser and exhausted animal. Brandy was used to revive her, but the consumption of nearly a bottleful by this bovine bather, must have produced a minimal medicinal effect, while the alcoholic content allied to shock should have laid her out completely! Well, the cow survived, but if anything happened to us, I had visions of someone having to follow its example. I personally had no desire to share an historical occurrence with a cow!

Nevertheless, one foolhardy weekend, with spotlight positioned and a bottle of brandy (just in case) the four Coppells cast off from their peaceful haven at Banknewton to sail to Barrowford. As we could see no way of avoiding it, we would have to go via Foulridge Tunnel; and we had it all worked out to a 'T', for tunnel! My action station was in the bow directing the light to an appropriate spot and fending off should we touch the sides; a cold, damp, thankless job I was soon to discover. Claustrophobic and inhibited in a stiff all-embracing waterproof with hood to protect Friday's hair-do, I waited. Dave was coxswain, and Alec was positioned, boathook at the ready, astern, where the height and width of the wheelhouse could become problematical.

After declaring umpteen times that the tunnel was just around the next corner, we rounded one — and there it was!

'Put the spotlight on, Pen,' shouted Alec.

We crept cautiously towards a dark, gaping orifice which had just yawned out two boats.

'Is it wet in there?' I called.

'Dripping,' came the succinct reply from a faceless anorak. To the accompaniment of our amplified heart beats we gingerly cross the threshold and the bar looks even closer. I grasp the light in a vice-like grip to hold it absolutely steady; dripping it certainly was, and it seems strange to relate that the only rain we suffered during that trip was inside the tunnel.

The spotlight's reflections make ghostly flickering shapes on the walls and the atmosphere is chilly and dank.

'A piece of cake,' I nervously murmur to myself when at the outset there seems to be ample room.

But as we edge further in, the tunnel roof takes on queer humps and bumps, forming grotesque, uneven contours; stalactites hang about waiting for the next hundred years to pass, and at one heart-arresting point the wheelhouse grazes the top; but we continue to push towards the pinpoint of light in the all too far distance. We shout childishly making funny noises and our laughter sounds eerie as it bounces off the tunnel walls to echo all around us. The air vents fascinate me and I strain my neck to look up to a circle of daylight as we pass underneath; my hands are stiff with cold although the lamp lies warm within them and the ceaseless dripping continues. A poem from my schooldays comes to mind . . .

> In Xanadu did Kubla Khan
> A stately pleasure-dome decree:
> Where Alph, the sacred river, ran
> Through caverns measureless to man
> Down to a sunless sea.

My keyed up imagination runs riot! We are on a journey into the deepest bowels of the earth; unknown, fearsome creatures are lurking in the menacing shadows!

'My God, what if the roof gives way? What if one of us falls in? What if Alec falls off the stern?'

When doing his version of a front crawl he goes backwards; so he would have to negotiate the tunnel in reverse! A bat swoops out of the darkness as if to attack us, silently sweeping over the boat again and again from different angles. Voices shout reassuringly from the stern, but I am not at all happy about that bat! He loses interest, thank goodness, and another air vent is passed. Half way! I glance down at a spotlight the vent has made on the water and notice hundreds of tiny fish swimming clockwise round and round the circle. 'Do they do that day in, day out, year in, year out?' I wonder. 'Round and round in circles all their fishy lives?' Rather like some of us humans I think!

Dave is doing a grand job, but we are all nervous about our lack of headroom.

'Look out! We're touching! We're stuck!'

We stop and move *Salidha* gingerly and gently by hand.

I decide that I am not fond of long tunnels and anxiously watch the small aperture of light at the other end grow steadily larger. As another air vent is passed our spirits begin to lift and over-confidence takes my hands off the light for a second; it shifts position and great shouts of consternation reach me, unintelligible, but their meaning clear. I grasp it quickly (my hands have taken its shape by now) and order is restored once more. The reflections in the water have a strange effect and are disconcerting at first, for the curved roof above mirrors as a tunnel beneath, creating an illusory effect of something which exists, but not as it is seen! Well, I know what I mean . . . !

Thankfully the end is near and blessed daylight is reaching in liberating fingers to draw us out from the depths into the normal world again. How warm the air feels as we emerge and what a pleasure to have the unconfined, immeasurable sky arced above our heads.

'Turn the light out Pen!' calls Alec.

What a busy trip SHE'S had!

We have been underground for three quarters of an hour; it seemed longer and I am glad to wend my dripping way back to the others after feeling cut off during this strange experience of our first canal tunnel.

Not far now to Barrowford, and we fully savour our transition from darkness into light as we complete our sail through the soft, intimate Lancashire countryside leading to the locks, where we are relieved to rest and discuss our epic cruise and tunnel-technique at great length.

Misguidedly, we asked Elsie and Stan to join us as extra ballast for the return journey. Elsie, five foot nothing weighing all of eight stone and Stan, an average sized fella made hardly any difference, so in spite of my desperate protestations, some water had to be allowed in. Consequently I felt only marginally safer with the extra clearance we gained for our second subterranean attempt.

By now Spring had matured into a blowsy Summer, whilst WE had matured several years. However, our ageing processes eventually found their 'norm' in time to prevent *Salidha* from being crewed by grey haired, senior citizens! And, one thing we absolutely knew in our hearts was that in spite of everything, this boating lark was definitely for us!

CHAPTER FIVE

And she shall have music wherever she goes.

(Nursery Rhyme)

I f you fancy a holiday during which you will be ship-wrecked, (almost), cold, depressed, tired, anxious, bilious, blown backwards, blinded in one eye and completely enveloped in black smoke, then come with us on a never-to-be-forgotten cruise up the historic River Trent!

We will offer interesting stops at navigation inns, friendly conversations, a few quiet moorings, one superb sunset, moments of great contentment, sunbathing (once or twice) on the roomy upper deck of *Salidha*, gallons of coffee, tea and hot soup, an infinite variety of thing to observe and a marvellous feeling of achievement and relief at the end of the cruise.

Included at no extra cost, is an opportunity for a spiritual awakening, for you will frequently pray to the Almighty for deliverance and offer fervent thanks when your prayers are seemingly, answered.

Before embarking on this expedition we must go back to the Autumn of 1971. Having parented *Salidha* for nigh on eighteen months we felt that it was time for her to come out of the water so that we could add the indignity of examining her bottom to all the other indignities already suffered at our hands. For this delicate operation we were to bring her close to home and our route took us without choice on a Yorkshire peregrination through Leeds,

Castleford, Wakefield and Dewsbury to Mirfield, where she was ultimately to stay.

The Leeds–Liverpool Canal ends, as one would expect, smack in the middle of Leeds where the Aire and Calder Navigation begins.

As soon as we left the leisurely pleasure boat canal which had contained all our nautical activities so far, the character of the waterway changed. Now we were hemmed in by dilapidated buildings, warehouses and wharves left over from bygone days. New, uninspired, box-like structures grew in abundance amongst the old, all with their inevitable piles of industrial rubbish. There were coal depots, oil depots, a bus depot and a smoke-belching power station, its imposing cooling-towers rising like clay vessels fashioned by a giant potter. We revelled in the novelty of sailing under the bridges of Leeds instead of driving over them and the commercial scene viewed from the canal was fascinating.

Just above Leeds lay a terminus for five-hundred-ton tankers, and we decided that a meeting with one of these mammoth, oil-drinking beasts could present quite an experience. As Leeds faded into the background the scenery became bleakly monotonous and although the enormous electric locks with their red and green traffic lights proved interesting, we were anxious to reach a junction at Castleford where our wake would make a right sweep up the River Calder towards Wakefield.

Castleford, at the confluence of two rivers, the Aire and the Calder, has always been a place of great importance. In Roman Days it was called Legiolium, and Watling Street ran through it enroute from Doncaster to York; so it is not surprising that, during the excavations on the Aire and Calder Navigation, many Roman remains were unearthed. Our curiosity heightened as we approached this historic meeting place of the waters and close observation memorised its layout for future voyages.

Salidha soon found her element within the deeper water and we let her have her head until our arrival at Woodnook Lock where the river slithered off following a tortuous course on our starboard side, and we entered the canal once more. The countryside improved as we pushed towards the famous Stanley Ferry Aqueduct which is identical in principle to Sydney Harbour Bridge. An entirely suspended tank carried us over the river now moving restlessly away over to our port side.

Elsie, Stan and Penny were part of the crew on this unusual excursion, but Dave had departed to follow more serious pursuits at university in London.

We were allotted our usual share of troubles. At Wakefield we encountered a lock full of debris, and as we emerged through polystyrene, drift wood, bottles and plastic containers, Alec shouted instructions for me to pull in. Although the rudder was hard over, she would not respond — not even to Alec's glares and frantic gestures — because a great white plastic bag had wrapped itself around the prop.

Luckily, we drifted alongside and after much prodding and pulling with boat hooks aided by a fair amount of bad language, we managed to free her. When pieces of rotting flesh floated, bit by gory bit to the surface, my interest livened at the possibility of our having uncovered some dastardly crime — but soon turned to disgust when we found the bag was full of abattoir waste.

This grizzly interlude held us up for over half an hour and, as we moved forward at last towards Dewsbury, the already unsettled weather began to deteriorate, sending squally showers to dog us and make progress uncomfortable, slow and difficult.

A frustrating hour was spent at Broadcut Top Lock when, having entered the chamber, we could not raise the water level high enough to open the gates. A cataract poured out through a hole in the bottom gates while unruly gusts blew the canal in noisy, chopping laps against the top ones. Although five exasperated crew members mounted a determined attack, no amount of shoving or heaving would budge the gates. When our physical powers were exhausted, we drew upon our mental ones — cleared the overflow of bicycle wheels, branches, tins and paper, allowed masses of water through and finally managed to level up.

These unforseen delays caused us to run very late. We had

ascended Fall Ings Lock, Wakefield at ten-forty and did not arrive in Dewsbury until after four. Five and a half hours to cover seven miles was a ridiculous performance even by canal standards!

Grey skies made the aspect gloomy, while the persistent wind would not leave us or *Salidha* alone as it tugged, pulled and occasionally dashed sharp pebbles of rain in our faces. We became overtired and our tempers were as ruffled as the canal's uneasy surface.

The climax of this now vexatious trip came at Greenwood flood gates and the climax of the foul weather also hit us at this point. We drew *Salidha* up to the gates where she nestled quietly, temporarily sheltered from her tormenter. Normally these gates would have been open, but nothing so simple was in keeping for us. No, the river was in full coursing flood and beyond the calm of the canal lay a vast expanse of seething water; the River Calder rushing eagerly headlong towards a wide, unguarded, foaming weir. I was alarmed to realise that, when we had passed through, the wind would be broadside onto *Salidha*, blowing like fury, intent on taking us towards and over the weir.

Rooted at the helm, I wished that I was anywhere else, for straightaway we struck a snag when a missing chain made one of the gates inoperable. Once again the strength of our heaving and shoving techniques were tested to the full and found wanting. Alec then decided that *Salidha*'s staunch bows would have to ram us to freedom — or disaster, as the case may be!

An extremely basic plan elected that all the crew, except me, would abandon ship and hold onto the ropes on our starboard side. Then I would move *Salidha* astern, give her the gun and force the gates asunder! To prevent me from being cascaded over the weir, the lucky ones on shore would pull like hell to bring her alongside once I had burst through. Apprehension and fear were my only companions, especially when Penny, showing considerable foresight, bawled above the wind.

'Take your anorak off Mum, in case you have to swim for it!'

My head was a jumbled mess of disjointed thoughts. This isn't happening to me — what am I doing here?— my last minutes have come — the water will be cold — the current looks strong — I hate boats — HELP!!!

Quivering hands removed the bulky outer garment and I took *Salidha* astern.

'You'll be alright,' assured a wind-tossed Alec, safe on the towpath. 'We've got the ropes.'

I put her in forward and she crunched nicely into the gates — which did not move! Back again, the same procedure, Alec shouting, the wind whistling, the rain raining, the river cold and uninviting racing towards the weir, and — crunch!

'You're not doing it hard enough!' he bellowed.

Back further this time and at what seemed a foolhardy speed she hit the gates — which only opened enough to let through a jet propelled canoe!

Alec then asserted his male authority and came on board. While I was screaming, in opposition to the wind, 'You're mad — you can't swim — we'll never do it,' and other encouraging phrases, he took *Salidha* right back and put her full ahead. I closed my eyes and CRASH, we were through the gates, Elsie, Stan and Penny pulling as though demented, the wind doing likewise and *Salidha* shuddering from stem to stern! To my utter disbelief we came alongside safely and, needless to say, Alec was extremely pleased with himself.

'I told you it would be alright,' he said, still white about the gills.

My thoughts were unprintable!

By the time we had reached Shepley Bridge, the night was as deep as the black water of the lock and a worn out, drooping crew voted for home, 'tele' and hot drinks by the fire. *Salidha*, bruised and battered, was deserted and left to lick her wounds at the British Waterways Yard until the following day, when Alec and I took her to Mirfield Boatyard where she was to be lifted from her natural habitat for a revealing inspection.

She wintered in Mirfield. WE wintered in Mirfield! During her stay she was stripped of all her possessions, lifted unceremoniously, swung and hung high in the air, shored up, and then, immediately, before she was even dry, her bottom was scrubbed with abrasive yard brooms dipped in strong, searching detergent. Unfeeling workmen made yawning holes in her hull, ripped out rotten planks and ribs with complete abandonment, and paint was scraped off, burnt off, Polystripped off, sandpapered off, chiselled off and fingernailed off! She was a haggard, dejected lady and I began to wonder whether she would ever recover from this major operation.

But after the enfeeblement of Winter came the rejuvenation of Spring and then *Salidha* began to have her parts put back: new planks to fill her gaping sides, new ribs to support them and a new rubbing strake made a world of difference to her appearance. We tarred her bottom — and ourselves, painted the hull — and ourselves and in the interest of *Salidha's* recovery we sweated, crawled, climbed, cleaned, painted, puttied, hammered and became bruised, blistered, black, back sore, buggered and bewildered!

Shipshape for Spring Bank Holiday was the goal we had set ourselves, but owing to various delays, we had to work flat out during the final weeks. The result was that, by 'Spring Bank', we were collapsing with fatigue while a transformed and rested *Salidha* was in great shape.

We planned a much-needed convalescent cruise during the four-day public holiday and this itself became a source of amusement because we were making for Sowerby Bridge — by car from our house, twenty minutes, but by canal, a few days there and back. On our way we would pass through Brighouse where I shopped regularly at the Co-op and I was anticipating the strangeness of sailing through such a familiar place.

The famous five were on board and Alec and I were thankful to be boating at last instead of working on the now gleaming, smug *Salidha*. By the time we had filled her full of food, sleeping bags, blankets, suitcases, Wellington boots, spare shoes, spare gas cylinders, spare batteries and spare everything else, we squeezed ourselves on board and were ready to leave at 10.00 hours on Saturday morning. We cast off in light-hearted mood, viewing even the very familiar landscape with new eyes, for the magic is that everywhere looks different from the canal. On the way to Brighouse we passed the partially constructed motorway bridge which was to carry the M62 over the canal and the River Calder. Here, when we waved, some workmen gallantly doffed their yellow safety helmets and called a greeting — which the breeze failed to deliver. Then at Anchor Pit Flood Lock, a broad Yorkshire dialect needed interpreting when we chatted with Arthur Crisp, the lengthsman and admired *Lucky Fella*, his trim Charnwood cruiser. We also met his petite, smiling wife Evelyn and borrowed a wooden 'spike' required to operate an unusual paddle mechanism which is peculiar to locks in these parts.

A crown-bedecked gas holder welcomed us to Brighouse Basin and an unanimous vote kept us there for lunch. Penny, engaged in some biological study at school, was (having the time of her life) collecting bottles of canal water and as I studied her first revolting sample, I was temporarily filled with apprehension, dreading what an analysis might reveal.

Brighouse Basin, not yet developed in the present day sense of the word, possesses great character and unspoilt charm. An extremely old lock cottage, dating back to the mid-eighteenth century, looks disapprovingly across the entrance lock at its more modern counterpart and then an irregular, pear-shaped pound, fringed with old stone walls, leads to another, more shallow, lock. An ungainly garage, decorated with corrugated iron, fits rather tipsily on the uneven cobbles, a working-man's club called (in downright, no-nonsense Yorkshire style) Brighouse Borough Band Club, is incongruous but rightly so, and an arm off to the right leads to a large oblong basin where boats nestle cosily near a noisy, spark-spitting steel works, which boasts a covered hoist left over from early days and a slipway that occasionally gives birth to the shapely form of a narrow boat.

Brighouse Basin has been the scene of many remarkable floods and on the garden wall of the old lock cottage, if you part the branches of a tree to look, is a flood level mark of 14 feet reached on November 16 1866.

A toll bridge (known as Halfpenny Bridge) which spanned the River Calder, was washed away in the flood of 1946 and during more recent influxes one could have sailed, had the four lock gates been open, straight out of the river into the basin!

The canal leaves this welcome sanctuary under an unusual double-roving bridge, that is one with two paths on each side, one straight and the other curved. Then a great mill dominates a scene which, if not architecturally planned, is most satisfying. Prior to living in Yorkshire, Brighouse had always interested me because of its famous brass band, which, when housed at the Brighouse Borough Band Club (where else?) must have wafted musical waves across the placid waters of the basin. Little did I imagine, when living in Nottinghamshire, that I would one day join the ranks of the Huddersfield Choral Society and be accompanied by the same Brighouse and Rastrick Brass Band.

Whenever I approach Brighouse by car, I pass over two bridges. One takes me across the rushing, tumbling River Calder and the other spans the quiet, cool canal; and I tend to dream about another Brighouse which offers serene riverside walks lined with sun-filtering trees and kaleidoscopic gardens. Not many places boast a river and a canal flowing side by side and I see a Yorkshire Llangollen where people can lean over bridges and gaze dreamily into the water or visit the bustling, colourful market place, and stroll clutching their wares, along a towpath fringed with lazing boats. They might even be drawn to a neat canal-side park, where a well-known brass band would entertain them with the lively strains of the good old Cornish Floral Dance.

As we broke up the mirror-like reflections of the mill, I entered upon this reverie once more, but a low bridge broke up my own reflections and we had to stop and push *Salidha* slowly, carefully, by hand, her wheelhouse just clearing the highest part of the arch.

A steep bank of trees waved us in and out of Ganney Lock and we enjoyed some pleasant canal scenery until a carpet factory made an intrusion by accompanying us to the next lock where we closed the separating gates upon it. A short straight sail further lay Cromwell

Lock and then the canal seemed, of a sudden, remote, softly pastoral and inviting; so much so that we remained there for the rest of the day and night. Opposite us spread a gently-rising meadow sprinkled with trees and myriad buttercups and daisies. Some distance away on our port side a large power station interposed, but we moored by a copious bush which screened it out of existence. Once again the magic could take over! A clearing sky allowed the sun's rays to find us and we lazed on *Salidha's* warm deck, luxuriating in our surroundings, about ten minutes away from home by car! No need to travel hundreds of miles — we were in a different world!

That evening we fancied a land expedition in search of an oasis, and after dinner set off, not expecting to be long but remembering to take a torch to lighten our return. We found a watering-place in the shape of the Colliers Arms, a piano stool full of old music and an ancient piano to accompany the same. So that was that — for the next two hours I was depressing discoloured ivories into such favourites as 'A Brown Bird Singing', 'We'll Gather Lilacs', 'Pedro the Fisherman' and 'The Lost Chord'. And I was thoroughly enjoying myself in the unaccustomed role of pub pianist. The music was rather blurred at the outset because I was obliged to borrow Elsie's glasses to see at all, and unless my eyes were positioned at a certain distance from the music, the notation kept going out of focus. Soon everybody was joining in and I suspected that, over the years, they had sung the same programme whenever an unsuspecting pianist hove into view. They sang lustily and after a few gins, the music remained permanently out of focus — but nobody cared, least of all me. Whenever I thought we'd had enough and made to rise from the stool, a forceful shove bumped me back down again and another classic materialised on the stand. Consequently, by the time we did leave, a very merry party found its unsteady way along a towpath which seemed much more uneven especially with an erratic torch beam to lead the way. Elsie and I were decidedly giggly and Alec, behind me, went all skittish ruffling my air with a long twig and telling me to look out for bats! Whenever Elsie stumbled (which was often) Stan cried out anxiously for her to be careful, but whenever Stan stumbled, Elsie giggled more. At one stage, when we thought that we had walked far enough, our impaired faculties conjectured that *Salidha* might have been stolen or sunk, but no, a few yards further on there she was, waiting resignedly for her inebriated crew to return from a happy run ashore! As soon as we had plunged tired feet into the depths of our sleeping bags, we plunged *Salidha* into darkness and shaded our bleary eyes with sleep.

We sailed at a quarter to ten next morning which, considering the previous night's revels, says much for our ship's discipline. Alec had to telephone the lock-keeper at Salterhebble who would operate a special guillotine gate, and advise him of our impending arrival. Unfortunately there wasn't any reply, so we had to go on and hope to find him when we reached this curious obstruction.

As *Salidha* nosed through the outskirts of Salterhebble, we were appalled to note that all the trees and bushes were dead or dying. Effluent from a nearby sewage works had overflowed its vileness to the neighbouring countryside and our sensitive nostrils confirmed this; in fact, the canal itself soon became a horrible, black-grey, sludgy consistency, while the stench where we halted by the guillotine gates was unbelievably foul. Elsie and I were left holding the ropes and our noses while Alec and Stan went off to seek the lock-keeper.

At his cottage, a large dog named (according to a sign on its kennel) 'Dunbarkin', barked loudly at Alec's approach, but of its master who had obviously 'dunworkin', there was no sign. Meantime, *Salidha* under the bridge, was staring belligerently at a great slab of steel which seemed immovable; although we had been told that hand operation was possible if you possessed great strength and had plenty of time. To help matters along, somebody had used the area as a lavatory, so we had to tread carefully and watch where our ropes were trailing. Elsie and I were really browned off. Stuck virtually in a sewer, short of drinking water, hunger mounting by the minute, (it was past our lunchtime but we couldn't eat there!), and waiting for someone, ANYONE to return and put us in the picture. Eventually, parched and starving, about to be overcome by obnoxious fumes, we abandoned ship to find some fresh air. Where was Penny? you might ask. Yes, you're right — she was collecting a bottleful of the vile stuff with a view to wiping out the entire staff and students of Greenhead High School!

With carriers at the ready, we set forth to locate a water-hole and find out what Alec and Stan were doing. Alec had found out that the lock-keeper liked his lunchtime pint, but had inquired at the closest public house to no avail. We split up (which was a bad decision) to search different points of the compass. I was sent to a likely pub a 'few yards' down a hill, but this turned into quite a trek, and when I appeared at The Punch Bowl at Sunday lunchtime in mucky canal jeans, rather windblown and smelly, the locals, engrossed in their beer and dominoes, regarded me as an alien from outer space. However, they calmed down after an explanation and confirmed the lock-keeper's frequent visits to the establishment. I also learned that he owned a bicycle on which he sometimes pedalled his thirst to another public house further away. So off I trundled, 'Punch'-drunk, fed up and ravenous, to meet the others who had had similar luck trying to overtake an elusive guillotine operator on his circuit of the local taverns. Elsie and I did divine some drinking water however, in an empty house with the front door conveniently wide open.

When we got back Alec was toying with the idea of opening the gate by hand. We all returned to 'Latrine Lock' to review the situation and just as he was about to attack the mechanism, the lock-keeper found US and 'open sesame', we were free!

We rose smoothly and swiftly up Salterhebble Locks where, although the air was far from sweet, we moored and fell upon our long delayed lunch. We also watered *Salidha* but had to traipse backwards and forwards with carriers because the tap was beyond reach of our hose.

Having warned the lock-keeper when we would be returning, we shoved off towards Sowerby Bridge, pausing on the way at a pleasant mooring near Copley Viaduct to have an untainted afternoon tea and take in the local football match. Under this picturesque structure, boasting twenty three magnificent stone arches, passes a road, the canal and the River Calder. From our position high on the hillside, springy, flowery meadows, sometimes slightly boggy, sloped down to the river's edge where a well worn path invited you to meander by the tranquil water. We were loath to leave but pressed on to Sowerby Bridge which was our final destination.

I was at once thrilled by our surroundings within a roomy, deep, clear-watered canal basin flanked by mellow warehouses and other buildings of the eighteenth and nineteenth centuries — all reflected far into the water on a calm, motionless evening. When the others strolled off to reconnoitre I remained on board and as *Salidha* and I enjoyed each other's company, the late golden light of day was counterpaning the silky water. A bright blue rowing boat tied to an old iron ring lay immobile alongside one of the warehouses and I wished that I could record a very special moment for posterity. Strains of a Mozart symphony floated from the radio and for a while time was suspended as the flowing, lilting music, the blue boat and quiet reflections became as one.

Salidha's clock also had an awkward habit of becoming suspended — even when fully wound — but I noticed that it was ticking existence away and soon the others returned and tea was the next item on the agenda.

Had we wished to sail further, we could not, because a submerged sill blocked the entrance to the Rochdale Canal while a busy road crossed it up in the town. We determined to walk the towpath towards Rochdale next morning and follow it as far as time would allow.

Next day dawned bright and warm and in happy anticipation we plodded off to seek the rudely interrupted towpath. We had heard of the beauty of this now unused canal and were anxious to discover it for ourselves.

We were not disappointed, for potentially beautiful it was but we were sickened that this fair waterway had become unnavigable and that people had misused their environment by dumping all manner of rubbish in it.

Opened in 1804, it was abandoned by an Act of Parliament in 1952; but someday, I thought restoration may return it to its former glory and then I must make my way to Sowerby Bridge once more, if only to pass through on a sentimental journey to this now charming Cinderella of a canal.

Imagining her former grace and refinement made for a nostalgic ramble which ended in a neatly-laid-out park where we collapsed on a bench to rest our weary pins. We talked to an amiable park-keeper who also regretted the demise of this gentle, eye-filling waterway. Then we retraced our steps to the waiting *Salidha*, tired, rewarded, thoughtful of what we had seen and pleased that we had made the walk.

After lunch we decided to return back a stretch towards home and moor for the night. Copley Viaduct was our obvious choice and after we had settled *Salidha* into her mooring, Alec and Stan trudged off to explore a nearby iron bridge. When they were away, some isolated, playful clouds selected them for a dousing and Elsie and I (most considerate of wives) giggled together about their being caught in the rain. However, upon their watery return, it was clear that, after waiting for half an hour beneath an arch of the viaduct for us to rescue them with raincoats and umbrellas, they were not amused! The fact that this course of action had not even occurred to us did nothing to remedy matters, neither did our rendition of 'Underneath the Arches' in imitation of another Elsie and Doris of music hall fame!

When they were talking to us again, we were not flabbergasted to learn that the village of Copley lay beyond the bridge, and after tea, accompanied by our still slightly-aggrieved spouses, we crossed over to see for ourselves. Our wanderings took us to an intriguingly lovely church, built as part of an industrial model village, and the soft, sun-screening woods which surrounded it kept us there until opening time. Otherwise the place was unimpressive and after a restoring drink we rejoined *Salidha* before darkness fell. A magnificent sunset in a stormy sky kept me gazing in pleasurable melancholy until lights shone on the hillsides and stars shone in the heavens.

Next day warm winds buffeted us when we pointed *Salidha* for home and revelled in a strenuous day's cruising. No visit to the Colliers Arms this time, for we had to reach Mirfield before nightfall.

However, we did allow two short stops to break the continuity of our passage, one for the consumption of burst bangers and mash, and the other at Anchor Pit Lock to return Arthur Crisp's spike.

Six of the church clock saw us moored back at Mirfield having thoroughly enjoyed our twenty-two-mile local cruise which lasted four days! *Salidha* had passed her trials with flying colours, while Alec and I, having recovered from OUR trials, were much refreshed.

In preparation for the Coppell's invasion of the River Trent we needed to move *Salidha* to Castleford in advance so as to begin our summer holiday from there. Alec, David, Penny and I put *Salidha* through her paces on the River Calder and completed this leg of the journey. Once again she gave a great performance in the deeper water and responded well to the extra power we allowed her; in fact she seemed to revel in it; which boded well for our epic voyage up the mighty Trent with its swirling currents and tidal dangers, with which we, as canal users, were not acquainted.

One mishap marred our trip — there has to be one! At Woodlesford Lock we pulled alongside to await the lock-keeper's appearance and when he obliged, a strong wind would not allow us to move away from the bank. Consequently *Salidha* aimed, and rather fast, for the curved, concrete approach to the lock, and although an alert Dave slammed her into reverse, she did not respond. The gear box had packed up at the vital moment. *Salidha* hit, wood against concrete, with a sickening crunch. Luckily damage was slight and after a long, anxious delay a resourceful lock-keeper produced a mechanic and soon we were moving again. As we approached Castleford Junction it was a relief to see welcoming traffic lights change to green and to glide into a safe mooring. *Salidha* was left resting peacefully on the unruffled waters of a sheltered basin under the surveillance of a crescent moon and a helpful Waterways employee. It was the calm before the storm both for her and for us!

CHAPTER SIX

Build me straight, O worthy Master!
Staunch and strong, a goodly vessel,
That shall laugh at all disaster,
And with wave and whirlwind wrestle!

H. W. Longfellow

Have you ever had the feeling that the fates were conniving against you? Events leading up to a particularly traumatic holiday certainly gave this impression; although subsequent happenings put these harbingers of our fortunes in a more favourable light. Carefully made plans had been completed and a departure date fixed, when Alec's mother, who lived in North Wales, was summoned to hospital for an eye operation. This meant a postponement for us and an unexpected journey to Abergele where Alec, then a jewellery representative for the Co-operative Wholesale Society, tried to cover some of his Welsh ground to prevent us losing out on the overall duration of our cruise.

All went well for Emily and in between visits to the hospital we lost ourselves in several of those beautiful valleys about which the Welsh are always singing. But then I was taken ill, and perhaps we should have realised that warning signs were telling us to stay at home!

We, of course, ignored them all and when I had recovered, we made ready to embark. Armed with a special chart of the Trent, (loaned by *Adagio*) which indicated everything above and below water, we still felt apprehensive but reasonably prepared as we cast off for unknown canals and rivers. On these occasions I always found myself frequenting the toilet and Alec usually made some rude observation about this manifestation of my inward anxieties.

'Well,' I kept saying to myself, 'If we run into trouble, we HAVE got an anchor!' At the same time I would dwell on a variety of possible mishaps: if the anchor chain was too short — if it broke — or if I (in a panic) were to throw myself over still attached — and 'How could that silly anchor hold a six ton boat, anyway?'

Every time I pictured that large expanse of tidal waterway, I was off to the toilet again!

Our first night was to be spent at Heck Basin; an unexpected, sheltered mooring full of pleasure boats which lies just off the Aire and Calder Navigation. Heck is a strange name, and as one of my favourite sayings is 'flippin' heck', I tended to be somewhat flippant about the place. The village itself is hard to find. This we found out when we motored over to make prior arrangements and passed through twice without knowing we had arrived.

To sail to Heck we parted the River Aire through mining country to Ferrybridge, thence to Knottingly, along the navigation and past Whitley Bridge. 'Tom Puddings' and pusher tugs ply these waters as well as other commercial craft and how well I remember a fully-laden oil tanker overtaking us on the first leg of our journey.

We became aware of this giant gaining on us and were not at all sure about the rules governing an overtaking vessel, so, after a heated debate, we pulled into the bank to allow him a good width of canal on our port side. Completely mesmerised, I watched his impressive bow-wave approach and was horror stricken to see all the water receding from the far bank as he moved along. Foolishly, I looked down at the water beneath *Salidha*, then at Alec holding the ropes on the bank, and wondered, if our water disappeared, would he be able to hold the boat upright until it returned. Was he strong enough? Would the ropes hold? Ridiculous thoughts flooded my mind. The skipper of the tanker didn't appear to be worried and gave a friendly wave as he passed. I waved back a tentative, quivering appendage and felt like throwing up on the spot!

However, the water did not disappear, I was not in fact, sick, and a playful *Salidha* bobbed up and down happily riding his wake. I learnt later that mooring on the main line of the Aire and Calder is forbidden because of the great wash from these tankers. Lack of wash, I have decided, would cause me more concern!

The Tom Puddings, or compartment boats are interesting, and unique to this part of the country. They were invented by an engineer named Bartholomew, one time General Manager and Director of the Aire and Calder Navigation; and they resemble a goods train, using a tug to pull a string of compartments or steel boxes capable of holding forty tons each. Sometimes pushed as well as pulled, they are emptied by being turned completely upside down, (out of the water of course) their contents falling into a huge hopper.

The first time that Mabel and Brian sailed through Leeds, they came upon several barges being unloaded at Shelton Grange Power Station where the more conventional system of a grab was being used. The fully laden barges were lying so low, that the canal lapped dangerously near to their tops. Mabel and Brian watched fascinated for a while, until one of the grabs overshot a barge and landed with a mighty splash on its far side.

'Good heavens!' cried Mabel in alarm. 'They've loaded that one so much that it's sunk!'

I will leave you to imagine Brian's reply to this classic utterance from Mabel.

We turned into Flippin' Heck about half past six, in nice time to moor up, have a cup of tea and then explore. A warm welcome awaited us, and an invitation to the clubhouse for the evening proved to be the full extent of our explorations. Here we did the usual things — swapped stories, talked boats, ate crisps, talked boats, downed a few drinks, talked boats, and then, at a fairly reasonable hour, downed our heads so as to be ready to weigh anchor early next morning.

At 09.15 we were untying our ropes, and a stiff, unruly breeze made the manoeuvre out of that crowded basin decidedly tricky. However, I am delighted to state that all went well, especially as some of the club experts were keeping us under close surveillance and waiting for me to make a cock-up of the operation.

The landscape was now rather flat and monotonous but we were soon to turn off into the New Junction Canal, and later into the Sheffield South Yorkshire Navigation which would take us up to Keadby and the commencement of our great adventure.

Waterways inns are generally pleasant to visit and the New Inn at Stainforth was no exception as we tied up at midday, where neat grassy moorings were provided for thirsty nautical customers wishing to sharpen their appetites for lunch. By this time stabbing twinges of pain in my back, which occasionally explored my left leg, were causing me considerable discomfort; so we searched for a chemist and bought some Deep Heat. I recognised the symptoms. For three months before our marriage I had suffered with sciatica; a very gnawing, painful complaint which I can only describe as chronic earache in the bottom accompanied by nagging toothache down the leg. When severe, it is crippling, and I had, after a two month diet of Codeine, become something of a martyr, resigned to the prospect of hobbling up the aisle with a walking stick as an accessory to the rather elegant outfit I had lashed out on for the occasion. However, a miracle happened two days before the wedding when I woke to find that the scourge had departed, not to return until this day — when I could least accommodate it!

A liberal application of Heat followed by vigorous rubbing, soon had my seat burning like a red coal fire. This completely took my mind off the original pain and allowed a reasonable, centrally-heated sail to Thorne. Here, outstretched welcoming newly-white lock arms caused us to blink at their brilliance, and hundreds of minute blue and white eyes blinked back from sun-warmed flower beds fringing the lock.

Three boatyards invited our more detailed inspection at a later date. One offered large, expensive, cocktail gin and whisky swigging pleasure cruisers; another, martini, sherry and beer consuming canal craft and chandlery; while a very busy ship-building yard was engaged in clamorous construction of sea-going tugs, lighters and barges — which would not remain teetotal for long. A dour line of tugs painted dull grey overall and destined for Cuba, lay resignedly alongside as we passed. Although our curiosity was aroused, a wish to stay longer was superseded by our eagerness to make directly for Keadby. We moved along straight unexceptional stretches of canal, spanned by occasional swing bridges. As we approached these, *Salidha's* then penetrating healthy horn would blast through the walls of the bridge-operator's house, interrupt whatever he was doing and cause him to walk a weary, circular way to allow us passage. Trains rattling by aroused our interest once or twice and train spotters would revel in this waterway which runs parallel to a busy railway line.

As non-spotters we waited restively at an electric railway bridge which, when operated from a signal box, slid sideways to allow us through. Ahead were the dark stern shadows cast by Keadby's Power Station's imposing outline and then beyond was a mooring behind a long line of boats pointedly facing the Friendship Inn. Alec was impatient to question the lock-keeper regarding our transition into the River Trent next morning and prior to this, a thorough check of the gear box was regarded as a 'must'.

I couldn't have agreed with him more, for when we strolled to a chilly, exposed vantage point beyond the lock I was appalled at the width and volume of the river and at our own foolhardiness in attempting to negotiate it. Fear flowed icily through my veins and the sciatic scourge added a nagging discomfort which showed no signs of abating. By now, every garment had become permeated with Deep Heat and *Salidha* smelled like a floating dispensary.

I drooped there, cold and depressed, gazing out on grey uninviting waters while Alec went to consult the oracle in his remote-control box. He proved to be a rude, unhelpful lock-keeper who caused an already diffident Alec to return glum and crestfallen. This man's uncalled-for bad temper put an effective damper on spirits which were already flagging, so we decided to gather some Dutch courage at the Friendship Inn. Described in the canal guide as a large pub with loud music — sometimes, the book failed to mention dozens of roaring, scorching motorbikes carrying teenage discothequers and VERY loud music indeed! But it lived up to its reputation of being friendly and we warmed within its congenial atmosphere for an hour or so, before the two-wheeled invasion began.

We had heard from a reliable source that when Brian and Mabel visited this inn, Alexander became absolutely pie-eyed on Bristol Cream Sherry and the landlady, obviously enchanted by this unusual exotic customer, wished to adopt him. All next day he suffered from a hangover, stroking his head with his foot and making pitiful 'sotto voce' squawks, especially if anyone dared to make a noise! Having witnessed Alexander's capacity for beak dipping, I can verify that he is an indiscriminate toper of the first order, so perhaps we should be thankful that Brian and Mabel could not bear to part with him, otherwise he would have become a chronic alcoholic and expired, prematurely embalmed, to an early grave.

Early morning wakefulness brought immediate realisation of the nearness of our attempt and all the old apprehensions flooded in with my usual internal results. By arrangement, a marine engineer came on board and by lunch time we had run out of reasons for further delay.

'Have a good trip,' he called as he departed waving cheerily. 'You should be alright.'

'SHOULD be alright?' questioned my subconscious, trying desperately to make its presence felt. Foolishly, I let it sink into oblivion.

Once more we were drawn to gaze over the challenging restless river and although the water appeared choppy, we thought along with the engineer, that we should be alright. If only we had turned our heads towards the smoke issuing right-angled from Keadby Power Station, we might have thought again.

At an appointed time we slipped our ropes, passed through a swing bridge and entered the lock.

'The point of no return,' I muttered, as the gates became wedged together enclosing us and two other boats within the deep chamber.

They were a reassuring sight — a steel narrow boat and a fibreglass cruiser.

'If they can do it, surely we can,' I thought.

So that you will not consider us to be complete fools, I must state that we DID carry some ballast — two oblongs of concrete, one each side of the bows! How were we to know that they would be hopelessly inadequate?

The distance from Keadby to Torksey is about twenty-seven miles and we had calculated our cruising time should be between three to four hours. We also nurtured naïve hopes about future speed-trials which would raise *Salidha*'s performance to unknown heights.

So there we were — map in position in the wheelhouse, Alec in position in the bows, Doris in sciatic position behind the wheel and the wind in gale force position around the first bend in the river, waiting for us! As we locked out conditions were breezy, but I relaxed temporarily as *Salidha* chopped happily through ruffled wavelets, and studied the chart before me, looking for the landmarks noted on it. At bends we were directed to keep to the outside because of shoals, while at bridges we were told to 'use this arch' and as I steered I endeavoured to assimilate all this enlightening information. Within a few minutes the outlook had totally changed, for as we rounded the bend a relentless procession of white-crested waves bore down upon us. In between the crests were deep troughs and *Salidha*, usually a smooth, graceful creature, changed into a tormented, lurching being as she smacked over the whipped-up tops and convulsively shuddered into the gullies beyond. Alec hurriedly left his forward position and came into the wheelhouse. Conditions became terrifyingly worse and *Salidha*'s extreme height above the water made every wave a nightmare of anticipation for me. The force, as her bows rose steeply and crashed down again seemed enough to disintegrate the whole boat and no doubt would have done if her recent overhaul had not taken place. Inexperienced, and quite unable to cope, distress gave way to dismay as every movable object on board was projected onto the cabin floor, adding further chaos to a quickly deteriorating situation. Then *Salidha's* steering locked and she swung broadside-on to the waves, rocking precariously, completely at the mercy of the ferocious elements. At this juncture Alec fetched our only lifebelt and I was in tears!

A small group of children outlined on the river bank watched with absorbed interest as we were blown towards them and the jagged rocks lying beneath the surface. Helpless, we waited for the inevitable crunch!

'Send for help!' we shouted on the wind and saw one of them run off.

They were standing among some tall, flexible reeds and these were being blown, like the smoke from Keadby Power Station, almost horizontal. By then we had recovered our senses enough to try and put a line ashore — while fighting to hold *Salidha* away from the shoreline with our long boating hook.

'Grab the rope,' we shouted, when we were within throwing distance; and after one or two attempts, small, eager, clutching hands had caught a dripping, muddy lifeline. We couldn't expect them to make it secure, so Alec dropped over the side through mud and water up to his knees, slipping and falling over the sunken, rugged bottom.

By this time, help had arrived in the shape of a local garage owner and although we were in a very precarious position, we were within reach of shore. After a brief appraisal he raced off to fetch several old tyres which we attempted to shove under *Salidha's* hull to prevent her chafing against the jutting edges of the rocks. The wind, of course, was furiously trying to dash us up against them and there began a battle of strength and endurance, with Alec, not daring to leave his station, fending off with all his might!

An inspection revealed that, although the rudder had been jammed full over, the steering was still intact and our only hope was to wait for the wind to drop and try to return to Keadby. Cold, tired, wet and sick with anxiety, we were convinced that our incompetence would result in the ultimate destruction of the fair *Salidha*.

More people arrived who were willing but unable to help — except by their comforting and encouraging presence. During the following two desperate hours we fought like people possessed against a vicious, demon wind which gave us no respite. At last, in an attempt to renew our diminishing strength, I went below, pushed the cooker back into place, recovered the kettle and made a cup of tea. Sandwiches along with this welcome hot drink, temporarily lifted our sagging morale but not, alas, for long. The water was now receding to expose more and more rocks and our sorely-tried spirits ebbed with the tide as we reluctantly acknowledged that *Salidha* was done for. Then the garage owner, vigilant on our behalf, returned to tell us about a wide shelf lying hidden below on which *Salidha* would soon be high and dry. This unexpected news brought us to the decision we had desperately been trying to make! Face to face with an unavoidable choice, we began to strive for *Salidha's* survival. She, of course, was facing the wrong way and in the prevailing conditions turning her was practically impossible; but with concerted action, amidst frenzied shouting and muscle-tearing tugging of slippery eel-like ropes, Alec sloshing and sliding amongst the sludgy, tyre-strewn rocks, and a totally disorganised, mud-covered shore party assisting with unlimited enthusiasm, the impossible was achieved!

The river was still a seething opponent and the reeds still salaamed before an indefatigable wind, but it was do or die now and if we could get away and around that 'bloody bend', conditions would improve. During our testing ordeal we had become quite friendly with our ever-increasing Band of Hope, and the garage owner, a resident of many years, admitted that conditions were, even for the notorious Trent, extraordinarily bad.

'Force seven at least,' was his comforting assessment.

However, his tyres had certainly helped save the day and now our excited onlookers were chorusing a round of 'good lucks' and trying to shove us off to our fate! Above the howl of a frustrated wind we were yelling back our thanks to them and, as I tried to ignore heaving waves of nausea, I became aware that my sciatic pains had completely disappeared; obviously due to effective shock treatment!

Our mucky ropes splattered on board, all hands pushed like mad and, as I offered a fervent prayer to the Almighty for deliverance, we were away!

The gale, hell bent, was behind us now and *Salidha*, intent upon winning, went like the clappers. Our loyal supporters, having promised to monitor our progress and report if we were in trouble, watched and waved — and waved — and waved . . .

'Who would they inform?' my muddled brain asked.

'The coastguard?' (Don't be stupid!) 'The unhelpful lock-keeper at Keadby?' (He probably won't let us back anyway!) 'Air-sea rescue?' A helicopter whirred into a maze of confused conjectures.

But we were busy now; fully occupied with steering a surging *Salidha*. And the bridge was looming hopefully near. Once under that, we would be rounding that vital bend and in the lee of the land. My heart lifted instead of my stomach and it made a welcome change.

Salidha's engine throbbed reassuringly and our excitement began to mount, while the waves, in answer to my prayers, became more subdued. We forged gleefully through the 'proper arch' and were soon within blessed sight of Keadby Lock — for about two minutes, that is — for Nature's henchmen hadn't finished with us yet! Ominous bass-drum rolls of thunder had shadowed our getaway, and now, with a terrific 'tutti' clash the heavens opened pouring down a torrential curtain of rain which made Alec on deck difficult to discern, let alone Keadby Lock! The windscreen wipers, limited in their efficiency even during a gentle April shower, were quite unable to cope, so Alec remained exposed to the deluge wiping the window with a sopping wet cloth. This greatly improved my view of HIM and I observed that he was rapidly reaching the wringing out stage himself! However, being wet was the least of our worries (especially mine!) as we moved tentatively towards where we imagined the lock to be, while blowing frantic S.O.S. signals on *Salidha*'s horn. Then, miraculously visibility improved, allowing us to locate the lock entrance, and what is more, the gates were slowly opening. Joyfully, I pointed *Salidha*'s bows towards them, opening the throttle with a burst of regained confidence — safe at last!

Not on your life! As the gates widened they revealed a massive barge ready to be disgorged. I disgorged my fairly limited supply of swear words while a tortured, dripping apparition on deck, performing a primitive ritual cursing all bargemen, laid tongue to a much-less-limited vocabulary. Round we had to swing again until the lock was clear — safety and landfall delayed once more. This time we remembered to sweep below the lock and sail upstream towards it — testing the theory that steering is easier with the boat facing against the flow of the tide. But as *Adagio* had instructed us on this tactical manoeuvre, I can't really be blamed for nearly demolishing the lock entrance on the way in! When the two great doors enclosed us in that quiet, deep, beautiful ravine, the relief was tremendous. I looked at Alec, dripping and bedraggled, and *Salidha*, dripping and bedraggled, and could not believe that our ordeal was over. That dirty, slimy compartment was a heavenly refuge and the sharply silhouetted power station looked sublimely symmetrical. After our ascent was complete and the lock gates pressed together in benediction behind us, we were profoundly grateful to be within the protecting arms of a grey, cold, untemperamental canal once more.

When *Salidha* was securely moored, our trying experience at once changed (from our position of safety) into a marvellous adventure. After a satisfying meal it was all hands for the Friendship where some poor unsuspecting soul had to suffer listening to our latest saga.

Next morning a dull sky reflected sobered spirits and deflation was high, for we had failed to navigate the mighty Trent and had, through sheer ignorance, nearly lost our beloved *Salidha*. For a while a morose Alec tinkered aimlessly about with her engine and then, silent and subdued, with our tails between our legs, we slunk back along the Keadby Canal.

Our desire was for safer, more sheltered waters, and we planned to journey as far as Doncaster or perhaps further, depending on what the canal had to offer. We moved listlessly for a short while, passing easily through a couple of swing bridges and without much enthusiasm for the sail; but as the sun gazed sympathetically down, our world brightened and Alec took up his favourite stance forward.

BANG!!!! The whole floor seemed to explode beneath my feet and the wheelhouse quickly filled with black smoke.

'Alec! Alec!' I cried in alarm, instinctively turning the wheel hard over to bring her into the bank.

'What's up?' he shouted in hasty transit back to me.

'What's up?' he reiterated superfluously, as he joined me.

'GOOD GOD! BLOODY HELL!' he cried on seeing a sooty Pakeha wife turned 'Maori', just before he became airborne on his way to secure us.

When an examination revealed that he had failed to turn on *Salidha's* cooling water, he sank into a slurry of self-condemnation.

'I've done the bloody engine in,' he chanted again and again over a scorched *Salidha*, having just escaped cremation.

This latest catastrophe overshadowed the shipwreck episode completely, for, with a new engine financially out of the question, our immediate future looked as black as smoke-filled *Salidha*. Now a tense waiting period began to allow her to regain her cool, when we would try to bring her back to life.

I suppose that water problems are a natural hazard on boats, but with *Salidha* we just couldn't seem to win. Either she suffered from too much water (as at Apperley Bridge), or too little (as in this instance), or alternatively, far too much without (as on the Trent)!

'Don't worry, it'll be alright.' I ventured unconvincingly. 'Let's have lunch while we wait.'

As I prepared a feast for the wake, Alec, foreboding masking his face, contemplated the 'remains'. And I also contemplated; for the dreaded sciatic pest, having recovered from earlier shock treatment, had reappeared with a vengeance and I began to wonder why we kidded ourselves that we were on holiday. Holidays are supposed to be carefree, sunlit, relaxing times, not sentences of deportation to unknown parts to endure all manner of anxieties and discomforts! Neither of us found any appetite for lunch and we were impatient for the time of *Salidha's* test — but fearful of trying too soon.

Alec had already connected a rubber pipe which had been severed from the exhaust, and after another fretful half hour we decided that the moment of truth had come. Neither of us dared to speak nor even breathe as Alec turned on the ignition; but what a whoop of delight we gave when that marvellous engine throbbed into life.

'Thank God!' breathed Alec, ten years of suspense falling from his brow. I too gave thanks — but with rather more sincerity.

'I told you it would be alright,' I crowed fatuously.

Our 'holiday' could now be continued and soon, in spite of all our trials and tribulations, the old magic began working again and we were actually enjoying ourselves.

Noticing masses of bulrushes thriving in some marshy land caused me to bring *Salidha* alongside sharply, and Alec started in alarm, fearing another crisis. I waded eagerly into the reeds gleefully flourishing a serrated bread knife to cut some. Then, when Alec wandered away along the towpath towards some old workings, I heard him cry out as he stumbled over something hidden in the grass. I was fetched from my sadistic slashing to view the ballast he had found; a great length of fist-sized iron links which looked, and were, tremendously heavy. Now you might assume that two reasonably intelligent people would have moved the boat to the location of the chain — because this would have been a relatively simple matter; but no — we struggled, fell, tugged and staggered all the way along an uneven towpath to an incredulous *Salidha*, who nearly rocked us and the chain into the cut as we sweated to lift it on board.

'Just what we need,' puffed Alec, red-faced but triumphant as it slithered and clanked onto the cabin floor.

'Just what my sciatica needed!' I thought, as it twinged a reminder of my condition.

'We could have done with that on the Trent,' said Alec meaningfully.

'We could have done with a lot of things on the Trent!' I thought.

We'd have been O.K. then,' he stated blandly.

I re-entered the bulrushes!

A promise to ourselves was kept that evening when we moored at Thorne Lock and spent a contented hour wandering in and out of boatyards debating which craft we would buy if ever we had the money. An unhurried chat to the lock-keeper accounted for another worthwhile hour, after we had recorded the presence of *Salidha* at his brightly blooming lock, with our camera.

Next day another lock-keeper (at Bramwith this time) waved us out of this arm of the navigation as we turned left into unknown waters. The River Don had already made our acquaintance along the way, reminding us of our pending arrival at Doncaster, the home of the famous St. Leger horserace, and now, massive cooling-towers landmarked our approach to the village of Barnby Dun, which seemed to have lost its identity within the ever-reaching tentacles of the main town. In an apparent bid to outdo the colourful welcome afforded us at Thorne, well ordered groups of flowers joined together in a floral dance as we entered the fully-mechanised, extremely busy, Long Sandal Lock. This was built as recently as 1959 especially to cope with the increasingly heavy commercial traffic of large motorised barges and Tom Puddings on this canal.

Here a railway line joined canal and river to form three snakes curving and slithering their way to Doncaster. As they moved together through bleak, uninviting ways, the canal, tiring of its austere surroundings, separated itself from the other two to seek a diversion along a small backwater which led to temptingly named, Strawberry Island. We sought in vain for strawberries but found instead an interesting crop of boats being reared and tended in this unexpected haven. Rejoining the main canal once more, we followed our snake to Doncaster Lock, which was hard to find amidst the criss-crossing steel girders of road and railway bridges. Not far beyond the lock, the River Don caught up and swallowed the canal for a while and shared its course through an unanticipated tree-covered valley. We glided into a delightful, shaded mooring at Sprotborough. It was obviously a 'Sprot' to remain overnight, for further on towards Conisborough, Mexborough or Rotherham, the latter's industrial atmosphere was always detectable two miles upwind when travelling on the M.1. motorway.

A distinct change in the weather became evident as the rather fresh wind (a boisterous offspring of our disastrous gale) became a calmer, more likeable companion. Warm probing rays were filtering through the foliage causing snowflakes of light to dance over *Salidha* and the surrounding water. Nearby a leafy lane invited us to wend an uphill way to the village, where the green and white of a cricket match on a ground next to a roadhouse called Ivanhoe, made us pause in our walk. Sprotborough, attractive and small, did not require lengthy exploration and we were soon back on *Salidha*, but planning another pause later at the Ivanhoe.

Encompassing warmth held us within its mantle, releasing all the tensions of the previous day, and as we indulged ourselves in the peaceful, secluded mooring, I was lost in wonder at the ever-changing diversity of the waterways. In fact it was difficult to believe that our near-disaster had happened at all.

'Could it have been a dream?' I mused hazily in the sultry sleepiness of late afternoon. I closed my eyes and allowed it to become so.

Later, when replete after a meal, we donned some respectable attire and trudged up the lane again; noting that the cricketers had pulled up stumps, but guessing that we would meet them inside the hotel. This proved to be the case and we passed an amiable hour plying them with our latest boating extravaganza, and ourselves, with whiskies and martinis. Afterwards we climbed back on board pleasantly mellowed and much more in holiday mood than we'd been during the previous traumatic few days. Too weary to commence all the business of getting our beds ready, we stayed up late and discussed the dramatic change in the weather. We both agreed that, given the present conditions, we could have been sailing the Fossdyke and Withen Navigation on our way to Lincoln, instead of burning the midnight oil at Sprotborough.

With senses and memories well and truly dimmed by confidence-injecting alcohol, we began to contemplate a second attempt; after all, we couldn't be shipwrecked twice — could we? On the law of averages that couldn't happen even to us — could it?

'We'll see,' hedged Alec, the cautious one. 'We'll see what the morning brings.

Already the probability was causing my adrenalin to flow, so it was just as well that one member of the crew had reservations.

'Yes,' I remember acknowledging, as my head finally dented the pillow, 'We must be mad to even think about it.'

The combination of fresh air, sunshine, martinis and perhaps a reaction to past events, put me out like a fused light.

Was it a coincidence, our simultaneous early morning wakening next morning? Can you imagine the beauty of the first searching gleams of sunshine amidst the delicate veiling mists in those Arcadian surroundings? Shining golden water lapped to the leafy sides of the valley, the whole bird population was singing, the toast browning and smoking, and the kettle singing along with the birds! We both knew without saying that, after breakfast, we would turn *Salidha*'s bows for Keadby once more. Of course Alec made his usual Fabian noises, but in our hearts we felt that *Salidha* must seek satisfaction from the foe which had so cruelly defeated her during their first unevenly balanced duel. Catching the tide at the right time was crucial, so once under way we kept moving, helped along by cuppas, Kitkats, butties and 'Co-op' soup.

Conditions were perfect when we arrived at Keadby, for the Trent, that raging mass of water of two days before was as flat as the proverbial mill pond, while an indolent power station gently puffing on a giant-sized cigarette, allowed drifting, curling smoke trails to rise into the atmosphere. Hoping that the lock-keeper would not recognise us or *Salidha*, we locked out and began our voyage up this marvellous historic waterway. The contrast was amazing; the river, picture-postcard blue, slipped easily past *Salidha* while Alec and I took turns to go forward and bask in the scintillating sunshine. For the first time, our camera emerged from the cuddy and we posed on deck as happy as millionaires sailing the 'Med'.

At the outset we scanned the banks for landmarks shown on our chart, but the scenery was of a sameness and we soon wearied of this 'spot the landmark' game. Confidence growing with every nautical mile assured us that ample depth lay beneath, so we ceased to study the chart for every little shoal and an enjoyable sail soon became a thrilling one, for *Salidha* was sporting a beautiful, curvaceous bow wave and leaving an impressive wake foaming behind her. The crescent shaped sweep of the river astern, the white, glistening turbulence from our prop and our red duster fluttering free, made a striking picture — and of course we had a slide to prove it. In fact we took many views in order to convince the sceptics among our family and friends, but, how a vast expanse of sky and water plus a red flag could prove we conquered the Trent escapes me now — but it seemed logical at the time.

A deepening, blushing sun lay astern as we drew into Torksey, where we tied up and waited for the lock-keeper to let us into the Fossdyke Navigation. While Alec sought him, I lazed on deck and fed a group of meringue-white swans floating gently on a strawberry-pink canal. They were beautiful to watch in the lengthening shadows and while I was relaxing in the peacefulness of journey's end, my thoughts progressed further along the mighty river to Newark. I had often strolled over a five-arched bridge there to gaze up at the remains of a 12th century grey stone castle rising sheer from the river bank. And then on to Nottingham, the city of lace, hosiery, cricket at Trent Bridge, the Goose Fair and Robin Hood fame. I knew them well, for, when Colin and I were reunited, we lived in Nottinghamshire, went to test matches, walked in Sherwood Forest and visited the infamous Nottingham Castle.

Having played the role of Will Scarlett in an operetta at Auckland Town Hall, I had a special interest in Robin Hood and his merry band. At the time I was a plump, gym-slipped, ginger-haired pupil of Auckland Girls' Grammar School and one rehearsal in particular remains in my memory. Miss Johnston, our strict, rather severe-looking headmistress was watching from the front row of the stalls and I was practising my big scene — Will Scarlett awaiting his execution in a cell deep in Nottingham Castle. My only prop was a low wooden stool and I, really acting the part, sat legs akimbo, leaning dejectedly on one knee singing a farewell lament. It wasn't easy in that position and I thought that I had done rather well. However, instead of praising me, as I expected, 'Johnny' rose, came forward, beckoned me to the front of the stage and whispered, 'Do be careful Doris. I can see your bloomers!'

Of course it was, as they say 'alright on the night' and my performance nearly moved ME to tears! In one scene I wielded a long wooden sword. Painted silver by my Mum, it looked most realistic — until during a fierce fight with the wicked Sheriff when it broke in half!

Poetic justice caught up with Johnny later — in morning assembly. Following an inflexible routine, the whole school lined up soldier-like in the big hall and when all was quiet and orderly, the assistant head tinkled a bell to summon Johnny from her study at the rear. As she strode purposefully along our port side I could hear titters coming from the girls. Getting louder, they travelled along with her until a mistress stopped her in her tracks, whispered in her ear and directed her into a side cloakroom. She had walked the whole length of the hall with her clothes nicely tucked into the back of her bloomers! Johnny emerged erect and straight-faced, mounted the platform, and, as if nothing untoward had happened, took prayers.

Alec jumping back on board startled me and soon broke up my schoolgirl recollections with the news that it was not journey's end. *Salidha*, hungry and parched, had to be refuelled and watered before we could act on the lock-keeper's advice and sail on to Saxilby, where, he assured us, a good meal would await us. As all the local shops were closed, this seemed a sensible course to follow, but time passed by, as it tends to do on the canals, and a sign stating 'FOOD' did not loom on our starboard bow until nearly eight o'clock. *Salidha* was swiftly moored and we changed in double quick time. I could have eaten anything; however, 'anything' proved to be a delicious four-course dinner which we demolished at speed, catching up and passing all the other diners who had started before us. Wending our way across a field of ghostly cows back to *Salidha*

in a happy state of contented fullness, we anticipated a pleasant sail to Lincoln next day. No temperamental rivers, just a good old canal trip, relaxing and restoring to the soul.

Famous last words of course, because during the night, the wind freshened causing Alec to be woken up by *Salidha* bumping about a bit and me, in turn, to be roused by Alec bumping about a lot trying to make her secure!

Next morning the wind was exulting in its favourite pastime, blowing like hell and being a nuisance to all boaters! Because we were on a canal, this did not worry us unduly, and after stopping in Saxilby, we pointed *Salidha* into the wind towards Lincoln. For a short while cars left us standing as the A57 ran alongside the canal, then at a place called Fiddlers Elbow, we caught our first glimpse of the magnificent Lincoln Cathedral. En route to Louth by car I had admired it many times, but never before from a boat. High canal banks tended to obscure an extensive flat landscape of indeterminate horizon, and the cathedral, raised high on a misty hill in the far distance, gave an impression of being suspended from overhanging clouds — only the superb triple towers being visible seemingly without any means of support. Thinly veiled and mysteriously indistinct, it was like seeing a vision — a miracle almost, so suddenly had it appeared. An unconfined Monet canvas lay spread before my incredulous eyes and I understood why so many artists sought to capture the cathedral's sublime proportions. Among a host of angelic voices (the sopranos of the Huddesfield Choral Society) I had sung in some of these mighty, echoing edifices, and during a few notable moving performances had felt their strong, inspirational power.

My eyes were drawn again and again to its ethereal presence which progressively became more tangible and earthly as we eagerly pressed towards the famous Brayford Pool. From there an enchanting city would later draw us up through narrow winding lanes to the top of a lime stone ridge on which this wonderful act of faith, in the form of one of England's finest cathedrals, stands.

As we passed the well-known Lincoln racecourse, fringed by tossing trees and bobbing pleasure craft, I imagined the busy scene on race-day; but our attention was soon focused on a lift bridge which, aided by an operator on shore, we were soon to negotiate. The bridge was occupying its normal closed position to allow cars and pedestrians across and because an ever-strengthening wind was presenting steering difficulties, we decided to tie up while Alec wandered over to arrange our passage. Upon his return I was informed that, when ready, I should give a hearty blast on *Salidha*'s horn and, 'Bob's your uncle' the bridge would rise and allow us through.

We cast off the ropes (our undoing in more ways than one!) and gleefully blew our horn, noting the usual startled looks from passers-by and other interested spectators. Expectantly and impatiently we waited for the bridge to lift.

'Open the bloody thing, then,' muttered Alec under his breath.

By now, the nuisance wind had seized a golden opportunity to blow us well away from the security of the wall.

'What's the silly bugger doing?' asked Alec rather more audibly.

Just then the 'bloody thing' began to lift — and just after, it stopped!

'CHRIST!' ejaculated Alec, 'He's going to let that bloody "dolly bird" over first.'

Sure enough, a smart young thing was coming from work and making for the bridge.

'JESUS!' said Alec, expressively.

I could have pointed out that she didn't look a bit like Jesus, but *Salidha* was by now a swirling Waltzing Matilda accompanied by bursts of forward and reverse to prevent her hitting the blasted bridge — and he wasn't in jocular mood. Alec, on the horn, was blowing like a demented motorist in a traffic jam and saying all sorts of complimentary things about the chap in the shed and the 'bird' on the bridge!

She tripped over without giving us a second glance and at last the obstruction began to rise. By this time *Salidha* was stern first onto it and, as there was no alternative, we sailed through backwards. My efforts to appear casual and add normality to this unusual tactic were completely belied by Alec who was swearing like a trooper, wild both in aspect and temper! The Lincoln swans became extremely curious about us during these unrehearsed gyrations, in which we could have, if effectively choreographed, included them in a gala performance of Swan lake!

After we had recovered from this morale-destroying episode, we took time off to admire our surroundings. This was more like it! We were secured at the edge of a large lake, which, flanked by old warehouses, commercial buildings, timber yards and many varied pleasure craft, presented a fascinating scene full of colour, activity and variety. Further along was the famous Glory Hole which consisted of a black and white half-timbered building astride High Bridge; inaptly named we thought, as it looked extremely low from *Salidha*'s point of view. We had had endless discussions with regard to going through the Glory Hole and I am sorry to relate that we, (self confidence sapped by the lift bridge incident) chickened out!

My sciatica was now a nagging reality which brought discomfort at every step, but I managed to hobble as far as the co-op shop, where I bought a new raincoat 'for my pains'. This didn't do my pains any good at all, and I became further concerned about my right eye which was feeling distinctly 'funny'. I kept telling Alec that there was positively something in it and, as he prodded and poked around, there certainly was!

Drayford Pool harboured us peacefully all that day and part of the next, and then, with the return trip down the Trent uppermost in our minds, we reluctantly turned *Salidha*'s back on the unviolated Glory Hole ready for our return to Torksey. The wind had dropped somewhat as we left Lincoln, and as well as enjoying the sights, we also managed (owing to the complete absence of 'dolly birds') to sail bows first through the lift bridge. Because of a very swollen eyelid, I was scanning the landscape through one and a half eyes, and had the exotic Alexander been perched upon my shoulder, I could have, sciatic limp assisting, easily outshone Robert Newton's and Brian's performances as Long John Silver.

Some navigable drains in this area had been highly recommended to us, especially one ominously named Catchwater Drain; but fearful of tempting fate by taking *Salidha* down a 'drain', we passed its entrance and sailed into the late afternoon to seek a night's mooring. Our speed automatically slackened at the sight of some boats queuing for opening time at the Pye Wipe Inn and we joined on astern of a handsome converted coastal lifeboat — not a passenger ship type like *Salidha*, but the real thing, steel hull and beautifully turned out. The proud owner was delighted to conduct two envious visitors around and would only allow us to leave when we had promised to join him and his wife at the inn later that evening.

The Pye Wipe Inn was no ordinary pub, for although isolated, appetising meals and a Saturday dance made it very popular indeed; consequently careering cars arrived from far and near, bringing people mostly much younger than us to transform our carefully selected 'quiet canal pub' into a seething mass of thirsty, noisy, smoking humanity. An atmosphere which caused my protesting eye to discharge as I shrank self-consciously in a corner, a concealing handkerchief pressed upon it, trying to ignore the continuous throbbing. But after a couple of gin-laced tonics, I renamed the place 'Eye Wipe Inn' and felt much better!

You might conclude from the number of public houses frequented that we are topers of the first order; the opposite is true, hence the need to redress this abstinence when on holiday. Owing to my painful condition, Alec's untuneful snores, and the nearness of a busy railway line, I spent an uncomfortable, restless night from which I awoke with an eye completely matted shut.

'I can't open my eye,' I cried, prodding Alec, who also opened one eye, said 'Ugh?' and turned over.

'No joy there,' I thought, groping resignedly for the kettle.

One bleary blinker discerned that it was early — hardly seven — but in order to catch the tide we had to lock out into the Trent before nine; so when Alec opened both eyes and focused them on the clock, he shot, jet propelled from his bunk and then I had to get dressed, bathe my eye and have breakfast all in the space of about ten minutes! Depressed and overtired, although the eye seemed less painful, I was especially thankful for another perfect day which allowed our sail down the Trent to be uneventful — except for one moment of stupefying anxiety at — where else? — Keadby Lock!

Again as we were nearing the entrance, history repeated itself and another craft lay ready to lock out. We had to perform our circuitous course once again and, without a thought for the fast ebbing tide, I executed a lovely wide sweep to line her up for our second approach. Alec, lookout in the bows, suddenly threw his arms pleadingly skywards and cried out in a loud voice, 'CHRIST!' Then, eyes glaring from an agonisingly distorted face, he began pointing vigorously down into the depths as if they contained a whale or some other phenomena. I was badly shaken to learn that this expressive display was a natural reaction to his horror when he saw the muddy river bed just beneath *Salidha*. We had avoided complete and utter disaster by inches!

Although unnerved by our narrow escape, we left the lock entrance and *Salidha* unscarred, and when the gates shuddered together to enclose us safely in the lock, it was quite a moment. However, despite my overwhelming sense of relief, reaction to our near miss soon set in, and for the first time in my life, I ascended a lock ensconced on a fast rising toilet!

The mood on *Salidha* was one of great jubilation, and at lunchtime, just dying for an opportunity to share our adventures, Alec and I (myself now fully-sighted) linked excitedly towards the Friendship for a well-deserved celebratory drink. This time our victim was chosen well, for he was Vincent Sissons of the *Warsop Guardian* and author of the navigational chart which had assisted our near-shipwreck on the Trent. A wholly-satisfying finale to our voyage was played out. A gay rondo of boating stories linked by drinking episodes, ending in an animated coda of hearty hand-shaking and parting good wishes, sending us light-heartedly back to *Salidha*.

Not surprisingly, a short encore proved to be something of an anti-climax when Dave, Penny and a friend met us at Thorne, where they listened in rapt disbelief to an improbable libretto dramatically delivered by a hero and heroine in the form of a highly embellished operatic duet.

From Thorne we sailed for Castleford again, managing to spend one heat-soaked day near Bramwith Lock where we tied up well away from some shading trees and allowed the uninterrupted comfort of a blazing sun to blanket us. Our resting place was remote and on this, our last day, we donned sunbathing gear for the first time and spent a thoroughly lazy, immobile afternoon reminiscing over an unforgettable fortnight.

Active bees buzzed contentedly and the water shone with an attractive lambency which brought the occasional dipping swallow and darting insect to its surface, where a silent, warming *Salidha* gently rocked two reclining mortals who had found peace at last!

Earlier, I presented you with an itinerary of what you could expect should you be foolhardy enough to join *Salidha* for a holiday cruise up the River Trent; however, if you possess exceptional powers of endurance, Messrs Brian and Mabel of *Adagio*, offer a very adventurous brochure of events. An experienced company — they have negotiated the Trent no less than three times — and I propose to join all three voyages together for your edification and disbelief.

First of all, your rather cramped craft will be absolutely ship-shape, for as you already know, Brian is especially particular about his boat. So, you can confidently expect *Adagio* to be freshly painted, sporting a new flag and even the boat hook will be silvered in your honour! The fact that you may arrive at Bingley at eleven in the morning and not depart until three in the afternoon need not distress you; just put it down to Brian doing a few last minute jobs which take four hours!

Progress may be slow even by canal standards. For no apparent reason (for Alexander is firmly secured) you will take two dragging hours to descend the Five Rise Locks and it is quite on the cards that you may not arrive at Hurst Mill Lock, a few miles from your starting point, until seven p.m. Lounge back gratefully after a tasty meal prepared by Mabel, (enthroned on the toilet remember) to absorb your favourite radio programme, and the ancient set may well go up in smoke! But never mind — the fact that you have missed both the news and the weather cannot matter one jot because you already know that it is helluva windy, helluva cold and bloody-well raining! And, just when you are in dire need of a compensating hot drink, the calor gas will run out!

Brian will then attempt to dispose of the ship's cook by throwing a rope which will curl around her neck, the knot hitting her viciously on the side of her face; then, not having succeeded in his objective, will later toss the cat to her instructing it to scratch her severely on the chest. Finding that he has not immobilised her completely, his next stratagem requires her to fetch some water so that she can fall when re-embarking and badly twist her ankle!

Given a lot of luck you may progress as far as Office Lock, Leeds, and spend a sleepless night listening to the noisy rattling trains and the reverberating station loudspeaker, until, crazed and no longer responsible, you contemplate stealing from your bunk to find the female belonging to the voice with a view to shoving a boat hook down her throat!

At the first electric lock the lights are, without doubt, going to be on red. Brian will prove that he never panics, steering in concentric circles and then entering while they are still on red. His next duty will be to raise the lock-keeper (intent on his cricket) and Mabel, Paul, Simon and you presumably, will also abandon ship to have a look around. As a result, *Adagio*, manned by two dogs, one cat and a parrot will begin to descend on its own and there will follow a mad scramble of arms, legs and bodies falling on top of the already fast-disappearing boat.

Passing the power station, Mabel is sure to amuse you with the 'over-laden coal barge' story and later your hair may turn prematurely grey, when, passing a large Esso tanker about one hundred and thirty feet long, it will become obvious that this particular bend cannot possibly accommodate both of you — and you might pray for *Adagio* to sprout legs on this occasion!

Should you survive all this you could actually arrive at Keadby and end up at the Friendship Inn, watching Alexander get besotted, and if you've any sense at all will get blind drunk yourself.

Because you are bound to be suffering from a hangover and past caring anyway, you are not likely to notice that the smoke from Keadby Power Station is maintaining its usual right angled position; but don't worry, the firm of Brian and Mabel do not wreck their boats, because they cannot possibly afford a new one.

By the way, Brian has, by now, had a flaming row with our favourite lock-keeper and once he's shoved you out into the Trent it will be futile to attempt to return.

When you do eventually lock out, a squatting Mabel will be busy preparing breakfast and she is bound to be surprised, upon glancing through the window, to find herself below water. Not deterred, (for as you know SHE never panics) Mabel will continue making her succulent bacon butties and handing them out to the crew above water. But you might be mildly surprised when you prise open your 'butty' inquiringly, to have the bacon whipped out by a Force Seven gale, leaving you open mouthed with only a soggy bread and butter butty to shove in!

Adagio is only a small boat and even if Brian wears his Captain's hat, the enormous waves might cause you some concern, and your face could possibly match Alexander's, which normally white, (or pink when pleased), has now turned green!

He must be regretting all the Bristol Cream Sherry downed at the Friendship Inn the night before, while you must be regretting any nourishment you've taken during the last twenty-four hours.

Look up, because by now the air-sea rescue 'chopper' is covering you, which could mean that things are distinctly dodgy and you might check on the number of life jackets on board, bearing in mind of course, that parrots, dogs and cats come first! But you will finally make it to Cromwell Lock and spend a happy time bailing out and drying your wet clothes and bedding.

At this point you may decide to leave *Adagio* and its entourage

— that is, if you're smart! Intrepid *Adagio*, however, will press on and reach as far as Nottingham, (don't ask me how) and her resilient crew will relish an imbibing visit to a friendly houseboat and stay out extremely late. On his return to *Adagio*, Brian, trying to erect a hood over the cockpit, will slip off the boat and crack his leg on an iron stanchion, fall betwixt boat and jetty and get a blinding pain in the process — wherever his 'process' is! After this he will be seen hopping about with a broom under his arm and, I hope, Alexander on his shoulder to complete the picture!

Don't forget that I have condensed three holidays into one; however, even divided by three, Brian and Mabel are certainly gluttons for punishment and you must admire their guts! What about your guts? Are you still on board?

If so, travel up the Soar Navigation with them and you will come to a very small lock which only rises one foot. Brian will consider its operation to be as easy as falling out of bed. A prophetic thought, for here he is to twist his ankle and from that day forth will steer with one foot submerged in a bucket of water. Although this injury causes him excruciating pain, he will remain steadfast in his determination to sail home at the helm of *Adagio*.

On the return journey they'll have to 'stand off' Keadby for a tanker emerging and Brian will have issued strict orders that *Adagio* must enter the lock looking shipshape with all crew members at their stations — especially Simon, as the keyman forward, holding a boathook at the ready. Coming up against the tide, Brian squares his shoulders and straightens his cap, every inch the skipper at the helm. The bows enter nicely enough, but the tidal flow catches the stern and swings her towards the lock side.

'Fend off astern,' shouts Brian, nautical and competent.

The only thing available astern is the mop, so *Adagio* enters with Simon at attention, boathook likewise, Brian head erect, practically saluting, and Mabel, shaking and giggling astern — fending off with — the mop!

Brian's discomfort will steadily worsen and it will become obvious that his injury is much more serious than a sprain.

Consequently, when they reach Leeds, Mabel will take pity on her spouse advising him to remain on board and take it easy.

'All you will have to do is sit on deck and catch the ropes,' she says.

Now, Mabel is not all that accurate with ropes and promptly heaves one which lands miles away from the boat and Brian; he gets up to fetch a boathook, stands on the mop handle, which rolls over the deck and pitches him into the lock.

'This is the end!' he thinks, as the succulent waters of Leeds Lock envelope him.

Upon surfacing he is capless and, as nothing is more important than that cap, he scans the water, sees his symbol of authority bobbing on the surface and swims towards it.

'Are you alright darling?' calls Mabel.

'Darling's' reply is unrepeatable but very edifying to a group of sea scouts who have left their activities to watch.

Mabel is, for once, in a panic and very grateful to the man who climbs down a ladder to heave Brian out. With water running out of his pockets and his cap back on his head shrinking visibly, (his cap I mean) he glares at the gaping scouts defying them to comment!

When they return home, Brian, crippled and walking with a stick, suffers a fortnight's agony before consulting his doctor, who subsequently despatches him for an x-ray. Later, at the hospital, he regards Brian quizzically through his half-glasses and informs him that he has a fractured foot. Then he tears him off a strip for neglecting it so long.

'BOATING!' he exclaims. 'You're not very good at it are you?'

Brian, momentarily abashed, mumbles something about unusual circumstances.

'You won't be going again will you?' ...

'Of course,' bristles Brian, 'It's my own boat ...'

'OH CHRIST!' interrupts his doctor, hands up in despair. 'I can bloody well expect you again!'

In addition to Brian being laid up, you will not be surprised to learn that *Adagio* was eventually lifted from the canal and also laid up in the front garden of a house high on a hill at Haworth. Her outboard motor and fittings were removed to a position of safety within a large garage, while she patiently awaited a major overhaul. Neither do I expect you to express amazement at the news that Mabel was also laid up, having her own major overhaul in hospital.

The season of the year was Autumn and the day just prior to bonfire night when Brian, making his weary way home from work, called at his local filling station. As he disinterestedly watched the gallons clocking up, he was startled back to awareness by the nearby wail of an air raid siren which summons the Haworth Volunteer Fire Service into action. The fire station, being situated opposite enabled Brian to cease watching the petrol gauge and start gauging the efficiency of the volunteers.

A flurry of cars and bicycles enlivened the scene and within two minutes the station was expelling one of its engines manned by breathless, clinging fire-fighters, and, as they seemed to be travelling in his direction, he tagged along behind.

As they rattled in convoy over the cobbled road, Brian commiserated in his mind with the victims of the fire, scanned the horizon for signs of smoke and flames and waited for the now fast-moving fire appliance to turn off so that he could carry on home, grab some tea, and visit Mabel in hospital. As the engine climbed the hill up which he journeyed every evening, Brian did not worry, for there were numerous routes which it could follow and even when they skidded around a very familiar corner, he was not unduly anxious, for his thoughts already had the local fish and chip shop ablaze! However, uneasiness did niggle a bit when they passed the 'chippy' which was not even 'frying tonight'. When the fire-engine screeched around the bottom of Hill Street, fear gripped him in sudden icy fingers — although he still reassured himself by assuming catastrophe for some unsuspecting neighbour. Tension and dread mounted as they climbed the hill and breaking-point was reached when the engine slewed to an ear-piercing stop outside his own house, where bonfire night celebrations were in full swing. Brian's flaming garage illuminated the whole area, while *Adagio*'s fittings, put there for safe-keeping, added fuel to the fire!

Had the lads been letting off a premature firework or two? Had they been having a crafty fag? A can of petrol certainly helped the pyrotechnics to get going with a bang and *Adagio* was indeed lucky to be situated in the garden or her days would have ended in a blaze of glory!

Mabel was kept in complete ignorance of the traumatic happenings at home, because Brian, considerate at last of her welfare, realised that even her amazing constitution would not have survived the shock. So Mabel and Hill House survived, and also *Adagio*, but bereft of all her parts which were consumed in the conflagration.

Maybe their exploits will make them as famous as the Bronte family who also lived on a hillside in Haworth. And perhaps, on a black, ominous, winter's night the ghost of Heathcliffe will meet Brian — unkempt, stumbling and desperate, searching the bleak rain soaked moors, crying out above a biting, howling wind, 'A . . . lex! A . . . lex!'

CHAPTER SEVEN

*And Noah he often said to his wife when he sat down to
dine, 'I don't care where the water goes if it doesn't get
into the wine.'*

G. K. Chesterton

During the winter which took 1972 into 1973 we began to
channel our thoughts along narrow canals and consequently
to narrower boats. Conversations with the owners of these
picturesque craft had whetted our appetites for waterways which
were inaccessible because of *Salidha*'s too ample beam. You may well
imagine that, after all our nerve-racking experiences, any normal
couple would have given up, but in our abnormality the opposite
was true, as we dreamed of voyaging to magical places such as
Stratford of the Bard, Llangollen of the Eisteddfods, Oxford of the
dreaming spires, and even London of the Queen! All we needed was
a narrower boat and all that stood in our way was money — or rather
the lack of it! Our finances underwent close scrutiny and we wrestled
with unpractised additions, subtractions and percentages until our
brains became as addled as our calculations. Even if our flagrant
betrayal and subsequent sale of *Salidha* provided eight hundred
pounds, most narrow boats cost three thousand or over. Short of
printing our own bank notes or doing a 'Bonny and Clyde', there
seemed to be little hope of realising our latest ambition.

By now we had become regular readers of a boating magazine
Waterways World, and I spotted an advertisement in which

Holidays Afloat of Market Drayton offered a thirty foot, ex-hire, narrow boat, *Drayton Duke* for sale at the seemingly reasonable price of one thousand six hundred pounds. Consequently, a resigned Alec, peace assured only if he telephoned the company, reluctantly made enquiries, and in the interest of a quiet life, found himself motoring south to Shropshire early the following Sunday morning.

Every mile I was forcibly reminded by him that we couldn't afford the boat and weren't going to buy it; but this resolve weakened after our arrival and Alec's subsequent conversation with Harry Machin, a former speedway rider and owner of the boatyard. Harry spoke in short, sharp bursts of the 'throttle' (just like a bike warming up I thought) as he gave us the *Duke's* pedigree. Soon we found ourselves hopping aboard an un-aristocratic but pleasant craft and, in company with quiet-spoken Alan, the boatyard engineer, gliding down the cut for a demonstration. Both Alec and I took turns at the wheel, found the narrow bridges disconcerting at first, but were surprised and delighted by the boat's easy handling. Unfair pressure was then brought to bear on a procrastinating Alec, until he found himself trying to negotiate a deal with an obdurate Harry Machin, who wouldn't allow any reduction in price.

We then found ourselves travelling speedily northwards to Yorkshire, Alec having stood firm, Harry having stood firm, and Doris feeling intuitively that she would win in the end. Her instincts proved to be correct when, much later that evening, a slightly bemused Alec found himself dialling Harry's private number to tell him we would like to buy his *Duke*.

We were now the owners of one large bungalow, two cars, two boats, various tellys, numerous radios, one grand piano and very little money! Harry, now highly co-operative, agreed on a deposit and settlement was to follow when we sold *Salidha*. Our Nationwide Building Society account (absolutely not to be touched!) was to pay in part, and a bank loan (definitely not to be entertained!) would make up the balance.

Feelings of regret and misgiving accompanied *Salidha's* rather cursory clean up prior to offering her for sale at eight hundred pounds. We had survived many trials together and parting was not going to be easy, so I was pleased when we negotiated an extra-ordinarily quick sale within a week and before we could have any serious second thoughts.

Having broken from our first love, we turned fickle minds and energies to our present acquisition and the all important choice of a new name. Conjecture was endless! *Coppelia*, was not regarded as a serious suggestion; with a view to changing *Duke's* sex, *Florence*, after my mother and *Emily*, after Alec's mother were considered; *Aotearoa*, (Land of the Long White Cloud) the Maoris poetic description of New Zealand, was thought too long and without relevance; *Kiwi*, was a hot favourite; *Tiki*, a close second and *Maori*, won the day. Our dream had been for a traditional narrow boat and *Maori* was a far cry from this but she was what we could, or couldn't afford, (according to how you looked at it) and now we planned an Easter visit to Market Drayton to repaint and re-christen her.

Subsequently, on Good Friday, two old and two young Coppells left Huddersfield laden with victuals, tins of undercoat, gloss and bitumastic paint, various brushes, putty, emery paper, rags, turps, old clothes, sleeping bags, pillows, hot water bottles and all the paraphernalia needed for a long working weekend. Penny, with impeccable timing, was swotting for her exams and excused from painting, but was made responsible for meals.

Harry Machin had already lifted *Maori* from the canal and painted her hull black to above the water line; at the same time he had replaced some rotten wood in the galley roof and now she floated in a spacious basin awaiting the Coppell onslaught. Many hours were spent sketching and experimenting with colours before I confirmed a complete lack of imagination by choosing a yellow superstructure above a black hull which was to be enlivened by brilliant red rubbing strakes. How eagerly we looked forward to that holiday weekend and our labour of love in the bright Easter sunshine! Did I say sunshine? Three bitterly cold days kept us dashing in and out between icy squalls to whip on a bit of paint — which the rain whipped smartly off again. Without hindrance, this wind came directly from the Arctic and carried everything except Eskimos, polar bears and penguins! How I longed to be of school age, taking my 'O' levels and stinking hot in the cabin by the calor gas fire!

'It's alright for you,' we would complain to Penny when she pressed her nose out of shape to gaze at three miserable bodies busily painting with frostbitten fingers — holding brushes of course! The nature of our work would not allow us great mobility, but an active *Maori* kept swaying like a poi dancer, making life difficult and painting a straight line impossible. We persevered though, and in spite of the weather's conspiracy against us, managed to persuade some paint to stick, albeit mainly to us.

On the evening of our first frustrating day, all hands adjourned to the local pub where we thawed by a blazing coal fire, drowned our sorrows, (mine in brandy) and felt better. On the second and third nights we continued the therapy — this being the only way to cloud the discomforts of each day and give us the will to continue.

Nevertheless, by Monday, *Maori*, against all odds, was actually beginning to change colour and resemble the badly drawn boat in my sketch. The yellow had dribbled to a few unlikely places and, here and there, the rain had created an unusual stippled effect; but we tried not to dwell on these depressing details. The lengthsman, whose house overlooked us from the opposite bank, shouted to ask how we were getting on. He had been monitoring our efforts — from inside his warm abode of course.

'It's beginning to look nice,' he called. 'I don't know how you've done it in this weather.'

HE didn't know!!!

That evening we crossed over to his side of the canal to view *Maori* from a distance and he was absolutely right, she did look nice from THERE! This revelation lightened our spirits, but we still felt an overwhelming need to lubricate our aching joints at the pub, and later, as three of us groaned into the succour of our sleeping bags, I prayed for a fine Tuesday morning to allow her and us to be finished off!

Tuesday, I will state guardedly, was reasonable. After three days of diabolical weather, ordinary awful weather becomes reasonable. To complete *Maori*'s transformation we needed non-slip paint for her roof-top and deck, but neither Harry nor nearby Ladyline stocked the colour we'd chosen. Refusing to be thwarted at the last, we agreed to act on Ladyline's advice and use undercoat laced with silver sand, but a miscalculated guess as to proportions required, resulted in a roof coated with difficult-to-apply mushroom, non-drip sludge! The finish, which resembled extremely abrasive sandpaper, was certainly non-slip and completely dispelled any ideas I might have nurtured of a reclining, bikinied, sunbathing body; but its appearance when dry was surprisingly acceptable.

Cheesed off, would describe our general state at low noon; flagging, the state of our remaining lettuce and salad; slightly sweating, the cold meat we consumed along with it; soggily limp, the tinned peaches and Carnation Milk which followed and, for once, we were greatly relieved to pack up and anticipate the far-away comforts of home. When we had filled all Harry's empty dustbins, we writhed and grunted into our rested car and, as Alec turned his back on our handiwork, I glanced over my shoulder at a brightly-decorated *Maori*, ready and restless for new hunting grounds, and thought that perhaps our labours had been worthwhile after all. Viewed in swiftly lengthening retrospect, the discomforts of the weekend began to diminish and, as the lengthsman had said, from a reasonable distance *Maori* did 'look nice'.

Alec, now recovering and relaxed at the wheel, seemed quite happy with our purchase; his one petty reservation being with regard to the toilet.

'I like *Maori*,' he kept saying on our homeward way, 'But how the hell am I going to manage with that toilet?' Or, out of the blue after a long silence — 'I wish that bloody toilet was bigger!'

What he really referred to was not, of course, the toilet itself, but the surrounding space. Being short-legged and female, it presented not too many problems, except to my rather well endowed upper half when standing, but for Alec, tall, boasting a corporation and male, lack of space was a decided drawback. A lengthy, mile-consuming discussion revealed that, in spite of a table hanging on the wall opposite the toilet, the 'standing up' operation was possible, but lack of knee-room when ensconced for a prolonged sitting, became for Alec quite problematical.

Many facetious, constipatory suggestions were volunteered, such as, perching garden-gnome-like with knees well up under the chin; or standing 'S' shaped, posterior hovering, for accurate aiming; but the favourite was, that when Alec needed to 'go', everyone else would abandon ship while he closed the curtains, opened the toilet door, sat side-saddle with unlimited knee-room and 'Hey Ho Silver!', all would be well! I agreed wholeheartedly with this procedure, especially on abandoning ship, for during the period when Alec was 'going', the only place bearable then and for some time afterwards, would be ashore.

Going to the toilet can become an embarrassing act if friends are on board. Provided the radio is belting full blast, a contented, thoughtful, undisturbed sitting can be sustained; but if everyone is restfully reading at some quiet mooring, the slightest tinkle emulates Niagara Falls and your temperature rises steadily to hot, sweaty heights as you picture them all sitting listening. I usually try to coincide my calls with extra loud music or a turned-up newscaster shouting the news; but if this proves impossible, sit slightly askew — this fools everybody and sets them, like you, wondering! Visitors have their embarrassing moments too. Having had the mysteries of the pumping system explained to them, they usually succeed in emptying a gruesome toilet-full into the boat, and we have to come to their rescue. This sort of thing either cements friendships or assists their termination, while, as far as husband and wife are concerned, it does little or nothing for romance or mystery!

With *Maori's* log to consult, I can state with certainty, that our first real trip in her began on Saturday the twelfth of May, 1973. She was still at her home town, Market Drayton, because we had decided to explore that area and in particular the Shropshire Union and Llangollen canals. A two-day initiation cruise was planned and joining the crew for the first time were Rodney, my nephew from New Zealand and his wife, Chris, then resident in Wales. Choosing to head south towards Tyrley Locks, we moved along in a very leisurely manner and were delighted at our easy negotiation of the narrow locks in comparison to the more difficult broad ones; no tying up, no threshing water bouncing you or your boat about, just a gentle, sedative uprising which at last, after three years, gave credence to Mr Kippax's idyllic description of peace and relaxation.

On our winding way a fresh, grassy bank sprinkled with yellow primroses, invited us to moor for a while. The boat behaved beautifully and our steady progress was so tranquil that it held, for us, a quality of benign unreality. This just wasn't our kind of boating at all and I attributed this agreeable change to the mythical, birdlike figures, known as Tikis, perched port and starboard upon *Maori*. According to Maori legend they bring good fortune and under their comforting spell we moved without one ripple of anxiety towards our destination and turning place at the Wharfe Inn on the Shebden Acqueduct. At this point I sincerely hoped that history would not repeat itself, as the embankment, one mile long and sixty feet high, caused great delays in the construction of the canal when, for a period of six years, it kept collapsing and refusing to hold water.

Dusk was fast disappearing into darkness when we drove our mooring pins home and secured *Maori* at this popular, spacious, tree-lined winding hole; therefore, we were not immediately aware of a large camping barge lying on the far side, nor of a pipe-smoking, bearded figure silhouetted astern, testing his engine with fierce bursts of the throttle. We were amazed to discern (once more through a sea of gloom) our bargeman friend of Banknewton fame, who, happy in solitude, and spiralling smoke-signals up into the cooling air, gave the appearance of a very contented character indeed. Competing with the pulsations from his throbbing engine, we held a noisy, disjointed conversation across the winding hole. Later we trailed, single file, through trees which had originally been planted to stabilize the banks, but now stabilized travellers along a well-trodden path to and from the Wharfe Inn where I remember being intrigued by the presence of a piano in the ladies' toilet. Appropriately, I couldn't resist having a tinkle (on the piano) and as it twanged its discordant displeasure, I realised the reason for its forced retirement to the 'loo'. Unfortunately, our bargeman did not join us for a pint and, much later, when, in inky blackness, we groped our way back on board, there wasn't a smoke signal in sight!

Our return journey was again unbelievably uneventful; that is if you can call sailing through Woodseaves Cutting uneventful! A deep, narrow, man-made canyon, spanned by high curved bridges and overgrown with lush vegetation thriving in a damp, shady, virtually undisturbed habitat, presented a fantastic location which inspired film director Rodney to leap off *Maori* brandishing his movie camera, and to prance along a squelching quagmire of a towpath to get a 'take' of us sailing towards him. *Maori* moved as slowly as Alec could allow, Chris and I sat bolt upright on the bows ready to salute, while Rodney staggered backwards, up to his ankles in mud, slipping and sliding over stones and roots of trees, trying to line up his uncontrollable camera. Against all odds he succeeded, and against all odds, the film was good — especially our giggling version of a pusser naval salute! Alec had trouble finding enough depth to pull in, but a triumphant Rodney eventually sloshed and dripped on board, shoes ruined, trousers likewise, but with camera and film intact. We made our still serene way back to Market Drayton, where we ended this incredibly placid voyage with reluctant farewells in the rain.

Because of the time consuming journey down the M6 Motorway every time we wished to sail *Maori*, we had, by now, scouted around for a temporary mooring nearer home but within striking distance of the Llangollen and Macclesfield Canals — both of which we were to explore for our annual holiday. Towards this end, on Spring Bank Holiday Friday, an excited party arrived at Market Drayton to move *Maori* to her new mooring at Bartington Wharf on the Trent and Mersey Canal and, as a diversion on our way, we were hoping to whet our appetites with a short intrusion into the beautiful Llangollen Canal.

Alec, Stan, Elsie and I were on board as we moved along a wide waterway flanked by 'truly rural' vistas and the new feeling of terrific relaxation was present once again. So much so, that Elsie and Stan wondered if they were on the right boat for they were not, when in our company, accustomed to such serenity of progress.

An attempt to raise some excitement by making ghostly noises through a supposedly haunted wooded section, met with no response, so, regretfully, I cannot record what our reaction to a real psychic manifestation would have been. However, this easy, soporific sail was to be savoured, for soon Adderley Locks, five in number, livened us up ready for later activity at Audlem, where there were fifteen!

Unfortunately we didn't have time to become closely acquainted with Audlem and had to settle for a quick shopping expedition to buy much-needed victuals and a large, delicious, moustache-encrusting icecream apiece. The reason for our haste was a pre-arranged rendezvous with Elsie's sister Eleanor and her husband John at Nantwich Basin. As the boat was already full to overflowing with four bodies, bedding and provisions, I reflected on the interesting effect that two more, plus their attendant clobber, might have!

Maori was built to accommodate only four people in reasonable discomfort, there being the 'cuddy' in the sharp end which sleeps two and allows only toes to make contact, and a narrow central cabin with two long seats facing each other which become beds at night. Normally, during the day, all items of luggage were shoved into the cuddy out of the way, but at bedtime, these had to be transferred to the galley. However, on this cramped cruise, Alec and I were going to sleep in the galley, where, in an emergency, a locker pulls out to serve as a double bed. This effectively fills the galley and makes access to the toilet hazardous both for the occupiers and any would-be night prowler trying to find relief, probably via our bed!

John, a naturally light sleeper, is perpetually complaining that he never sleeps; then stating ambiguously, that when he does, someone drops a pin and wakes him up! In order to contain this restless spirit, he and Eleanor were allocated the cuddy, where, with heads far apart they could, if wakeful, play feet, and where, by closing an intervening door, we could isolate John from the general snore-up which reverberated through the cabin during the small hours.

I forgot to tell you, that after an eight-day conference, we had evolved a complicated system of juggling cars so that upon our arrival at a fixed destination, there would be a car waiting to fetch another car left at our last point of embarkation. So, when we moored at Nantwich, John's car whizzed back to Market Drayton to fetch Alec's car and escorted it to Hurleston Junction, which lies at the beginning of the Llangollen Canal. John's car then returned to remain at Nantwich, while *Maori*, bulging at the seams, pointed her red-streaked nose towards the famous Welsh Canal. We slipped ropes at quarter past eight and, accompanied by birdsong at eventide, took our ease during a warm, calmative sail to lock into the Llangollen Canal at half past nine, having taken well over an hour for a journey which takes minutes by car. John observed that he didn't think that he could stand the pace, but admitted to enjoying his first 'ride' on *Maori*. Alec, however, was only just recovering from his recent unnerving ride with John, who tends to press hard down on the accelerator, seems surprised when he arrives at a junction and then rams the brake pedal through the floor to avoid hitching onto the car in front!

A brilliant evening sky boded well for the next day's cruising as we moored a short way along the canal and well away from a traffic bridge so that John could not complain about noise disturbing his non-existent sleep. However, passengers or pedestrians who glanced over the bridge may have been startled by loud banging noises emitting from a sharply heeling boat during the fiasco which occurred when the ship's company decided to turn in. Mountains of luggage became airborne out of the cuddy to land on Elsie and Stan's bunks or on the floor of the cabin, where we all squatted in utter turmoil while Eleanor and John made up their beds, disrobed, searched out their sleeping attire from the jumble, pumped water to have a wash, attacked their molars and, under strict instructions, whether willing or not, visited the toilet and fought with our unusual plumbing arrangements. Then, to the accompaniment of oo's and ah's, while they struggled to wriggle into their sleeping bags and onto the bunks, (which John was already declaring totally impractical) Elsie and Stan repeated this retiring ritual, dumping everything in turn in the galley. When they were safely cocooned, one each side of the cabin, it was our turn to throw all the remaining gear back on top of them and attempt to extricate our bed. A locker chockablock with toolboxes, ropes, mooring-pins, paint tins, bottles and fenders, required several disc-displacing heaves to leave four inches' width of floor-space for us to perform our ceremonious bedtime ablutions and manoeuvre into our receptacles of repose.

The whole crew had been unanimous in their desire for an early night, but preparations lasting an hour and a half had pushed the minute and hour hands together at midnight. John kept shouting out asking when all the racket was going to stop so as he could do what he never does — sleep! But during that night the loudest noises of all issued from the cuddy, and unless Eleanor has a masculine snore, it must have been John. However, next morning he hotly denied sleeping at all, having been kept awake all night by the frustrated bellowing of a randy bull!

Alec and I were first up — we had to be — and, absenting ourselves from the heaving chaos of everyone rising on *Maori*, we strolled a short distance along the towpath into a world of unbelievable beauty. 'Morning had broken, like the first morning', heavy dew encrusting everything with diamond droplets, which the sun, already gloriously shining, had set blinking at its brightness, while extrovert songsters, eyes shaded among the leaves, voiced their joyous approval.

John, still harping on about his terrible night, could not grumble about the weather and was soon lying uncomfortably on our ultra-non-slip roof out of earshot of Eleanor and Elsie who talked nineteen to the dozen catching up on each other's news. Their pleasant chatter faded into the background as I withdrew, completely absorbed with the hundred and one things that make canals special for me: a fleeting effect of sky dropped into the water, the wind patterns on its surface, the shy creatures seeking cover at our approach and the ever-changing flora moving with the swish and swell of our wake. For once I had unlimited time to observe, and occasionally, just one small flower brought a great sense of wonder and humility to discover such perfection of thought.

Mind you, while I was admiring all these wonders, I noticed that, because of a freshening wind, an empty chair perched on top of the engine hatch looked in danger of being blown into the cut.

'Is that chair alright?' I shouted to Alec.

'It'll be O.K.,' he answered, just before it blew off and gurgled merrily down into the depths of Baddily Lock beneath his dis-believing gaze!

'Curse that bloody wind,' said Alec, (and did) while he waxed busy with the boathook.

John, reacting swiftly, jumped off onto the bank to steady *Maori* by hanging onto a hand rail along the roof and much swishing and prodding by Alec in the general direction of the sunken chair, caused her to rock gently away from the side. More violent stirring and poking moved her out much further and John stretched into a bridge between towpath and boat towards a fast approaching point of no return.

'Let go,' shouted Alec.

'I can't,' shouted John.

'Let go you silly bugger!' cried Alec, not realising that if John did, he would execute a neat header into the lock and if he didn't, would end up hanging from *Maori* with his feet dangling in the water. Luckily, someone on the bank acted, bringing John and *Maori* back to the towpath just in time; and just as Alec, who had been pushing on the boat hook, up-ended it to display a dripping nylon chair hanging on the end. Great jubilation followed but with an undercurrent of near-unintelligible mutterings from John about silly buggers fishing for chairs!

We lunched at Wrenbury, and here, the female members of the crew took part in a harmless conspiracy against their male counterparts. We thought that, for a change, when the meal had been eaten, we would make an excursion ashore to find a pub and leave the men to wash up; after all, we manned the boat in addition to doing the chores, so why shouldn't they man the galley occasionally! Consequently, three jokers looked more than a trifle nonplussed when we announced our intention and quite taken aback, when three little maids arose from the table and tripped off to the Cotton Arms for a quick one. Nevertheless, the clearing up had been completed by the time we returned, but the atmosphere was, I thought, unusually strained.

However, negotiating an old-type wooden lift bridge was soon to demand all our attention and Stan's and Alec's combined weights to raise the contraption high enough for us to pass underneath. It was quite unnerving to have a large, wobbling bridge poised above one, ready to crash down at any moment should the crew ashore mistime its descent; so I was much relieved when we emerged safely on the other side.

Wrenbury is a picturesque place, and the bridge reminded me of Van Gogh's painting, 'Bridge at Arles', which features a horse and wagon passing over a bright blue canal, the surface of which is disturbed by a busy group of gossiping women as they dip and rub their laundry near to a sunken vessel.

Our sky also, was as blue as Van Gogh's which made us regret all the more that time was advancing too quickly and our turning point must soon be reached. Although we longed to take *Maori* further on to savour the more spectacular reaches of this promising canal, we put about at Marbury Lock and sailed to my favourite mooring place, (which can be anywhere) a quiet, beautiful, secluded wooded stretch of water in the middle of nowhere.

John, Eleanor and I found no signs of civilisation as we took a peaceful stroll along the winding towpath through woods made mysterious and shadowy by the deepening sun and I hoped that the owl population wouldn't hoot all night and disturb John in his somnolence. An idyllic spot became less so as flies buzzed us and gnats made reconnaissance flights into my hair, while John, imitating

Alec's flexible windmills, declared that he was being eaten alive by mosquitoes!

On Monday the wood-pigeons cooed farewell as *Maori* got under way to return us to Hurleston Bridge, where, if you remember, Alec's placid car was patiently waiting. And while lunch was being prepared, it journeyed resignedly to pick up a less placid companion for a drive to Middlewich where John's protesting, screeching vehicle was deposited at our next port of call. Before we finally locked out of the Llangollen Canal, Alec's car was left at a garage close to Hurleston Bridge to await yet another collection.

Maori, rather disdainful of all this feverish rushing, made her unhurried passage towards the Middlewich Arm and was soon negotiating a rather awkward right turn beneath a bridge and easing along a straight stretch of glittering, cerulean waterway where many boats, all shapes and sizes formed a colourful guard of honour to an equally colourful visitor.

There are some lengths of canal which one journeys of necessity to get from A to B, and they bring little joy, but the Middlewich Arm boasts rolling meadows, a marvellous mooring high above the River Weaver, one village only, (but well worth a visit) and some spacious, eye-catching views of the Weaver Top Flash as one draws near to Middlewich.

John's car was waiting quietly for us there but soon changed back to its old erratic self as John swerved off to collect Alec's car, leaving those left on board to ponder on the possibility of dining out. Eleanor and John were to leave us 'before he collapsed from lack of sleep', so a farewell celebration seemed in order. After 'phoning the Golden Pheasant at Plumley, where they promised to try and fit us in if we turned up, we didn't turn up; for I remembered the Good Companions at Holmes Chapel where my cousin was once head-waiter and we decided to join up with J.B. Priestley's famous characters.

John, eagerly anticipating his soft, welcoming bed, was in good form, especially after a couple of drinks as we waited for our call to the dining room. After a third and fourth found us still waiting, we were relieved when the present head-waiter ushered our rather unstable party through the hunger-assuaging portals to consume a splendid dinner.

When Eleanor and John departed in their slightly merry car, the depleted party remaining on *Maori* expanded, took full breaths and rejoiced in the knowledge that the toilet was available during the night without disturbing the whole boat. In spite of the fact that John hadn't slept a wink and Eleanor's unusual sleeping position had given her a bad back, they had (they said) enjoyed their trip. But we hadn't entirely finished with them yet, for on reaching our final destination we were to summon John's car from the security of its garage for a last liaison with Alec's long suffering motor which would then return us home!

Our cruise from Middlewich to Bartington Wharfe was, once again, devoid of any major crises and very rewarding, for straight away the navigation wound its sinuous way up the lovely Dane Valley through parkland and arching trees and here Elsie borrowed my glasses — which Alec promptly knocked off her nose into the canal. This caused a slight disturbance during our smooth sail because Elsie became very upset; but while everybody was commiserating with HER, it occurred to me that I should be the one who was upset, as my glasses were lying virtually unrecoverable in the mud at the bottom of the cut!

There was great excitement when we met a horse-drawn hotel boat, which, while looking gay and picturesque, threatened to push us into the far bank and some soft, sucking mud there. *Maori* rocked violently as all hands rummaged for their cameras and raced to grab vantage points on an unstable craft which made focussing, in the short time available, impossible. The hotel was sailing from Lymm to Llangollen and I wondered if the man leading a resigned, docile horse, walked all the way!

There was more animation as we entered some wide silvery lagoons, frequented by many water fowl, fishermen, partly submerged skeletons of old wrecked hulls, and on this special day — our first canal heron. Displaying a magnificent wing span for our benefit, it became airborne on an extended circular flight which ended far away from *Maori* and her pointing, excited crew.

During this interesting sail we also watched a boat descend a lift! This unusual event happened at Anderton, where we arrived about noon and saw, for another first time, an absolutely amazing piece of engineering which has become recognised as one of the wonders of the waterways. We tripped, single file, along a narrow catwalk to find an already familiar operator whom we had met recently at Middlewich. We were privileged to receive a first hand demonstration and explanation of the controls.

This lift links the Trent and Mersey Canal to the River Weaver, where sea-going ships ply back and forth, and it consists of two water-filled tanks made of iron, enclosed by guillotine gates; a giant framework on giant legs houses the tanks, which worked, as far as I could see, on the principle that as one went up the other came down, and this indeed happened as we watched a narrow boat arrive to make its descent. Our friendly informant shed some light on the fascinating mysteries of hydraulics and counter-balances and told us that, once operated by steam, the lift was now all electric. We could only stand and gape, spellbound by the assemblage of pulleys, weights, wheels and controls of this gentle leviathan which lowered its cargo fifty feet to the lower level of the Weaver with all the tender care of a mother placing her baby in a cradle. Our need for food, finally dragged us away from this Victorian marvel — an ugly looking structure I thought, but beautiful too in its well oiled movements and phenomenal co-ordination.

Later, a prolonged argument took place as to whether the tank of water weighed more when occupied by a boat than it did without! Some declared against, as they reasoned that the boat would become weightless and therefore the tank would weigh the same. I cannot remember who was for and who against, but the heated discussion certainly raised the volume inside *Maori*, just as I thought the liquid volume must surely be raised in a tank housing a displacing boat!

This interesting discourse continued until Barnton Tunnel blacked it out and then a superb view from a steep hillside to the enormous Saltersford Lock on the River Weaver kept our interest once we had emerged. Saltersford Tunnel soon intervened, after which, still on the hillside, we could follow the river pursuing its many diversions along a fertile spacious valley. Rather abruptly, for we had been wholly absorbed in the sail, we rounded a bend in the canal to arrive at Premier Boats and a sudden end to our cruise.

With incredible swiftness we were brought back to earth both mentally and physically, with Alec already disappearing to contact John's car so that we could fetch ... well, you know the drill by now! Then the usual packing up, locking up and carting up to the car took place with four bodies plus dirty clothes, half-eaten food, milk bottles, water carriers, bedding and rubbish, having a cramped, somewhat smelly ride back to Huddersfield to the luxury of a steaming bath and a toilet where one could comfortably swing a cat! Home HAS its compensations.

Maori now rested happily at her new mooring on the Trent and Mersey, disturbed only occasionally for short, weekend excursions and once by Emily, who had moved from Abergele to Brighouse and was persuaded, against her better judgment to chance a ride.

An unconventional boarding, involving being lifted bodily, had Emily (but not the trip) off to a flying start; for her dignity had suffered a mortal blow at the outset. However, pleasant weather heralded a hot summer and when we were under way, she sat upright on a nylon folding chair within the shelter of *Maori's* cockpit, completely recovered, acknowledging passers-by as regally as a queen on a royal barge and thoroughly enjoying herself. That is, until we entered Preston Brook Tunnel. The transition from bright sunlight to damp darkness took her by surprise and, anxious for her comfort, we suggested that she might prefer to be inside. Emily, somewhat hard of hearing, informed us that we were inside, and despite her obvious discomfiture in an unusual environment and her repeated inquiries as to 'how much longer?' she doggedly stuck it out, all one thousand two hundred and thirty-nine crooked yards of it, to the bitter end. Long tunnels always make me apprehensive, but once we are swallowed into their depths, they hold a strange, almost hypnotic attraction. However on this particular day I was impatient, for Emily's sake, to be disgorged from the realms of sunlessness as soon as possible.

Emily did not understand our amusement when she asked if our return journey took us through the tunnel, and our second penetration was achieved with Penny and Grandma ensconced inside the cabin, inside the boat, inside the tunnel supping tea and playing 'snap' with all the lights on! This was her only excursion with us.

'It was very nice,' she conceded, not wishing to offend, 'But I didn't like being lifted on and off with all those people staring!'

There hadn't been a soul in sight, but that was her reason and she steadfastly declined to set sail again.

Even if we had wished to bring *Maori* back to our mooring at Bingley, we certainly couldn't have sailed her there then because a serious breach in the Bridgewater Canal had occurred on August 2nd, 1971 at Bollin Acqueduct near Altringham. The canal, some thirty-four feet above the River Bollin had washed a hole ninety feet wide in an embankment. Discovered as early as twenty past seven in the morning, by eleven thirty, log dams at each end of the breach had sealed if off; the canal in Manchester dropped fourteen inches but by August 3rd this had been made good with water from the River Medlock.

Curious as to how reconstruction was progressing, we took off on a weekend sightseeing excursion as far as the breach. Vacating our mooring at Premier Boats on the morning of July 7th, we headed north and once again nosed into Emily's favourite tunnel, Preston Brook. We were intrigued by a stop lock just before the entrance which lowered the canal only six inches, and where I stood immobile holding *Maori* while Alec did all the work. He, impatient to be through, struggled to part the gates by brute force instead of waiting for the water to level, and succeeded, but the forceful flow shot *Maori* out like a cork from a bottle and I staggered along behind taut ropes, *Maori* pulling me instead of me pulling *Maori*!

Salidha with four captains on board

'Mt Everest' in the form of Bingley five rise locks

Swing bridge on the Leeds-Liverpool Canal

Summit of the Leeds-Liverpool canal — Jim's house

Adagio held steady by Brian (and son) in a crowded lock

Salidha' at the top of Banknewton locks

The largest mooring pin in the world (according to Jim)

'Salidha' – shipshape

Banknewton locks

The Colliers Arms

Guillotine (latrine) lock

Scene along disused Rochdale Canal (now restored)

'Drayton Duke' — later 'Maori'

'Drayton Duke' becomes 'Maori'

Mary (Shroppie Fly) and Doris locking 'Maori' up in the Yorkshire Dales

'Maori' at Stratford Upon Avon

Jenny Wren with mum in Karangahape Road, Auckland

*Marriage to Yeoman of signals Colin Wood Evans at Pitt Street
Methodist Church, Auckland. Sub-Lieutenant Gherkin as best man*

*Robin Hood and his merry men. Will Scarlett left of Friar Tuck.
Auckland Girls Grammar School. Performance at the Auckland Town Hall*

'Cow cockies' reunion. Joan, Merv Fernyhough, Doris and 'Win'

'William Hennell' launched at Mirfield in 1950, registration number 371, with a load of 75 tons of coal en-route for the Thornhill Power Station (photograph by Peter Smith)

The Coppells: Conversion means fulfillment of their dreams
(Photograph reproduced courtesy of the Huddersfield Daily Examiner)

'Shivering in all me Timbers'! Driving 'William Hennell'
through Greenwood Flood Lock. Weir on the right

'Maori' at Norbury Junction

Calder House at Shepley Bridge

Double locks at Shepley Bridge. Nora's cottage on the right

View from my bedroom window

The Weir in full flood — River Calder

Dry dock at Shepley Bridge

Skating on a frozen canal — Shepley Bridge

Ice cracking on the canal

Once through the tunnel, the Trent and Mersey was behind us and we were parting the waters of James Brindley's masterpiece, the Bridgewater Canal. Engineer extraordinary, called the 'Father of British Waterways', he joined with the Duke of Bridgewater and John Gilbert (the Duke's agent) to construct Britain's first arterial canal from Worsley to Manchester. Opened in 1761, its amazing success led to thousands more miles being built.

While we ordinary mortals cannot hope to match the imagination of such a genius, there are some who try to enhance our environment and as one travels the canals, it certainly shows. Whenever we sail through Daresbury, I am lost in admiration at the immaculate grassy banks belonging to (of all people) the Nuclear Physics laboratory which slope gracefully to the water's edge. Inviting iron rings await our mooring ropes and arouse a strong desire to stop for a while. Lewis Carroll was born in Daresbury and some of Alice in Wonderland's friends, inanimate on the stained glass windows of All Saints Church, are obviously just waiting to come to life and partake of another crazy tea party.

This particular weekend was sun-soaked and we wallowed gratefully in its enveloping warmth. For what is more tranquillizing than potent high summer, when minds become hazy and nervous systems melt away in the heat? The bliss of mooring in some secluded place, feet up, eyes lidded, food near at hand and Jim Swanton's unhurried, commentary feeding you the test match between England and the Aussies — 'England two hundred and twenty-one for four!' — what more could one ask, even if one is a New Zealander?!!

But idyllic afternoons are not, alas, unending, so in slow motion we coiled limp ropes and moved lethargically on to Lymm; a charming town, old, unspoilt, with an uneven cobbled square which boasts some ancient wooden stocks that in bygone days held fast the local miscreants.

Following an unwritten law, we slid wakeless past an interminable line of moored craft belonging to the Lymm Cruising Club and gently parted a broad, clear waterway beneath a wide blue sky dotted with butter-pat clouds. An immobile, oblivious fisherman hardly lifted his eyelids as we came alongside where the canal had been blocked off. Later we experienced the strange sensation of strolling along a canal bottom, which on this balmy airless day had become a solar oven, to make our way to the actual breach above the River Bollin — where we went off on our own separate explorations and lost each other! I reflected that, if it hadn't been for the diligence of two small boys who detected the breach so early in the morning, events could have been very serious indeed; even so, a whole canal system was disrupted with the Leeds–Liverpool and the southern canals disconnected. Its repair was imperative for us and many other boat owners who were stranded south of the breach, for *Maori* had to come home to Yorkshire later in the year.

The cause of the breach was a complicated leaching process of fine sand particles from the bed of the canal which continued over the embankment's two hundred years' existence, and the problems in dealing with an old structure were manifold, not the least of these being to decide where to draw the line between repair and renewal. The materials being used were, as far as I could see, mainly concrete and steel and the cost of repairing the leak eventually amounted to twenty-five thousand pounds. Some leak!

The fisherman hadn't altered his stance when Alec and I were reunited on a sunbaked *Maori* rocking, as we boarded, on a multi-coloured canal reflecting a brilliant Turner-like sunset. Our attention was diverted for a while to the preparation of a meal and when we emerged to eat outside, the angler had noiselessly slung his hook!

The evening was too perfect to waste in the nearby pub, so we passed it tending *Maori* and proving that 'There IS nothing half so much worth doing as simply messing about in boats.'

Sunday was anticipated with pleasure, for some other boat owners, Eileen and Rodney Bass, were to join us at Lymm to view *Maori* and sail back with us to Premier Boats. As I parted orange curtains to the morning, the blinding glare of the sun caused me to blink and rub my eyes, surprised to see the fisherman, who had once more materialised, his position and demeanour unaltered. His weighty considerations obviously required solitude, so, hardly daring to start *Maori's* engine, we cast off keeping our voices low until out of earshot. To wait can be pleasant in certain circumstances; and so it was when we moored at Lymm and watched for our passengers to arrive. When the kettle was whistling its coffee commercial, they made a timely appearance, brandishing their contribution to Sunday lunch — a bottle of homemade apricot wine. Rodney, Yorkshire, down to earth, not a man of miracles, can nevertheless turn most things into wine with the aid of some complicated equipment designed to concoct extremely potent end-products. Homemade bombs often explode inside their garage and these discharges sometimes forewarn of the effects of the potions on unwary tipplers among their friends!

They are the proud owners of a forty-foot Mindon steel narrow boat named *Dragonfly* and, although *Maori* belongs to a lower social class, we were happy to present her for their admiration and approval. Remembering a pretty, shady cutting at the attractive village of Walton encouraged us to delay our lunch until our arrival there, and as the mooring pins went in, the apricot wine came out, and being thirsty and liking the taste, I sloshed mine in double quick time into the empty well of my waiting stomach. Dinner, which had been cooking along the way, soon appeared on the table and meat pie plus vegetables followed, helped down by yet more virulent vino. The sweet as I served it swam before my eyes and when I finally strove to rise from the table, the boat rocked violently and I keeled over first to port and then to starboard. Helping hands grabbed and assisted me out onto the towpath where I collapsed into a chair and passed out! Half an hour later I woke with a start and, wondering what the hell I was doing there, inquired what had happened. Because nobody else had been affected by the explosive liquid, they unkindly suggested that I had hit on a good way of getting out of the clearing up!

There is no hope of my living down the incident and for a long time after, I viewed with suspicion a bottle of Rodney's cowslip wine reposing in a wine rack at home, pointing ominously in my direction. When I did partake, I made sure that I was comfortably replete after a meal, in sympathetic company, and reposing on a soft, receptive sofa.

This was the last short cruise before our main holiday and I recall it as among the best, in spite of being knocked out by Bass's secret weapon!

CHAPTER EIGHT

The barge she sat in, like a burnished throne,
Burned on the water; the poop was beaten gold,
Purple the sails, and so perfumed, that
The winds were love-sick with them, the oars were silver
Which to the tune of flutes kept stroke, and made
The water which they beat to follow faster
As amorous of their strokes.

William Shakespeare

W hen not actually boating, we were thinking boats and visiting boatyards. Occasionally, at weekends we would (for a change) ride three miles to Mirfield Boatyard where *Salidha* had been repaired, and 'gongoozle' at friends slogging away on their boats, offer them unwanted advice, eat their sandwiches and sup their tea. One fateful Sunday, when doing just this, we came upon a large coal barge which was having an overhaul in the dry dock. It was a West Country barge with voluptuously curved irresistible lines and a romantic appeal which neither of us could ignore. Rudely we eyed her from all angles, praising her and debating on the exciting possibilities she presented for conversion. Departure there and then would have been the wisest move before Leslie, who ran the boatyard, sowed fertile seeds with information about Hargreaves Canal Carriers inviting tenders for two such vessels. My conscience, which persistently questioned our need for an enormous coal barge, tried to surface but was (as usual) drowned in a fast rising tide of naïve enthusiasm.

As when we first viewed *Salidha*, and then later, *Maori*, I was absolutely carried away; imaginary pot plants sprouted all over the sun-deck where we lazed on comfortable loungers, sipping cool refreshing drinks and entertaining our less enterprising envious friends. Nothing to do but raise a languid hand in greeting to a passing wayfarer, soak up the sun, flick off the flies and sigh contentedly into the embracing cushions. One could even tend the garden while lying down — plucking out a weed here and there and tossing it overboard to float away, wind-blown along the canal. Exhausting holiday arrangements would be at an end. Life would become one long vacation, serene and fulfilling, with the ever-changing living water on one's doorstep and time to pursue whatever interests one wished — painting, writing, listening to music, reading, uninterrupted conversations, or just sitting. 'Heaven on Earth,' I thought at the time.

The barges offered for sale, *Gwendoline* and *William Hennell*, (both West Country Yorkshire Keels) were smaller than others working on the North Eastern Waterways and practical to our local canals and therefore, in our state of illogical fascination, practical to us!

Over the years, when age or toil had disfigured their appearance, Leslie, acting as personal cosmetic surgeon, had become intimately acquainted with these handsome vessels. We eagerly sought his expert advice to assist our choice as a subtle change in attitude took place and we began to discuss which, not if, we should buy! Although *William Hennell* had sustained damage astern, Leslie advised us in its favour.

During his life-time, Leslie, small, dark, unhurried and quiet of speech, has passed on many pearls of wisdom to aspiring boaters; but his observations, because they were dropped so casually, could easily be missed by the preoccupied listener. Les tended boats; lived surrounded by boats; spent most of his holidays close to boats; ate, dreamt and drank boats and was lucky to be indulged by his more flamboyant wife, Doreen, whose life was also ruled by boats. Because their Yorkshire-stone house stood in Mirfield Boatyard, their privacy was invaded most weekends by those requiring chandlery, a particular piece of wood, a certain screw, or an answer to a knotty problem; and Les could usually produce anything from a nail to a ship's bell out of some dark, secluded, dusty corner of that ancient boatyard. There, an object may have lain unused and seemingly forgotten for many years — but not by Les!

The beginnings of Ledgard Bridge Dockyard, as it was called, are somewhat obscure, but because of its proximity to the River Calder it seems reasonable to assume that a boat-building yard existed even before the canal was made. That boats have been built at this yard for hundreds of years is certain, for when removing a stone doorstep, which itself was worn down by uncountable ups and downs, Les found another one underneath eroded in exactly the same manner.

When discussing the *William Hennell* in private, I was once again the impetuous one and Alec the more cautious; but he indulged me and (I suspect) himself, by agreeing to view the barges. Consequently, on an appointed Sunday morning, Alec, (feelings suppressed) Penny, (questioning our sanity but interested) and a highly excited Doris, piled in amongst Alec's business samples, collected Les and were soon being checked in at the gate of Thornhill Power Station, where we had arranged to meet a representative from Hargreaves. He arrived, and after exchanging pleasantries through the car window, we careered after him to the coal wharves. There, a crane was noisily employed, its huge, gaping grab swinging over to scoop up a mouthful of coal from the bowels of a waiting barge and then returning to spew it out in an impressive cloud of choking black dust. The crane-driver looked surprised at our early morning arrival but stopped work until we were safely out of range of the scoop. Our guide, while polite and informative, was I suspect, more than a little amused at the idea of us buying such a vessel. After all, a craft fifty-seven feet six inches long, by fourteen feet two inches wide, is not everyone's choice. Mooring, for instance, could present problems with regard to space and depth and *William's* size made accurate steering through bridge-holes and into locks, absolutely vital. The engine, compared to *Maori's*, was enormous and I pictured non-mechanic Alec approaching this intimidating giant with much trepidation and withdrawing completely flummoxed.

The hole in the stern allowed a shaft of daylight to reveal its greasy mechanism and although Alec turned her winding-handle with ever-increasing momentum, he couldn't get it going. I was confused and kept referring to *William Hennell* as 'her', feeling it should be 'him' and ending up with 'it'! When considering costs, the 'easily mended hole' (according to Les) was the subject of the most speculation, and, unable to reach a satisfactory conclusion, we decided to return home to our dried-up Sunday lunch and chew things over.

The *William Hennell*, named in honour of the man who designed and supervised its building, was no ordinary coal barge. Conceived and formed at Ledgard Dockyard, its growth from an incongruous skeleton on the canal side, into a handsome West Yorkshire Keel, must have been fascinating to follow. Leslie's brother Wilfred, who, from a young lad, had been under the wing of the master-builder, was mainly responsible for its construction. Made of solid, well-seasoned English oak, it was fashioned by Yorkshire men who maintained high standards of workmanship. 'They don't build boats like that these days,' is sadly true in this case, for the last West Country barge was built in 1955, a 'she' named *Isobel*.

William was launched in April 1950 and the procedure leading up to this important event was quite complicated. The vessel had first to be raised by using barrels and wedges under the bilge, after which three pitch-pine baulks were inserted and secured by spurshores to overhang the canal by about six feet. Stern end and forward were then packed with oak pieces laid across each other, called Bostick-packings and held by one pin at each end. Eight men took approximately two hours to complete the whole operation, which raised the barge six to nine inches to provide enough slope for its slide into the canal. To ensure an easy transition, the plankings were greased with soft soap.

Launching day was always an excuse for noisy celebrations, when, after the event, all workers were awarded the remainder of the day off. The owner of the vessel was privileged to bear the cost of the traditional 'shout' at the Navigation Inn, conveniently adjoining the boatyard.

William's launching was no exception. Mr Hennell, another intrepid boatman, had decided to launch his namesake from on board and experience the thrill of an exciting splash as twenty-five tons smacked sideways, at a frightening angle, into the cut.

On this particular day, a (then young) Leslie was a 'striker' and the *William Hennell*, his first 'knocking-off' job at the yard. To explain — just before launching, nearly all packing and supports were removed and only two vital pins remained to be knocked off. When the foreman, Wilfred, shouted 'All clear — packings out!' the strikers knocked it off its pins (so to speak), and away it slid over the soft soap, baulks flying up in the air, its bulk displacing a great deal of canal and causing a spectacular wave. Foaming champagne flowed over the stem from a bottle enthusiastically smashed by Mr Hennell and with bunting flapping and people cheering and waving, congratulations were exchanged for a job well done, after which all hands invaded the Navigation Inn — to push the boat out yet again!

What a gay, lively scene it must have been and what an unforgettable day for those directly involved. According to Leslie, when ladies performed the naming ceremony, they usually did so from the canal side, but I have deluded myself into thinking that I would have had the courage to remain on board, if ever such an honour had come my way.

Smooth launchings were the general rule, but one wayward individual, *Bradsylda*, objected to being knocked off and slid stern first into the water, striking the wall on the far side of the canal. In spite of some protective sacks of sawdust, which hung over this vulnerable part of her anatomy as fenders, she was severely damaged and her immediate dry-docking prolonged thirsts and delayed celebrations.

The mental and verbal wrangling which precedes an important family decision had begun and perhaps William Hennell turned as restlessly in his grave as I did in my bed. Alec retained valid reservations but was intrigued with the idea of converting the barge;

I wanted to go the whole hog and sell our bungalow to transform *William Hennell* into the most luxurious vessel on the cut. To this Alec would not subscribe, and in retrospect I suppose that he was right. But we agreed to submit a tender and, if successful, convert the barge in spare time (which we didn't have) with money (not foreseeably available).

An ideal mooring was found at Cooper Bridge Lock on the Calder and Hebble Navigation. It was close to home, and we were delighted to meet up with Arthur Crisp and his wife Evelyn, now living there in retirement. As we outlined our ambitious plans, they matched our enthusiasm and a long and valued friendship stemmed from this unexpected encounter. Final approval rested with Alec Millais, an Area Inspector, and we were lucky to have his interested co-operation and permission for the mooring. Having negotiated this major hurdle, we entered a tender for four hundred pounds, cleared our minds of coal dust and turned clarified thoughts to a much-needed holiday.

Maori's log, which I kept faithfully at this time, tells me — and you — that, in spite of a flat battery, we left at a quarter past ten on Saturday July the 28th. As we quitted Premier Boats, the morning air cooled our faces and a low cloud ceiling hung above us. But we were feeling carefree, for our holiday cruise, which promised to be a most stimulating one, was just beginning. A well-studied route was to carry us further along the Llangollen Canal and over the famous Pontcysyllte Aqueduct which, judging from the stories we'd heard, would provide us with a hair-raising experience and invite all manner of disasters. Then *Maori*, if she survived, was hoping to find fresh hunting grounds along the Macclesfield Canal and eventually some idyllic spot to moor, so that Penny and her friends could transistorise her for a week's holiday.

So there we were, parting the deep waters of the Trent and Mersey Canal once more and relishing a lazy lock-free sail on this broad, interesting waterway — an impressive swan-song by the designer,

James Bridley, who did not live to see its completion. Originally a commercial enterprise built especially to serve the pottery industry, the canal has been utilised by many and has also greatly benefited the large areas of agricultural land through which it flows. The tunnels are funny, crooked structures, and although *Maori* experienced little trouble in finding her way beneath their humps and bumps, our emergence was always welcome — especially at Saltersford, where genial graceful trees beckoned us out of dark confinement.

Leaving the cool morning behind, we sailed into a warm sunny afternoon — which allowed the mass of industrial eyesores connected with salt production, to become more acceptable. It was difficult to believe that someone had actually designed such a hotchpotch of nightmarish shapes and connections. I pictured a maniacal sculptor starting off with a pipe or two, and then, from his confused twisted mind, concocting a memorial to humankind's torment on Earth! Queer vapours hissed out of unlikely places, as if from the bowels of the earth, the Devil himself was letting off steam unwanted even in Hell! They seem to be the epitome of all that is ugly and undesirable in our environment, but are an integral part of the canal scene and a reason why it exists, so I suppose we must try to accept them. While industry spoils and pollutes the waterways, some mellowed mills, warehouses and wharves enhance them and a cooling tower rising in its magnificence to dwarf your small craft can be an awesome sight.

We arrived at Middlewich well contented with our first day's sailing and ready for the added satisfaction of a good meal. As we walked through the town, I thought that a place of great character had once existed — until changed by that obliterating process called 'progress'. Nevertheless we found some excellent shops and later that evening a tiny café in the High Street served up a superb dinner. However, the size of the café was not reflected in its charges and, with the holiday now off to a rousing start, we acknowledged the need to conserve our limited funds.

At Middlewich, a famous signpost at a canal junction points three ways and we followed one which indicated a right turn under a bridge and up a lock, to travel the attractive Middlewich Arm yet again. After gliding through a hump bridge we temporarily entered a fishing competition, for dotted at regular intervals were areas of flattened grassy bank, each arrayed with a basket, a fishing net, an umbrella, a protruding rod and line, a seat and a fella. 'They stretched in never-ending line along the margin of — our way', and we, fearing their absolute immobility and concentration, crept along like late-arrivals at a funeral service; intruders in a holy place!

I am not going to describe this holiday in daily detail because I cannot remember it that way; but I do recall an extremely shallow canal which in places caused us to scrape, rather than sail to Llangollen. We possessed an unrivalled talent for finding submerged objects and at one point became air-borne when hurdling *Maori* over what proved to be a huge metal drum.

Learner drivers in hire-boats acting as if they owned the canal, were unwilling to leave the deep middle channel and often forced us aground, usually when I was driving. On these joyous occasions we practised our various techniques for getting unstuck. Racing the engine furiously in forward and reverse was particularly advantageous to the muddy bottom of the canal, which it aerated while allowing us to settle deeper into its murky mire. Alec, on shore, vigorously rocking *Maori* with me jumping up and down on the opposite side, bottom well extended over the cut, was entertaining to passers-by and sometimes effective. But, far more sensible was Alec ashore armed with a sturdy pole, levering *Maori* and me to a precarious angle, which did the trick nine times out of ten — until I then had to come in close to pick him up — and we were stuck again!

I also remember, on a quiet stretch of waterway, seeing a long narrow boat becomingly bedecked with relaxing, bikinied, sunbathing bodies, proceeding serenely towards us. Next minute it was slewing crazily across the canal to the accompaniment of shouts and panic-stricken gestures from the now highly-activated bodies. Not expecting our inoffensive appearance to have such a dire effect, I was amazed to see it ram the bank with terrific force and shudder to a stop, completely blocking our passage along the canal. The reason, I am reluctant to relate, was a learner woman-driver! Poor Mum, having her first go at the tiller, panicked at the sight of *Maori*, peaceful native though she was, and could not remember on which side she should pass, so tried both! Taking pity on her plight, we offered our well-tried and tested canal churning tactics and, half an hour later Mum, demoted below decks to the galley, went her disconsolate way and we went ours.

Another day I remember with complete pleasure began with a perfect midsummer's morning. I love warmth. If the sun is pulsating its rays at full strength to the earth on a timeless, hazy day in July; if the insects are humming and hovering on the heat and the air is motionless save for their movement through it, I am happy. If afloat, I am in Paradise! On this Tuesday we were very close to a paradise of sorts — at least I thought so.

We arrived at the Press Arm mid-morning and, having read of the beauty of this now disused canal, decided to moor up and see for ourselves. I was not prepared for the enchantment that this walk offered, for Nature, the supreme horticulturist, had taken over and fashioned a garden of rare charm. The unwanted but lovely sight of water-lily cups covered the canal surface, their leaves making natural platforms for all manner of insects and birds; from a distance wild flowers became diffused into a sea of colour and I feasted my eyes on a three-dimensional impressionistic painting, sensuous and shimmering in the heat; even some workmen, intent on repairing a rare old, skewed bridge, became transformed by the lustrous light. An old man and woman (both toothless) emerged from their cottage to take a gander at us, and the man, rather bristly about the face (like Blake), gave the appearance of having reverted to nature. The old woman disappeared abruptly as we approached — to retrieve her molars, I thought at the time. However, having found us to be friendly intruders, the man nattered time away discussing the canal's demise and I was very touched when he nearly over-balanced into the water in his effort to pluck a particularly rare flower for my bouquet. Alec made a pointed remark about lunch, and although I was loath to leave, the call of our empty stomachs returned us to the boat.

Lunchtime! Time should be made to stand still on such precious occasions. God started this business by creating night and day, and we, not content with light and dark, had to measure it second by second by inventing clocks with which to rule our lives. We seem to be possessed by time: the time we were born; the time we get up; the time we eat; the time to go to work; time for the news; how to achieve the fastest time; time to go to bed; time to die!!?? TIME LADIES AND GENTLEMEN PLEASE! Time, time, time! Time we stopped thinking about time I think!

Now it was TIME to move on and make our way towards Blake Mere. We had expected to travel much further during the afternoon, but when we reached that blissful spot, it was a must for a night's mooring. Just across the towpath a glassy lake, framed in a canopy of trees, spread before us; a placid habitat for ducks and other wild birds which could be seen swimming far over on the other side, where steep wooded banks rose us from blue-green water to blue-white sky. Other wild creatures were swimming on our side, children splashing and laughing with the complete abandonment of the very young enjoying a hot, carefree holiday.

That night we were treated to a spectacular display of lightning as a thunderstorm passed over the lake and transformed the scene from one of sunlit tranquillity into dark, dripping, ominous shapes and shadows at times brilliantly illuminated by vicious forked tongues of electricity. Completely absorbed, I viewed the tempest through the boat window and early next morning, when I simultaneously opened my eyes and the curtains, the lake was smoothly cool in the morning sun, and everything was newly washed, clean and refreshed, *Maori* included.

A special morning heralded a special day, for we were to arrive at Llangollen that evening after having sailed across the Pontcysllte Aqueduct. Excitement mounted as the miles between us and this amazing tank (over one hundred and twenty feet above the River Dee) narrowed.

A 'taster' came first in the form of Chirk Aqueduct, which is spectacular in its own way, but is overlooked by a taller railway viaduct. A passenger could (if he or she'd a mind) sing from the carriage window, 'I'm the King of the castle and you're the dirty rascal,' to us lower beings on the canal. We serfs could (if WE'D a mind) visit Chirk Castle, a two-mile trek away — but we declined this time. This trough of water transferred us from England into Wales and the scenery, as the mountains enfolded us, became exceptional. To 'Climb every mountain' must be thrilling — but how about SAIL every mountain??!!

Pontcysyllte was something of a mountain to us, for it represented a high peak in our canalling experiences. Although the air about us was warm on this bright brimming day, it was also active, disturbing the undergrowth, whisking the canal surface and fluttering *Maori's* triangular flag. All that we had read, all that we had heard, paled into insignificance when we approached and caught sight of a choppy one thousand and seven foot long tank of water which, suspended high above a deep luxuriant valley, presented a sheer drop on our port side and a reassuring towpath on the starboard. Alec was at the wheel and as we edged forward, our brows puckered with apprehension, *Maori* suddenly seemed much higher above the water-line and terribly vulnerable in the strong cross-wind which knocked her, with gnawing persistence, against the side of the sheer drop. Hair-raising it certainly was! Alec kept urging her towards the centre. But no! we banged and bounced, steel against steel, all the way across, not daring to look down but totally hypnotised into doing so!

A facetious remark of mine which observed that it would be too bad if somebody pulled out the plug, turned out to be quite feasible, for apparently a plug is removed when the structure has to be repaired and a spectacular waterfall to the river below results.

Having arrived safely on the other side, we breathed sighs of relief and completely messed up the ninety degree turn into a narrow neck of canal which was to lead us to Llangollen. Reacting quickly in the presence of interested 'gongoozlers', we pretended that we weren't making for it at all and moored-up in the boatyard.

At this point one is advised against going further if your boat draws more than twenty-one inches. As *Maori* draws twenty-four, it is not surprising that we excavated the canal bottom all the way to Llangollen.

How can I describe the magnificence of this watery way which meanders gently around tree-covered mountain sides like an enchanting slow movement weaving towards its final cadence. I am no Welsh bard to enlarge on what has already been expressed in verse, story and song; even the hypersensitive brush of the painter cannot record all nature's moods; but there is no need, for an exultant work of art exists for you to see.

So much unadulterated beauty induced a state of emotional inebriation and I spent the remainder of this fantastic journey intoxicated by my own heightened feelings. That is, until we curved around under a sheer rock face where a slim, slithering canal does not allow even narrow boats to pass and where I had to act as scout by running on ahead. We were, of course, aware of the great musical festivals held in Llangollen and I half expected some full-throated Welsh choir to line the towpath and mark our arrival in song. As it was, we made our entrance totally unnoticed, and tied up content to anticipate a non-sailing period in this wholly delightful place.

Being fairly ordinary folk, we straight away took an ordinary tour of the shops, bought some ordinary picture postcards and, for a while, gazed down on a rocky river bed which tormented the untamed River Dee during its downward surge. Here, our elbows helped to wear down the stones of a 14th century bridge, as did many other leaners and peerers who were also attracted by the water's troubled turbulence.

That evening, at a non-ordinary barn which had been converted into a pub called the Royal Oak, pre-dinner drinks plus vino with the meal nicely took the edge off everything, and we blissfully wended our woolly way to a lazing *Maori*, to rest enclosed in gathering shadows under shapes of hills. 'The black and folded town fast and slow, asleep'.

Very romantic you might think, and so it was, although boating (as a whole) is not always the most romantic pastime in the world. A hard day's sailing, working stiff locks and awkward swing bridges in foul weather, with muddy ropes hitting one in the face, is not conducive to nuptial bliss. When you are throbbing all over, hair-do bedraggled, all in all buggered, fed-up to the teeth and falling out with each other, your only wish is to crawl inside a chaste sleeping-bag and zip up against all boarders; ten to one your partner is buggered too, hates the sight of you, and has zipped up before you!

However, there are moments of sweet communication; and what happens? If there are only single bunks, you lie together hanging on like grim death, unable to move in case you fall over the side into a narrow passage which wedges you indivisible. (They're not called narrow boats for nothing!) Move an arm to make a fond caress, catch the front of the locker, and down swings a heavy door and wallops you on the head. By now you'd settle for a cup of cocoa and forget the whole thing!

If you are very forward and squeeze into your spouse's sleeping-bag, there is NO WAY that it will zip up over your ample proportions, so a ruddy great draft plays on your back and your thoughts centre solely on whether it's lumbago or sciatica you're catching!

'Are you alright "luv"?' he will ask, trying to ignore the bulkhead cracking half his ribs.

'No, I'm not bloody-well alright,' you want to cry out, but your reply is a series of 'oo's and ah's' as cramp viciously attacks one of your legs.

Imagine a honeymoon on such a boat. If she wasn't a boaty type it could be absolutely disastrous. Imagine the wedding night! He will probably take a late towpath walk to water the canal while she hastily undresses and covers herself (and the boat) with her favourite talcum powder. She hunts for her creased nightdress, (still in the suitcase) and arrayed in all her glory, awaits his return. The boat rocks and the door opens.

'Bloody-hell,' he says sniffing energetically. 'That sodding calor gas is leaking again!'

After that they would have no chance at all on a bunk two foot six inches wide and the honeymoon might not even run its full course!

During our non-sailing stay we boarded a horse-drawn boat to sail just that bit further along the canal in company with a large party of Senior Citizens. Their delight was obvious. Even embarking and disembarking was an adventure for them, especially when the boat rocked. This unreserved, child-like enjoyment was infectious on a warm, encircling afternoon as we drifted through leafy glades, the horse clip-clopping an accompaniment to the happy, twittering passengers.

On our way back to *Maori*, we hesitated at a pontoon-boat called *Earl* and found there a would-be canal artist and his wife who lived on their boat. Suckers for a souvenir, we purchased one of his works of art — an 'original copy', for every painting was identical, depicting a surprised-looking castle against a back-drop of deep blue sea and a blancmange shaped cloud — the whole presenting a questionable, thought-provoking perspective! *Maori* objected to this embellishment being pressed upon her and rejected it again and again. However, the contents of a maltreated tube of glue stuck really fast to my fingers which finished up, after scouring pads had scrubbed them, practically skinless. Nevertheless, by the time our newly-made friends came to visit, the castle was insecurely in place. Sherry and talk mingled the evening away and I dreamed of a water gypsy's wandering existence as they outlined their nomadic way of life. Next morning we left our artist, his castles and Llangollen, to sail to Ellesmere for a sentimental stay at Blake Mere; but first of all we entered Ellesmere Basin for supplies and to telephone a pressing invitation to Elsie and Stan.

Had John been with us, he could have moaned for days about a large dairy factory, which not only churned out endless rattling crates of milk for great, hulking chaps to sling with crashing enthusiasm into endless revving lorries, but its machinery reverberated, a wireless reverberated, *Maori* reverberated, and everybody inside the factory and out, shouted to make themselves heard above the incredible din.

I assumed that the hellish operation began at some ungodly hour of the morning and, unless John had retired on a bottle of whisky and several sleeping tablets, his chance of a reasonable night's sleep would be nil.

The telephone wires from Ellesmere to Huddersfield also reverberated as Alec, my own adjectives interpolating, expounded on the beauty of Blake Mere and the disused Prees Arm. Elsie and Stan (their sweet sleep just broken by a reverberating alarm) were dragged many sodden reverberating miles on a wet cool day, for cold meat and salad, tinned fruit, reverberating jelly and Carnation milk, during a grey, drizzly trip, which made all the wonders we had described, dripping and dismal.

Next day a grateful *Maori* headed back towards deeper waters and Middlewich, this time to follow another arm of the signpost, south, to climb the innumerable locks of 'Heartbreak Hill', a penance required for our passage to the Macclesfield Canal. Unusual double locks, some fallen into disuse, made our ascent interesting as we tried, upon our approach, to guess which were operational. Dark ominous clouds sailed the sky after *Maori* and occasionally emptied themselves upon her, while the sun took a couple of looks, didn't like what it saw and went back in.

Someone's mistake at Thurlwood, in the shape of a massive, grey steel lock, made me avert my eyes from the ugly structure, which, complicated in design, proved no less complicated to operate. We were unable to decipher instructions displayed on a notice board, gave up and went up the conventional lock next door.

About a dozen locks later we arrived at Kidsgrove, sailed through orange washing-up water to Hardings Wood Junction and sought the entrance to the Macclesfield cut. As we were facing South and the 'Mac' lay to the East, you might assume that a left turn off the Trent and Mersey would seem reasonable. Not so, for at the junction we turned right, right again, and right again, crossing over the place we'd just come from by means of the Red Bull Aqueduct.

We were at once in a more intimate canal, the sort which I prefer. Pleasantly neglected, Nature had reached out for her own, and now reached out for us, as we happily became lost in the countryside. Some impressive hills made us aware of their presence and we congratulated ourselves on choosing to sail this delightful waterway. A high fell, called The Cloud, rose and dominated the scene as we wound and unwound to the foot of Bosley Locks, where we moored late into the afternoon, on a straight steep embankment. Far below, the River Dane flowed through a nave of trees flanked by transepts of ever-rising, daisy-eyed meadows, and as the departing day gave way to a perfect summer's evening, we added other earthly pleasures — a glass of wine and a leisurely meal. The soporific effects of these may have caused my total submission to an overwhelming feeling of dreamy contentment; a yielding to beauty within, engendered by unspoilt natural beauty without.

Next day, when night-narrowed eyes emerged to squint into the bright morning light, a lock-keeper trimming bee-buzzed hedges, looked a very contented man indeed. We arrested his shears in mid-air to ask for a long term mooring when our holiday was over, and, he promised to accommodate us. We ascended his rising and falling water garden, skirted by tadpole-infested exotically overgrown ponds and freshly-shaved grass. Yellow musk, ragged robin, marsh willowherb, prize clover, cranesbill, vetch, parsley and water drop wert, all competed to get into the picture. The morning expanded as early enveloping mists gave way to hot dispelling sunshine and our sensitive noses also expanded to intermingled fragrances from grass cuttings, honeysuckle and wild roses.

As the haze rose, so did we up the locks. I became baked in increasingly hot lock-ovens, while Alec, stripped to the waist, performed endless turns of the windlass to assist our ascent. That night we walked a mile to make two telephone calls: one to Penny, who informed us that we had not yet acquired a coal barge; the other, to Poynton, advised a colleague of Alec's, Ken Daniels, of our presence on the canal and our eagerness to accept his generous invitation to a meal out. We arranged to meet at Higher Poynton, which gave us a long languid day, to sail at an elevated five hundred feet above sea level to Macclesfield and then, in splendid isolation, to follow the deep winding contours of an incredible beautiful waterway as far as Bridge 18, which just happened to be in close proximity to the Miners Arms. Because of a canal made deep and wide by coal mining subsidence, fishermen and fish are plentiful here and that evening at the pub we surreptitiously slipped in amongst these men who normally sit motionless as we pass. They were far from motionless on this occasion — their elbows working overtime and their imaginations also. Little fish grew longer as time together lengthened, and I could hardly believe that these boozing, chattering, gesticulating beings inhabited the same planet as the inanimate introverts along the canal, who seemed to communicate solely with fishy creatures and each other! I, (seeking an explanation) inquired about their dedication, to be told, against the clamour and fog of a noisy, choking, eye-watering, smoke-filled bar, that they sought peace, fresh air and communion with nature! Unsatisfied, I persisted, hoping to glean their innermost thoughts, but most of them admitted to lack of thought as they sat and 'just enjoyed being there'. This seemed to me a blissful state indeed, almost one of transcendental meditation, and I envied them their uncluttered philosophy.

True to his word, Ken, accompanied by his wife Kathleen, came to motorise and nourish us the following evening and the thought of a night away from the canal became increasingly inviting. They had to hop on board to view *Maori* and, of course, we spliced the mainbrace (rum unavailable) with a couple of draught sherries apiece! After being conditioned for ten days to three or four knots canal crawling, fifty miles an hour seemed a foolhardy speed; but I sank back to take in the beautiful Cheshire countryside, and at one high point quitted the car to gaze across a broad, stretching plain to where the myriad lights of Manchester flickered star points into the gathering dusk. Ken indicated the very tall Co-operative Insurance Society building and then, thinking of the un-calor-gas-cooked nosh to come, I was transported to the Redway Inn at Kerredge.

The pub, as we drew up, looked cosy and friendly and we had another preliminary drink, this time a gin and tonic for me. Yet another round went down the hatch before we actually sat down to dinner.

As it was a special night out, and, as Ken was in the chair, we decided to go the whole hog so to speak. 'Hog' was the operative word, especially where I was concerned. Ken insisted on a bottle of wine, which worried me a little, because to 'recap', two sherries and two gins and tonics had already gone down. Two courses with white wine followed and my stomach, in sympathy with its owner, also became worried by this unaccustomed onslaught.

'Hog' ordered chicken cooked in — what else — red wine, and when that slid into the inner regions, deep volcanic action began to make its presence felt. My head started to spin, my stomach churned like a concrete mixer, my eyes wouldn't focus and all the while I endeavoured to be pleasant, exude enjoyment and make interesting conversation.

'God in heaven!' I prayed, 'How shall I manage the sweet?' and I stared in glazed horror as Ken filled my one glass (which kept dividing into two) with yet more white wine. Desperation reached 'g'astromonical heights after the main dish and when Ken excused himself, I gratefully rose and made an intoxicated un-beeline for the 'Ladies', which was, mercifully empty. Everyone showed genuine concern at my pale-green return to the table, but I pleaded a headache which would soon depart and decided not to enlighten Ken about all the expensive food I had flushed away before he'd even received the bill!

In fact, the sweet was the only course I did enjoy, when my stomach, empty and untormented, allowed it to enter in relative comfort. Ken was quite put out when I declined a Gaelic coffee with my cheese and biscuits, and, as I relish the same, I was put out too. Ken is Alec's senior at work, and this was our first social outing together, so while wondering what sort of ghastly impression I was making, I was also hoping that our hosts were three sheets in the wind too and that their perception was dimmed as a result.

This must have been the case, for Ken and Kathleen dropped us off at *Maori* having accepted an invitation to bring their grandchildren, Robert and Stephen, to Bosley Locks the following Saturday. Stars winked knowingly at each other as a pearly moon lit our way back on board, where a calor gas lamp hissed us into the privacy and succour of our sleeping-bags.

'What a night!' I thought, bitterly regretting my fall from grace since I had, as a teenage chorister at Pitt Street Methodist Church, inspired by the Reverend E. T. Olds, signed a pledge of abstinence at Band of Hope meetings — three times! My throbbing head jarred into the soft pillow and Alec blacked out the light.

Maori's log records a late-ish start on the morning after, but we had ample time to call at Macclesfield for supplies and to be delayed at a delightful spot called Oakgrove, where we experienced some trouble with a swing-bridge. Perhaps our late-night revels had weakened us — I know that I was decidedly fragile — but whatever the reason, the bridge, despite all our efforts, would not budge. Eventually every man and his dog were pushing the obstruction and when we had exhausted all available helpers, a little frail old lady volunteered the information that it was always happening. Alec decided to contact British Waterways.

We did not mind waiting in this pretty hamlet among the hills, with its attractive public house aptly named Fool's Nook — Alec and me being the fools that couldn't open the bridge. Soon a blue van arrived and slammed out three Waterways men equipped with levers, who, somewhat to our discomfiture, had the bridge open in no time at all; in fact, an obviously smooth and well-practised operation totally confirmed our elderly informant's observations — it WAS happening all the time! We noticed that a few minutes work in the heat by the men required a longer cooling-off period at the Fool's Nook and I wondered, suspiciously, if this could be the reason why the bridge hadn't been repaired. Not such fools!

A holiday sadly drawing to an end leaves little else to relate, although one telephone call proved to be rather significant. Upon our arrival at Bosley Locks we contacted Penny, who staggered us with the news that we had become owners of an enormous coal barge. I suppose that, in our heart of hearts we hadn't dreamed that our tender would be accepted and I vacated the 'phone box in a mild state of shock, while Alec, turned pale and quiet, was probably having similar second thoughts.

Next day, Ken's grandchildren rocked *Maori* at her mooring, and when his car, at high speed, followed a long, questionable route to fetch Alec's, Kath and I, children in tow, wandered down the ever-inviting locks. An amiable boat — I forget its name — took Stephen and Robert aboard to ascend two or three stairs and grandfather, on his return, was met by an excited reception committee eager to relate their adventures. Then the usual disconsolate un-loading and loading commenced before we made for home and *William Hennell*!

As a coda to this chapter, I must tell you about a flock of migrating 'birds' who were released from Huddersfield and dropped onto *Maori* for a week's stay. Carol Poppelton, Susan Knapton, Jane Price and Penny, (individuals all) suddenly vibrated *Maori* and covered her with glamorous, bikinied bodies — a transition which must have taken the quiet place and the equally quiet lock-keeper, by surprise. As their idea of a holiday is, except for the occasional application of suntan oil, lying absolutely immobile, they took an extremely dim view of the mile and a half trek involved for nightly liquid refreshment and daily victuals.

Chris Coles, an unsuspecting windband colleague of Penny's who visited this brood, caused some comment in the local bus-queue about a visiting Casanova who kept passing them on his motorbike, sporting a different bird on the pillion every time he roared to the pub.

Carol Poppelton, tall, attractive, deep-copper-haired, but in Penny's words, 'a walking disaster area', excelled herself by using the unit where boaters empty their chemical toilets — instead of the conventional lavatory next door! On her return to *Maori* she observed that Waterways toilets were 'funny', and then later that same evening, when ambling back from the pub, was chased by a 'mad' dog and ran straight into the canal! Jane Price, lethargic, blonde and blue-eyed, after emptying the ship's dustbin, conserved her energy by leaving it amongst others belonging to British Waterways, for obliging refuse men to remove.

Dave undertook the unenviable task of joining this motley crew for three days, during which time they all took turns at driving *Maori* — because we weren't there to stop them! However, even Carol failed to cause a disaster and they reached Middlewich more or less safe and sound, although Dave was in a mild state of nervous collapse when we collected them.

Later in the year we brought *Maori* home. Thus, when she slid into *Salidha's* old mooring for her winter respite, 'Drayton Duke', a Southerner turned New Zealand native, became a Northerner and 'Yorkshire'.

CHAPTER NINE

'If seven maids with seven mops
Swept it for half a year,
Do you suppose,' the Walrus said,
'That they could get it clear?'

Lewis Carroll

Upon our rapid shift from boat back to bungalow, *William Hennell* occupied our thoughts and conversation more than somewhat, and there were grave misgivings when we realised the magnitude of the task awaiting us. Although time remained for us to back out, (and all logical arguments pointed to this) we were quite irrational, almost possessed; alike to a lover, fated if he remains but unable to withdraw. Inexorably the wheels turned towards our ownership until we were totally involved in a love-hate relationship with *William Hennell*; captivated, but afraid too, questioning our own capacity in the clandestine affair.

It was not to remain a secret for long, for soon all of Huddersfield knew, the word spread to Leeds, Manchester and even to London, as incredulous friends learned of our latest folly. We were, to say the least, a little out of our depth and the transition from a thirty-foot narrow boat to a fifty-seven-foot barge, was somewhat worrying. So we were greatly relieved when Hargreaves arranged for *William*'s former skipper to accompany us to her mooring at Cooper Bridge and provide a crash course in her handling. Captain Oates had trained his craft well and reduced even difficult manoeuvres to child's play. During a brief two-hour passage he tried to endue us with the experience of a lifetime and in his hands her considerable bulk became regal, graceful and magnificent.

He encouraged us to try our skill. Alec and Dave were the bravest and steered first. Then, (shivering in all me timbers) I stood at the wheel, felt her gentle response, felt like answering 'Aye, aye sir,' to all the Captain's quiet orders and alternated *William*'s gender almost every other sentence between 'hers', 'his' and 'its'. Captain Oates did not seem to notice my dilemma and when I had successfully inched her through a flood gate, his 'Well done,' fell upon me like an accolade from the highest in the land. She just fitted the locks, just squeezed under some of the bridges, and it was just as well that Captain Oates was in command or we might have left several demolished lock approaches and bridges in our wake.

Nerve wracking? Yes, but exciting too, for as we progressed, our confidence quickened and doubts were pushed away by her broad shapely bow. We became part of her throbbing heartbeat, part of her existence and she part of ours. Cleopatra was welcome to her burnished throne, silver oars and flutes, even to Anthony; we had our bisexual and occasionally asexual *William*!

And a thick-skinned individual she proved to be; quite capable of enduring any knocks or grazes we might inflict on her. In fact she was double-skinned, built with a lining of short planks inside her hull which could be removed for inspection purposes; and, during her years of coal carrying, a multiplicity of black nuggets and fine dust had slipped into the cavity between the two. Beneath her engine she had deposited a considerable amount of thick, gungy oil, which rolled about during her movement, and which, along with the coal deposits, it would be our undoubted pleasure to remove.

Alec, now realising that we had purchased a load of filthy, unattractive, unpaid work, arrived home one Friday with three sets of overalls, for him, Dave and me respectively. The former two fitted quite respectably, but mine, because of a six-inch overhang at all extremities, looked downright ridiculous and inspired an effective scarecrow dance around the lounge when I donned it. Penny didn't require any. Once again perfect timing had her studying for more exams and craftily absolved her from our self-imposed slave labours. Our immaculate overalls soon changed from blue to black as weekend after weekend was spent mining for coal and drilling for oil. And what a laborious business! Before it could be disposed of, coal had to be raked, prised, brushed and shovelled into buckets, ready for a dangerous ascent up a rickety ladder out of the bowels of the barge onto the deck. Volunteer Arthur Crisp would sometimes take pity on us, stand on deck to receive the endless conveyor belt of buckets and add the contents to his own store of fuel. When he had enough, we built up the towpath and filled all kinds of receptacles to transport it home; a ploy which invariably filled our choking, disgusted car with coal dust as it angrily snarled around a sharp corner. Every weekend our faces darkened, our shoes, socks, feet and hands went into mourning and our nostrils blew black. The bathroom floor changed from 'peacocky' blue to coal-dusty black and the bath, after three immersions, was 'disgustipating', while our towels would not show their faces in any self-respecting launderette!

There were occasional compensations. Sometimes, to dispose of general rubbish, I would light a fire in the open grate of the forward cabin and then emerge to watch the flexible tendrils of smoke issue from a chimney which protruded up from the deck. Great clouds of billowing smoke below would not allow re-entry, and then I was able to collapse on the 'sun-deck' and dream my former dreams of total inactivity.

Eventually the local press was onto us, and a reporter, photographer in tow, arrived at Coopers Bridge to view *William* and interview us. The photographer, who nearly stepped backwards into the cut when adjusting his sights, asked me to pick up a hammer and 'look as if I was doing something'. As I was in a state of shocked exhaustion from teaching, carpentrying, house-keeping, decorating, gardening, excavating and worrying, I could easily have done something to HIM! However, commonsense tempered my first violent reaction and finally it was Alec who posed with a small hammer poised, while I, for some obscure reason, struggled to hold a thick heavy plank. In fact, the picture was quite impressive, but the article relating to a middle-aged couple who dreamt of living on a romantic old barge, (me, allegedly, playing a grand piano all day!) was less so. Nothing could have been further from the truth at that particular time, for our morale had reached bilge-bottom and we were just about pooped-out. But respite came in the form of (how can I think it?) welcome Winter, when we only visited *William* intermittently to sweep up late fallen leaves and pump out unwanted fallen rain.

The Spring of 1974 saw us, with purified lungs, strength and enthusiasm revitalised, attacking *William Hennell* once again, with the result that *Maori*, a stranger in a strange land, was left lonely and dejected at her mooring at Bingley. However, the illogicality of possessing two boats which never sailed, coupled with a low in our finances, temporarily suspended our attentiveness to her big brother and we happily downed tools to join the Airedale Boat Club for a cruise to Gargrave during Spring Bank Holiday.

So with our yellow A.B.C. pennant streaming aft, we left Bingley on a fine, frisky, Friday evening and pointed a delighted *Maori* towards the Dales once more. The air nipped at us as we moved gently through silky water, disturbing momentarily, the white bridal veils of the May trees trailing into the canal.

'Isn't it lovely to get away?' I sighed to Alec.

'But I haven't got away — you're still with me,' was his romantic reply!

The buttercups and I shivered a little as the receding sun began to draw away the day, and sensitive daisies curled pink tips up tight against the searching, cold night air. To warm the rising moon, the sun sent smoky flames tipped with crimson, flickering across a darkening sky, and as he gathered up the embers, distant lights pierced the gloom of a gentle subsiding valley. We subsided too as *Maori's* exertions ceased, and moored nostalgically where Alexander had made his famous bid for freedom — but there wasn't even a ghost of a macaw or another human being in sight. Traffic was non-existent;

even the wind had ceased its plaguing; and as darkness delicately descended it deepened into an unfathomable silence.

Not for long though, because a meal still had to be prepared, the news had to be heard, washing-up had to clink cutlery and swish rattling pots, and bedding had to rise out of entombing lockers, (the lids of which crashed down at the slightest provocation). The kettle had still to whistle its goodnight song for our goodnight drink, our toothbrushes had to follow their abrasive courses, and the toilet had to suck out its final spoils before lights clicked dark and bunks exhaled under bodies, heavy inside nylon bags. Then muffled 'goodnights' put us off the air and allowed magical silence to smother all.

A cuckoo clock in a nearby tree awakened me early next morning, and lying cosily inert, I listened to its insistent call to rise and make friends with the day. And a friendly, warm day it became, as we ploughed towards Silsden (of the not-so-friendly swan). This time it was already engaged with another boat, luckily well protected by many tyres, the objects of savage, biting dives accompanied by wide, frightening, flapping wings. We slipped by unnoticed and watched him attack four times before a bend turned us and our heads to the way leading to Kildwick, where the canal hugs and squeezes the hillside and lazily licks some attractive stone buildings perched thereon. Here, everyone lives in a 'house on the hill' and some of them have to labour up crooked steep gradients to reach them. But then they can pause to gaze back at a spectacular view and replenish their lungs — that is if the panorama doesn't once again leave them breathless!

On hearing my first cuckoo of Spring, both heart and head had lightened and I found myself warbling 'Morning Has Broken' along with all the other warblers giving voice amongst the greenery. Purple cliffs of cascading rhododendrons fell to the water's edge and some sticky buds expanded their containing skins, just bursting to get into the picture, while indolent sheep were content to stand about and let fully-rounded dandelion-clocks blow time to the winds. Ambitiously, I changed my tune to Haydn's, 'With Verdure Clad' and the statuesque wool-gatherers blinked in surprise as I executed a famous ascending 'run' to a high note.

Funnily enough, from the age of eleven, ascending to a high note now and again had been a regular occurence in my life. Inspired by my mother who, in the thirties, learned to play the piano as therapy after a nervous breakdown, I begged for the chance to learn and later, when someone decided that I had a voice, singing tuition followed. Vic also played and my dad, a light baritone, had a go at the odd Victorian ballad. A strong Irish accent acquired during youthful days in Ireland coloured his 'rendition' (as he called it) and in a particular favourite called 'Absence', 'Thinking I hear you call' always came out as 'Tinkin' I hear you … ! !

All in all we were quite a musical family and because the vibrations from our flat in St Kevin's Arcade wafted out over Myers Park in Auckland and ultimately penetrated the caretaker's house at the Baptist Tabernacle, a life-long friendship began. Ma and Pop Fernyhough and their family lived there and prior to our meeting they had, for months, wondered who was belting hell out of a piano during Vic's realistic interpretation of the Anvil Chorus.

With no television to distract us, musical evenings were frequent and everybody did their party piece. And there was no getting out of it either. Trying to disappear into a corner, I waited for the dreaded moment when Dad would announce, 'Doris will play for you' or 'Doris will sing for you'. Sometimes he would issue the ultimate embarrassment 'Doris will sing AND play for you!!' Now and again Vic and I joined in piano duets; Schubert's March Militare or an arrangement of Rossini's famous William Tell Overture. Practise times were always confrontational when we raced to see who could finish first or alternatively — play loudest! Physically stronger, Vic would gradually shove me sideways along and off our elongated piano stool. Then Mum would come in and read the riot act!

Not everybody appreciated our artistic efforts and, in the flat below, Robin Wood, broom in hand, would thump loudly on the ceiling when he'd had enough. A pianist of some ability himself, his signature tune was (believe it or not) The Robin's Return; so you can imagine the rude remarks made by us 'Cappas' when he played that particular classic.

Myrtle Poole, who greatly impressed me with a brass plate at her gate and letters after her name, lived at Royal Oak and taught most of the Capper clan to play or sing — or both. Every Friday night I waited outside the Tivoli Theatre (affectionately known as the 'Tiv') on Karangahape Road to catch the Onehunga tram and spent a rattly half-hour ride, doing my music theory homework, which had been set at the last lesson.

Mrs Poole (I wouldn't have dreamed of calling her Myrtle) always greeted me with a charming smile which transformed a serious, slightly hook-nosed, heavy-lidded countenance into a warm welcoming one. Her approach to pupils, while wholly professional, was also innovative, and the regular student recitals at her home were highlights of the year. Mums and dads, if the slightest bit musical, were also roped in to sing part songs, excerpts from Gilbert and Sullivan operas and, once, a concert performance of Schubert's Lilac Time, at a local church hall. In this the characters, Tilly, Willy and Lily (I was Willy) wore long, frilly frocks made of lilac shot-taffeta which cost threepence three farthings a yard and Salvation Army bonnets (borrowed with difficulty) covered with the same.

I came to enjoy all of these activities and my love of the piano and joy of singing grew side by side as I expressed all my awakening youthful emotions through music. I found these times to be, like the halcyon days spent on Blake's boat, the best of my childhood.

At this time my parents earned a reasonable living as caretakers of St Kevin's Arcade and the flat went with the job. Dad also made a bit on the side as a part-time barman at the Naval and Family hotel on the corner of Karangahape Road and Hobson Street. I don't know whether it was a mecca for theatre managers but, for whatever reason, free access to most of the local cinemas turned Dad and me into avid filmgoers, and filmstars into my heroes and heroines. When I plonked down on a hard seat at the Prince Edward, the Empress, the Arcadia or the 'Tiv', I entered another world and became part of it. So it was natural for me, when a fourteen year old soprano enchanted everyone from the screen, to emulate her and dream my dreams of similar success. In a national Deanna Durbin singing competition I 'rendered' Toselli's Serenade well enough to become a finalist. On the stage of St James Theatre, Auckland, as a runner-up, I received an enormous bouquet, an enormous box of chocolates and an enormous boost to my morale.

On the strength of this success I later persuaded reluctant parents to let me audition with Ted Croad's Dance Band, landed the job, and was billed as Auckland's Nightingale. I sang twice weekly at the Orange Hall on East Street for ten and sixpence a song! Deanna Durbin with a hundred-strong symphony orchestra had nothing on Doris Capper giving her all (under the bouncy baton of Ted Croad) dressed in (Mum's choice) an enveloping black velvet evening gown, singing 'Little Old Lady — passing by', into a crackly microphone.

Sadly this also 'passed by' when Mum decreed that it was interfering with my school work.

Once, on holiday during a visit to the world famous Waitomo Caves, I laid claim to fame again by testing the acoustics of the Cathedral Cavern with an aria from Handel's Oratorio, Joshua — Jubal's Lyre. For this the other tourists gave me a standing ovation — mainly because they couldn't sit down. Later, as we glided along in a small, open boat through the glowworm cave, there was no applause when Winnie Elliott and I, stuffing handkerchiefs into our mouths to stem an uncontrollable fit of the giggles, exploded and put out all the lights!

Back once more in the 1970's, in broad daylight, gliding along in *Maori*, Alec also failed to applaud my vocal gymnastics, but blinked (like the sheep) and refrained from comment.

Suddenly, our interest was caught by a bright, flashing bevy of canoes manoeuvring near a swing bridge some distance ahead, and a cautious Alec instructed *Maori* to stalk these unknown natives at a stealthy crawl.

'I wish I had a canoe,' he said, turning towards me and heading straight for one of them.

'You will have in a minute,' I cryptically remarked!

At one point a busy road raced alongside the crawling canal; a noisy, jostling companion on our port side, while on our starboard, a sylvan wood rose from a bluebell-scented bed — trees stretching as in wakening but still dreamy, with sunlight filtering through to rouse their hidden, misty depths.

Skipton Basin opened out to receive us, and there, replete after lunch, we followed a jingling, jangling, fluttering group of be-ribboned Morris dancers to explore a deep secluded cut where a magnificent Norman castle reflected its battlements into the canal. In this bustling Dales centre we rubbed shoulders and other parts of our anatomy with haversack-heavy hikers, can-carrying campers, fresh-faced farmers, bargain-seeking boaters, meandering meal-seeking motorists and shoving, shambling shoppers. On the canal, the duck population seemed to have suffered an explosion and hundreds of operatic quacks, all varying in pitch, combining in a totally improvised chorus, made us untie our ropes and leave before the finale. Silent, sympathetic members of the swan ballet escorted us to the swing bridge exit, saw us through and returned resignedly to their noisy companions.

The canal, reluctant to leave its surroundings, would not allow us quick passage, but unwound its arm slowly, from soft breast-shapes of hills separated by moorlands and lush grazing pastures.

Rumour had it that water was short, but we discounted this until, after having ascended two locks at Gargrave, a lengthsman confirmed it. By now the Airedale Boat Club had turned up in strength and our Commodore decided to dispose his fleet at the base of the locks, in order to conserve the vital element. We turned and came down to join a motley line of boats: *Lois*, over-dressed with bunting, clinker built, independent and sea-going, proudly carried Commodore Ken and First Lady Nadine.

Their tall mast overlooked fibreglass cruisers — large, small, dirty and clean, and converted lifeboats in various stages of completion or degradation. Also solid dependable steel and wooden narrow boats and other craft which did not easily fall into normal categories. *Adagio*, laid up at home for minor repairs, had sick leave, but Brian and Mabel joined a special Saturday night supper for all hands at The Grouse, and here Alexander enhanced his erstwhile reputation as a very boozy bird by dipping his beak into everybody's drink. Glasses clinked, and smoke and boat talk filled the air, the former limiting Alexander's visibility as he made short flights from shoulder to shoulder and from slurp to slurp.

Eventually, all ratings, overfull with floating pies and peas, followed a merry macaw, drunk as an owl, out of 'The Grouse'. Slurred 'goodnights' were exchanged and a promise was exacted from Mabel and Brian to rejoin the fleet on Sunday for an eagerly anticipated barbecue.

Next morning Alec's shaver wouldn't work and the toilet threw an untimely fit of temperament. Consequently, Alec, bristly of face (like Blake) and likewise of temper, spent most of Sunday head down, behind up, sorting out the plumbing. Actually, for accuracy's sake I should state that the toilet really sorted Alec out by refusing to go back together after he had completed his autopsy. Little washers and nuts seemed to possess endless interchangeability, and as Alec could never memorise which sequences he had already tried, I began, after two hours to get quite worried and fidgety — mainly because I wanted a 'wee'. The blame for missing a blast from Lois's horn, which signalled the start of a treasure hunt, fell squarely on my shoulders, because Alec had his head down the 'loo' at the time. For a while we wondered why 'silly buggers' were jumping aboard, shouting for, and taking all our Brillo pads! Realisation dawned, and abandoning the toilet mid-operation, we hared along an animated towpath, grabbed a paper waved at us by an excited Nadine and dashed around trying to collect the listed treasure objects, only to find by then an acute shortage of everything — including Brillo pads! We did well in the quiz though, mainly due to our possession of the

Leeds–Liverpool Canal booklet and our undeniable ability to look up the answers.

This temporary diversion from toilet trouble gave Alec fresh heart to renew his surgery and after a blood-pressure-testing hour, the toilet was reassembled and working. However, post-operation complications left the pumping mechanism terribly stiff. If it didn't actually rupture the operator, the energy required necessitated a lie down after every visit.

At dusk, crates of 'pop' and beer appeared on the towpath and from one craft there issued mouth watering vapours of frying bangers and onions, while from another came bread cobs slit from ear to ear to receive them. In our turn we waited to receive THEM and soon openers were flashing and many beer bottles were upended over receptive, gurgling throats, while children dashed excitedly about, pop bottles permanently protruding out of their 'gobs'. The cows in an adjoining field looked interested and slightly envious, but then took the huff and moved away to a far corner, dejectedly chewing their monotonous milk-producing cuds while perhaps fancying our fat-producing, frizzling sausages. Mabel and Brian materialised into the crowd and Alexander, scarcely recovered from the previous night's revels, found it difficult to get his beak into the bottles but consumed his fair share of hot dogs.

Later, when we were recuperating back on *Maori*, they came on board to help drink our dwindling sherry, but not until they had first depleted the alcohol on another boat, where Mabel, during an inebriated exit, had slammed the door shutting the owner's keys inside and the owner — outside. Almost immediately, Alexander presented us with his calling card on the cabin floor, and as Mabel departed, she stood on the end of the gangplank causing it to shoot up and tip her off, luckily INTO the boat. *Votrekker* joined us and then *Debonaire*, and, as many boating experiences were swapped, our entire stock of Brighouse Co-op draft sherry was consumed. A wholly satisfying and pleasurable evening from every point of view.

This entertaining trip made us less and less inclined towards weekends of toil on *William Hennell*, and the frustration caused by limiting finances contributed to our general disquiet. I even began to write a book (this one) with the naïve notion that I could, overnight, blossom into a female James Herriot and raise the money for *William*'s costly conversion. However, the 'best laid plans of mice and "mine" gang ever aft a-gley', and this was not to be.

Other financial problems arose. My Fiat, having undergone extensive cosmetic surgery for body rot, was by now more fibre-glass than metal and although its disintegration had been temporarily arrested, a possibility existed that it might soon deposit its occupants on some remote country road and go sailing on without them. This major worry, plus other minor income-consuming setbacks, took the heart out of our wearying exertions on *William Hennell*. However, events during one particular weekend necessitated its abandonment to make an enforced dash on *Maori* to seek distant deeper waters.

Friday is usually hair-do day, and after an exhausting cleaning and baking morning I relish my visit to the hairdressers, where I usually collapse into a chair and sleep blissfully for half an hour under the coma-inducing hum of a drier. On Friday, June the first, I had done just this, and as I clicked the front door open, the 'phone jangled a summons. It was Alec.

Following up various water shortage rumours I had, that morning, contacted British Waterways and received ominous news about the Leeds–Liverpool Canal's possible closure. Alec listened in stunned silence to my tale of woe which would put paid to a well-planned holiday sailing the Staffordshire and Worcester Canal, the River Severn, (God help us!), the Worcester and Birmingham Navigation, and then, as a fitting climax, the Stratford upon Avon Canal to see 'King John' at the Shakespeare Memorial Theatre. We'd even bought the tickets!

I had anticipated a frustrated reaction, but when he suggested an immediate departure to transfer *Maori* over the Pennines and past Wigan Locks, I caught my breath, which just gave him time to say, 'Think about it!' and hang up.

'Think about it?' He had left unco-ordinated wheels crashing about in my head as I thought of Mabel and Brian expected that evening, Eileen and Ted motoring over from Nottinghamshire on Sunday, Grandma (whose shopping still had to be done) due on Saturday, having to arrange a day off from the Polytechnic where I taught, the transfer of all my students to another day, food for the journey and for Penny who would, no doubt, remain restfully at home.

'THINK ABOUT IT!!' he had causally said.

After a numbing, inactive few seconds, a couple of wheels clicked into place and Penny's head and mine met over a Waterways map to decide if a flight to freedom was feasible. It was — if we could start that evening.

We now had to wait for Alec's return, and as I imagined him breaking all the speed limits, a screech of brakes and a simultaneous slamming of the car door had him attending a quick conference in the hall. It was the quickest in our history; a rare decisive vote of two out of two occurred and the trip was on!

Feverish activity followed and within minutes, a clean, tidy house was reduced to a state of utter chaos. First of all 'phone calls (nearly all long distance) crackled hurried explanations, excuses and promises along the wires; then shopping lists were scribbled so that Alec's still-warm tyres could scream off to Brighouse Co-op; suitcases slid from under beds, clothes flew out of drawers into their depths, sleeping bags fell out of elevated airing cupboards, water carriers filled up and cardboard cartons grew heavy and bulging. Never before had they materialised so quickly.

I tried to remain calm, but couldn't. It was exhilarating really — a race against time — an unexpected adventure! Somehow, by five o'clock we were away, and after several near misses through the rush hour, we were lucky and relieved to arrive at Bingley. One minute a meditative *Maori* lay gently at her pleasant mooring and the next was being molested by two frantic humans leaping onto her rear end. They dumped cases and cartons aboard as if their lives depended on a fast getaway — no time for her to gradually warm up, no time to stow away in an orderly fashion, no time to check water, oil or fuel. Ropes, callously flung, struck *Maori's* person as we hastily shoved off, and it was no wonder that she showed her displeasure by bellowing black smoke at us when we pushed open the first swing bridge. Angry she certainly was and we were quite upset by this show of her injured feelings.

Except for us, all was calm, the scent of May trees making the air heavily still. A freshly-varnished canvas reflecting sun-dressed powder puffs of cloud lay beneath us until *Maori's* bows gently rippled it away; an inquisitive swallow dipped and swooped a wing-tip to the water in a nicely timed manoeuvre and we breathed more deeply as the old magic took over once again.

The obstacles to our progress were, of course, the swing bridges. But people seemed to sense our haste and many were swung in advance when they saw us coming. Luckily they opened in the direction we were heading, so when helpers were unavailable, *Maori* beguilingly nosed up to them in a native greeting and nudged her way through.

As we approached a particularly remote bridge, a man (obviously from a boat moored nearby) was contentedly circling around in his rubber dinghy. Our sudden appearance caused him to pull madly for the shore where he practically capsized when trying to alight from a flexible, wobbling craft which, after two or three heaves, he managed to get onto the bank. All this just to swing a bridge for two people he did not know and who had utterly destroyed his sweet moment of tranquillity. We shouted heartfelt thanks and Alec suggested that, if he paddled very fast, he could beat us to the next one!

The sun had become a ball of red pulsating fire hanging in a peppermint-pink sky and we scissored cleanly through a shot-silk surface, selfishly hoping for warm weather to assist our passage, when we should have been praying for biblical rain so that all the 'Noahs' on the Leeds–Liverpool Canal could keep their arks afloat.

Sometimes, contours of the land would create an optical illusion of a canal sloping uphill and *Maori's* engine would seem to labour as she chugged up these imaginary gradients. She had not completely recovered from her unceremonious departure and was still emitting an occasional rude back-fire; but our progress was steady and as we relaxed further, I disappeared to organise a coffee which I passed to Alec now casually poised at the wheel. Lulled by our idyllic surroundings into a false sense of security, he lifted the steaming liquid towards his welcoming lips just as hundreds of midges converged on him from all directions and an unobserved shadowing swan (probably an off-spring of our Silsden friend) attacked from behind. *Maori's* even, purposeful course changed to one of crazy zigzags and Alec's contortions, as he attempted to control the boat, grab a boathook, drink coffee and ward off midges, had to be seen to be believed!

Approaching Silsden, we mounted continuous watch for our old adversary but on this occasion he respected the urgency of our mission and swam ahead to ensure our safe, uninterrupted passage. We took this change of heart to be a good omen and as night came to meet us and lights began to sprinkle on in the misty distance, we urged *Maori* on to further efforts. Gliding under a hump bridge, she rubbed close to a moored boat called *Chalfont*; a gaily tattooed lady completely covered in colourful roses and fairytale castles. *Maori* slowed down to gawp at this splendacious personality and we exchanged greetings with an artist busily sketching on the towpath, wondering if she was responsible for the flamboyant works of art on this narrow boat.

Journeying right into the night had tired our eager souls, while the mixture of gloom and chilliness made us thankful to finally moor at Kildwick and take our rest.

Saturday dawned dewy, calm and steamy with promise of heat to come as a misty sun began the daily climb towards its zenith. I woke troubled by a blinding headache which throbbed above an extremely sore neck — the result, I supposed, of unusual positions adopted to apply yellow paint to the 'zenith' of an awkward, sloping ceiling in Dave's bedroom. Inevitable reaction to the previous day's excitement had set in, the bloody toilet was acting up again, and I had forgotten to pack any tea. As if being without our life-restoring cuppa wasn't bad enough, I had also forgotten my make-up and a change of underwear; so, wherever our destination lay, I would arrive undisguised, looking my age and worse still, possibly smelly!

Needless to say, Alec was full of the joys of Spring — they always are what you're not — but I cheered up somewhat when it was evident that *Maori* had ceased her tantrums and was no longer putting out her black smoke-screen.

The owner of Snaygill Boats hardly had time to stifle his early morning yawns, let alone scrape his toast, when we arrived at 0800 hours demanding diesel. We had been sharpened wide awake by the astringent qualities of a seven o'clock departure, but his slow tread told of recent deep sleep and an unwillingness to emerge from that blessed state. However, as the pink liquid gurgled down *Maori's* throat he became quite chatty and was, in the end, loath to give us leave. But if he had all day, we hadn't, and we departed rather abruptly, finishing our conversation over an ever-widening expanse of water.

In spite of our inward anxiety and the need to press on, there was so much to admire. Renoir meadows (without paths) rose up and away from us, splattered with florescent colour and alive in the wind; a large, toffee-nosed, white cat padded, back arched, tail erect, over a bridge parapet, his demeanour questioning our right to exist at all as we chugged underneath him. Skipton's horse-chestnuts bloomed a welcome brighter than any fanfare and the sun honoured its early-morning promise as we wallowed in the expended energy radiated during its sweltering climb up the sky. Great excitement occurred when a large pike swam alongside in a crystalline section of canal. Adhering to the four-knot rule, *Maori* and fish kept pleasant company in their common element until old stone warehouses, hung about with iron mooring rings, cast deep shadows into which he disappeared.

So prolific were the helpful 'bridge swingers' during the remainder of our sail to Gargrave, that our feet barely touched dry land, and we were hardly surprised, therefore, when the last one seemingly opened itself, only sheepish bystanders being present at the time.

The factory catering for babies bottoms (and other parts) was a welcome landmark as we moved, swing bridges now astern us, towards the first lock, which was (of course) empty and waiting for us. Our well-oiled lock drill went slightly awry when I tossed a mop-tangled rope up to Alec, who was startled to see it rocket into the air, curve over and do a neat mop-header into the lock. This handy implement had been purchased on the Llangollen Canal, so for sentimental reasons as well as practical, I grabbed a boathook to retrieve it. Yelling to Alec not to open the ground paddles, I recovered the mop and dropped the boathook; then I reached for another, much shorter boathook to fish for the first one and an impatient Alec, windlass at the ready, shouted down to ask what the hell I thought I was doing. As I was totally dependant on him at the time, I was grateful that he ignored my ill-timed directive to 'Get lost!' and we locked steadily up to Gargrave, did not even call at the Anchor, the Waterway's toilets or rubbish disposal, but forged on towards that special place where you have moored before, Banknewton. The sun had achieved its zenith and when we reached this favourite staircase we had achieved, in five hours sailing, the same distance a car would have travelled in half an hour!

Rising up Banknewton Locks on that particular Saturday morning bore no resemblance to our first idyllic ascent. Thirty minutes had been allocated for lunch when we reached the top of the flight, so as well as steering the boat, fending off and throwing ropes, I was also employed opening tins, boiling eggs, throwing a salad together and making tea. Once again fate, in the welcome shape of a friendly lock-keeper, Don Pearson, was kind to us as he joined *Maori*'s crew at the second lock and assisted us through the rest. This speeded up operations and ME quite considerably! Into the galley to slap some butter on — out to throw a rope; in to cut my finger on a tin — out to fend her off; in to toss some lettuce on the floor — out to drive the boat; in to over-fill the kettle — out to pull her in; in to get the table up — out to get the boat up; in to lay the table — out to lay *Maori* alongside and tie up! Alec couldn't understand why I was so breathless when we reached the top, for as he pointed out, he and the lock-keeper had done all the work!

But what did it matter? Banknewton was as beautiful as ever, the straight lines of the canal converging to an old, stone hump bridge over which horses' torsos and their riders occasionally clopped; a neat row of moored boats rubbed up against a protective grassy bank where the yellow and orange poppies had once more achieved their prime in the annual cycle. Nothing had changed — the intimate delights remained when the eyes weren't sweeping greater distances over roller-coasting hills; the rocket was, as ever, high on its hill-top pointing towards the unknown, and when we pointed *Maori* towards some other very well-known locks at Greenberfield, Jim the keeper was positioned to lend a hand.

Jim, brown and weathered, swore a hell of a lot, played war games, and kept the whole German army and navy (two Bismarks included) in some old tobacco tins. He wore a battered felt hat which looked as if stampeding cattle had passed over it and often donned a broad leather belt held by a large 'pirate' buckle. A swashbuckling character himself, extremely pleasant and helpful (at least to us) but just now and then daggers drawn when sorting out some of 'those bloody silly buggers' who misused his locks. Approach his cottage by the wrong gate, and you could be butted by a charging goat, or, have your legs bitten by some ferocious geese; a guard dog caused some concern even if you chose the right gate; but successfully face and negotiate all these dangers and bottles of pop and sweets were your rewards.

Safer by far to invite Jim and his wife Margaret on board for an evening drink and listen enthralled while he deployed his armies to re-enact some ancient battle. As he faded out of the present into the past, Jim changed the whole course of history with his reviewed plans and stratagems (made brilliant by foreknowledge of what the enemy might be expected to do) and his omniscience with regard to these conflicts was amazing. Unfortunately, his adjectival fluency tended to capture your attention and so a valuable history lesson went for a Burton!

On this trip, however, our thoughts were engaged with our own battle — against time, but looking forward to using the Waterway's amenities I asked Jim if there was any toilet paper inside.

'Toilet paper? BLOODY TOILET PAPER? NO — THERE BLOODY ISN'T. Every time I bloody-well put a bloody toilet roll in the bloody toilet some bloody fool pinches the bugger!' We commiserated with him for we knew all about 'bloody toilets', used our own toilet paper and then took our leave.

Our next 'short' stop was to buy tea and other provisions at Barnoldswick, where I was put in mind of Mabel when my search for an open shop resulted in a conducted tour of a rather sordid estate, where grubby, net-lidded windows gazed heavily out of dreary countenances into toy-strewn, neglected, balding gardens. Here and there, amongst the drab, sagging, gone-to-seed community, shone a lively cared for home, clean and smart with neat flower beds, hedges shaved to shapely smoothness and fences painted and secure. Sadly, the other side of the hedge usually remained unkempt, lacking in order or design, while the trim erect palings would hold hands with badly disfigured companions on either side. MY good companion was an extremely kind lady (badly bruised on the face as the result of a fall at Great Yarmouth the previous week) who escorted me for at least ten minutes, took me into her confidence on various matters and discussed the state of our society in general. She turned to starboard and port with well practised navigation, and it was clear, when she retraced her steps after pointing out the shop, that she had gone well out of her way so that I might buy some 'Yoohoo Typhoo' tea, a garish lipstick, a bottle of 'paralysed' milk and a loaf of yesterday's bread. After making one or two wrong turns, I negotiated the maze of identical streets and panted back to the boat which was already untied to assist fast propulsion out of Barnoldswick and its environs.

Alec did not ask me what the hell I'd been doing, so I filled the kettle, applied my new lipstick and made a welcome cup of tea. Image somewhat restored and two steaming hot beakers reposing on the cabin roof, we settled down to sail confidently towards our next objective, which you, because of your recent familiarity with this stretch of canal, will have guessed to be Foulridge Tunnel.

'I suppose I shall land the damp job of sitting up the front again,' I reflected rather pensively, as I sniffed the interesting combination of May blossom, newly mown grass, cow 'cacky' and exhaust fumes!

As we crossed over the border into Lancashire, a field, absolutely alive with buttercups, shone pure gold in the melting heat — except at its edges, where it was fanned by masses of waving bluebells and cooled by the canal's long, lapping tongue. Every turn of the screw brought new experiences and aromas; and fresh breezes, now changed into strong head winds, causing the water to lick more cravingly, were making our chances of reaching Barrowford Locks before six o'clock closing time, touch and go. Already the hands of our glassless clock had semaphored five o'clock and the tunnel still had to be negotiated — if we ever came to it!

Maori pushed hard against an unseen, restraining barrier, while the sky, lately a playground for racing, fluffy clouds, admitted a dark, disapproving presence, which chased them away becoming more and more forbidding by the minute.

'It looks as if the arks might stay afloat after all,' I thought, as we rounded a bend and the tongue slid us into the open throat of Foulridge.

As the reason for our journey was a prolonged drought, I wondered, when perched in my favourite spot, where the hell all the drips were coming from, and formed the opinion that the hill above us had reservoired its rainwater to await our arrival. This time a narrow boat had entered before us, so we were ingested slowly into the inner regions, our passage wearisome for a while, until they, at last aware of our chafing presence astern propelled up some effervescent Eno's and speeded up their progress and our final expulsion.

'How could that damn cow survive in that cold, mucky water?' I asked myself and a disinterested Alec. 'I wonder what breed it was? Well, whatever it WAS, it certainly ended up a Friesian,' I chortled.

Alec, chewing on a 'Topic', groaned!

Neither was he amused to learn that our six o'clock arrival at Barrowford meant we could not descend the locks; but I was happy to kill *Maori's* engine and throw out the mooring pins onto a grassy bank bordering the toilets and rubbish disposal. Turning my back on the Waterway's amenities, I gazed from our starboard windows over a gold lamé canal to fresh, emerald green meadows dotted with trees and cows, where a young boy, enveloped in a very sloppy jumper (probably his dad's) lay flat on his stomach fishing with a tea strainer tied insecurely onto the end of a stick. My eyes swept further around to the locks and admired immaculate black and white approaches; which reminded me that I must look out for Elsie, Barowford's own Dickensian lock-keeper — a character from her head to her not too distant toes. Rotund, ageless, her speech slightly blurred and difficult for me (a foreigner) to understand, always sounded as if she was finishing a mouthful of icecream, which she sold — but not to us, as we always arrived when stocks had run out.

During our last icecreamless call she had mentioned a pending visit to hospital to have treatment or possibly an operation for a complaint which I failed to decipher but gleaned that it had to do with legs, and now I was anxious to inquire after her welfare. When I knocked on her cottage door and heard a muffled shout from inside, I took this as a signal to enter and found Elsie lying on a couch. She remembered me, bade me welcome, stated that prior to her stay in hospital she could walk, but now, after an operation she couldn't, called them names for making her worse, said that they were now treating her husband and would probably make HIM worse, that the icecream man was coming in the morning but if I wanted any pop I would have to help myself! Concerned, I asked how she was coping and heard all about a useless assistant lock-keeper who had made matters worse when, after chaining and locking the locks, he had dropped the key into the canal. Elsie, horizontally irate, had given him a right ticking off and then handed over the spare key — which he promptly dropped in as well.

'And would you believe it?' she stated in an aggrieved tone, 'He didn't tell me! He just buggered off home without me giving him a second telling off!'

Eventually the chains had to be cut off the lock.

When she had finished her fascinating saga, I cut off back to *Maori*. During an unhurried meal, Alec bemoaned his lack of raspberry ripple, but then thinking aloud that we had achieved a fair day's sailing, he relaxed and burped loudly on Elsie's pop.

Sunday dawned ominously with dark, rain-dispensing clouds sweeping arrogantly across the sky. We kitted up in our North Sea fishermen's gear and prepared for the worst. A shallow pound below the first lock needed refilling and while we waited for Elsie's favourite lock-keeper to come and set us free, I engaged in scintillating conversation with someone in a woolly hat on *Gordale*, a desirable narrow boat belonging to Yorkshire Dales Cruisers, which was also hoping to be released.

'Good morning,' ventured my sou'wester.

'Good morning,' answered the woolly hat.

Silence!

'Stinking morning, isn't it?' I contradicted myself.

'Yes,' agreed woolly hat.

Silence!

'Still it could be worse,' I declared with originality.

'Yes,' he said, nearly causing me to fall overboard when he continued. 'There's a bit of blue sky over there.'

I followed his pointing arm to a minute speck which was hardly discernible.

'My Granny used to say that if there's enough blue sky to make an elephant's waistcoat, the weather will be fine,' he enlarged.

I measured the speck against an imaginary elephant.

'Oh yes,' I rejoined brightly. 'Well, we'll find out if your Granny was right.'

Just then the butter-fingered lock-keeper arrived and windlasses began whirring to fill the lock and allow water and us through to the first pound. The weather, in spite of Granny's prediction, worsened, and as we descended the second lock, as well as being rained on, I was 'peed' on by little jets of water issuing out of the lock wall. Not that it mattered very much to a person already acting as a watershed, with five locks to go and past caring! However, in spite of appalling conditions, many agile woolly hats from *Gordale* made our descent easy and I was soon being 'peed' on again in the last lock of the flight.

As we passed by the conglomeration of small villages which have become Nelson, industrial squalor depressed our already dampened spirits, but must have suited a family of swans who had chosen to live there. Then, as a lady from an upper window of a terrace house smiled and waved a gay yellow duster and the Co-op milkman lifted a 'pinta' in greeting, I warmed to the friendliness of the town where Evelyn Crisp had been raised.

She occupied my thoughts as we stole through her past and I imagined her running out from one of the terraced houses which marched up regimented streets on our port side or, skipping in the playground of Whitefield Common Council School, still standing on our right. As I wind to avoid debris floating on the water, I see her drawn, as are all children, to play by the canal she loved. Later, when only twelve years old, as one of a family of ten, she toiled half-time at t'mill and half time at school, a practice which was normal in those days. How strange that her husband should become a lengthsman and bring her in later life to live in a Waterway's cottage on a lock side, where canal and river were her constant companions.

A large plastic bag catches my attention and causes me to swing *Maori* rather violently, and Alec, ensconced on the stern awakes from his reverie as I do from mine.

Having returned from the past, the present demanded coffee to be the order of the day, and as I drank the warming liquid and admired the symmetrical beauty of tall mill chimneys against the sky, I noted that the sun had at last broken through a chink in the clouds, so perhaps Granny was going to be proved right after all!

As industry flourished on our port side, the countryside flourished on our starboard and we enjoyed the best of both worlds; until we rounded a blind corner that is, to find a large unattended working barge straddled across the canal. *Maori* was reversed to a sharpish stop, which, had she been a car, would have set her screeching. *Gordale*, not far astern, shocked to come across two frantically signalling ratings standing on *Maori*'s engine hatch, promptly sailed into some reeds and became stuck. As it was obviously time for decision making, we decided on a barge boarding party. As I manoeuvred alongside, our party (Alec) took a flying leap, landed insecurely and swayed over the bowels of the barge, where receptive sludgy gunge, which had once reposed on the canal bottom, awaited him. For a timeless moment he tottered on the brink but recovered to pick up a mile-long boating hook, which nearly overbalanced him again. This superb canal-churning implement was very much to Alec's liking and he soon had the whole area bubbling like a thermal region, while the barge stayed put.

A better decision involved attaching a line to some chains on the barge and throwing it ashore — but there wasn't anybody on-shore for we were both on the other side of the cut. As for *Gordale*, they were busy trying to extricate themselves from some particularly glutinous mud and the chances were that we would have to rescue them as well. Just as we had hit on an obvious plan to sail a line ashore, *Gordale* sucked itself free and all of a sudden the towpath was enlivened by cowboys and cowgirls, coiling and tossing ropes with the enthusiasm of competitors at a rodeo.

As the barge was being secured, I noticed that more blue sky was becoming visible; enough for a waistcoat — and pants as well. Good old Granny — she knew a thing or two!

An uninhibited *Gordale* now forged ahead, leaving only a wake for us to follow and by the time we had reached the outskirts of Burnley, even that had disappeared. However, while the brightening day had, by now, fully clothed the elephant, it had divested us of our hampering waterproofs and with a beaker of asparagus soup each to warm our vitals, we settled down to contemplate some general canal dereliction. In particular, the eyesore created by an incongruous group of broken-down garages, all shapes and sizes, which no respecting town planning authority should have allowed to exist. But then, as *Maori* moved, hemmed in by houses and industry, we received quite a shock at the contrast afforded by a soft grassy border made dark green beneath large arching trees. This caused us to look further to where some rowdy children and a hairy dog chased a ball around a pleasant park which sloped away on our right hand side. Once away from the lee of the trees, I was aware of an uncomfortable, freshening wind, a very bright sun, and also a pile of dirty dishes in the sink; but we were drawing towards the very famous Burnley Embankment and the washing-up could wait.

An extensive Lowry scene opened out and absorbed us as we sailed sixty feet above the patterned rows of terraced slate roofs and lines of smoking chimneys. Lowry-type 'match stick' people, who were hurrying about the daily act of living, boarded matchbox buses, entered toy shops, pulled minute children and dogs, walked deformed by heavy bags — leaning into the wind, and were seemingly unaware of our eye in the sky entry into their environment. Later, some romantic old warehouses just begged to be transformed into luxury apartments — with (a coquettish thought!) connecting bridges astride the canal. A little Venice in Burnley!

Now the Calder Valley opened spacious views over to looming Pendle Hill, the setting for *The Lancashire Witches* which I had recently read. It told of a suspicious, uncompromising community which tried and executed many so-called witches.

I resembled a witch myself when, as we skirted an open hillside the wind whipped up the canal into small, energetic waves and my waves into a tangled mess. *Maori*, her inflamed, running nose pressed hard against the water, had to travel almost sideways to maintain her course. Some exposed swing bridges lying further on occupied my thoughts as I anticipated all sorts of difficulties in our duel with this blustering opponent, who, disregarding our need to reach Johnson's Hillocks Locks by five o'clock, had taken over and rearranged our itinerary. In fact progress became so laborious that we could not even be sure of our arrival at Blackburn for that time. But we achieved it and four smoking monsters dwarfed us into our rightful perspective as we passed a large power station which, I supposed, lit the homes of Blackburn, kept its mills working and warmed and fed its one hundred thousand inhabitants. Unfortunately, Blackburn uses its canal as a dustbin and I waited for usual excessive vibration caused by something round the prop — happily in vain this time. From a high embankment I counted many spires rising out of smoky, populated depths to breathe a purer air, and the vista, as bright sunlight caught their pinnacles, was momentarily one of great beauty. Freshly grassed banks and newly planted trees added their message of hope and even architecturally austere mills and chimneys were compatible to the character of this interesting stretch of waterway, where six extremely tidy locks dropped us, with the enthusiastic aid of two very untidy boys, over fifty-four feet.

Banks of houses now lined the canal on our port side and each bore witness to their owners' interest or disinterest in them. One garden, terracing down to a fine stone landing stage, flaunted multi-coloured frills to entice the eye, while next door a rusty corrugated iron barrier fell over the canal, weighed down by its burden of weeds and household rubbish.

At one point, a huge collie dog ejected itself from a house, went berserk at our unexpected appearance and careered back and forth along the soft margins, leaping, skidding and barking, his superior speed enabling him to harass us until he ran out of gardens to trespass. However, with his front paws submerged, he paused on a grassy prominence, looked questioningly at the water, thought better of it and only barked his annoyance at our getaway until we chugged out of sight.

Because we had been travelling non-stop on a diet of coffee, soup, tea, sandwiches, cakes and 'Crunchie Bars', we were more anxious to arrive at a square meal than our destination Johnson's Hillocks; but some satisfying canal scenery had to suffice as tall, mature trees temporarily held the wind at bay and allowed a short, restful sail through a velvety jade surface, bordered with delicate pink campion, fragrant bluebells and fresh green bracken.

But the biting, tugging wind pounced gleefully back on us when we emerged from our woodland shelter, refused to lie down with the dying day and demanded its last pound of flesh for the rest of the way. This flesh became progressively tired and goose-pimply and even the superb views could not atone for a hungry, uncomfortable sail which we were grateful to end, tied astern of *Gordale*, whose ship's company had already adjourned to a nearby pub.

After a meal, we trudged (upon direction) uphill to a telephone box farthest from the boat, gaspingly inquired of Penny if SHE was alright and tottered back to collapse into the Top Lock Inn and with a brandy and a Guinness respectively. Although *Maori* lay only a few yards away, it required maximum effort to stagger back, undress and make our beds, before finally falling into them and flaking out.

Monday morning arose gloriously, but I arose ingloriously (requiring at least ten hours more sleep) when shaken awake at six thirty. But later, after loads of steaming tea and high calorie buttered toast and honey, an unromantic image (in a poetic setting) looked more or less human when it emerged one hour later to visit the Waterway's toilets. There, I recalled, dreamily our last ascent of these beautifully situated locks. At sunset, we glided through liquid gold between smooth, green banks and margins of wild flowers, the locks transporting us from one entrancing aspect to another. Then, as we neared the summit, the sky subjugated all with a brilliant display of crimson, pink, bright blue and orange, splashed like a rough sea around the great fiery disc of a sinking sun.

As *Gordale* had already watered, we did likewise, and when they entered the top lock we followed. Granny's hatless, topless Bill (we had actually exchanged names by now) was at the helm. During a slightly more relaxed conversation we discussed the possibility of locking down the formidable Wigan Flight of twenty-three 'drops' together. Because of our hasty departure from Huddersfield we had not arranged for a lock-keeper's assistance and, as *Gordale's* crew members were younger, stronger and more numerous than *Maori's*, togetherness seemed (to us) the logical thing.

In spite of the various setbacks, our schedule was going well, but this was the vital day when, barring disasters, (never to be ruled out) we hoped to proceed along the Leigh Branch and find a suitable, safe mooring. If successful, our race against time and tide would be won and our pending romantic voyage to offer homage to King John at Stratford, would be assured.

An annoying incident caused a delay in the fifth pound, which had developed its own minor water shortage. Allowing *Gordale* the deep, middle channel towards the next lock, I pulled *Maori* too far to starboard, entered the shallows and found some mud. With Alec out of rope-throwing range on a distant towpath and Bill likely to land in the same predicament if he attempted a rescue, I was completely marooned, so I sent up a hasty prayer and put *Maori* hard astern. Lovely, muddy ripples churned from her rear end as she wallowed in a succulent, black mud-bath. Unlimited advice from the towpath soon had her floundering like a beached whale and me shouting like a fish wife, until Alec (having seen a great light) opened all the available paddles above, so that buoyancy restoring water could cascade to our rescue. This left the previous pound tenaciously turbid for the next unsuspecting boater! Poetic justice caught up with us though, for after being freed from the bottom lock at eight thirty, nine o'clock saw us stopped dead in our tracks by an enormous clinging plastic bag which had been drawn to tangle with our brassy, scintillating propellor. Alec automatically stripped to the waist and then climbed down into the access hatch, where his feet became lubricated by water and floating oil as he hung, eventually suspended, head down over the prop shaft, hands fully extended to reach the unwanted pick-up. In his haste he became too enthusiastic and I was summoned (a comfort stop unexpectedly shortened) just in time to pull him out.

Soon, two totally different modes of travel criss-crossed each other and a roadway sign on the M61 surprised us with the information that Bolton was thirteen miles away, Manchester twenty-three and Rochdale twenty-eight. We were so close to home by car and already I had lost my bearings, become disorientated and a different mortal. As we stole, eyes looking up, beneath the great concrete structure which vibrated with heavy-goods-vehicles and a never ending succession of cars, I was grateful to be insignificant and slow on the canal and happy when the bleating of sheep took over from the interminable roar of battling beasts from some other undesirable world. A large, picturesque mill invited admiration, as WE did from some of its employees who, as they lounged on some seats along a grassy sunny verge, observed that 'It was alright for some!'

Along the way, as our wake played up to the edge of a small park, I waved vigorously to a little girl topped by bobbing sunlit curls, who skipped, small hand in large, alongside her grandfather. They stopped, but when he urged a response, shyness buried her head in his knees, where, in spite of great encouragement she remained hidden, content to regard my bird-like flapping out of the corner of one suspicious eye.

The wind, having risen late, was making up for lost time and freshening by the minute, so I sheltered down in *Maori*'s well and chased the sun (as a winding canal kept altering its position in the sky) by changing my position just as frequently. After a few peace-disturbing moves, Alec could stand it no longer.

'Bloody hell, "Doh",' he ejaculated. 'I wish you'd bloody decide where the hell you want to sit!'

An interesting old milestone carved the message that eighty-seven miles lay astern towards Leeds and forty ahead to reach Liverpool, but we were to branch off at the bottom of the Wigan flight. The few miles approaching this heavily industrialised town are very attractive and a pre-Tudor mansion superbly positioned in acres of partially wooded parkland, made one imagine sedate, formal garden parties, polite conversations and croquet. The lawns, adorned with huge posies of purple rhododendrons and fanning trees, swept with unrestrained gracefulness down to the fondling canal. In fact, the house is open all year for the public at large to enjoy golf, have a picnic, take a nature walk or ride in a tractor-drawn trailer. Or, if invited — you can attend a wedding reception.

Wigan's tall office oblongs and industrial smoke stacks soon stood out from a murky haze way down on our starboard beam, for we were flying high on a hillside above the pulsating town and making for the bare, wind-swept locks and pounds which were to lower us over two hundred feet, to within hearing and feeling of its heartbeat.

We began our breezy, dishevelled descent with *Maori* leading the way into the locks and Granny's Bill following after. This system worked well for a while, although I became somewhat alarmed by the speed at which Bill aimed his craft at the locks. However, the boat seemed to be capable of shuddering to a stop within a few yards, so my fears were temporarily allayed — until the eleventh lock that is, when it all happened. In spite of resistance from the strong wind, I had already sailed into the chamber and awaited Bill's pleasant company. He, in order to frustrate increasingly erratic gusts, aimed *Gordale* at speed towards the space that remained and I took up my now habitual stance on the engine hatch anticipating his usual emergency stop and waiting to fend off. Fend off? As Bill completely mistimed his manoeuvre, *Gordale's* enormous prow struck the lock entrance, bounced off and aggressively headed straight for *Maori* and me! Nothing I could have done would have halted that massive hunk of steel, so in the interest of self preservation, I fell into the safety of the well just as a sickening crack and splintering of wood had *Maori* shaking from blunt end to sharp and me from head to toe. Bill was beside himself with remorse, but luckily *Maori's* engine hatch was stoutly built and the damage, when surveyed, amounted (unbelievably) to only one fractured cross-beam. After the accident I suggested that *Gordale* should enter the remaining locks first, so that I could have a go at THEM, and we proceeded to the pound just above the famous Wigan Pier without further trauma.

At the twenty-second lock we turned left into the Leigh Branch, waved farewell to *Gordale* and also to our fears of a water shortage. I felt a few cheers would have been in order, or a celebratory dressing of ship, but as four-twenty leered from a clock-face high on a nearby church tower, (which didn't even ring a bell for us!) we curved apathetically around a similarly unimpressed power station, to descend our last two locks into a dreary no-man's land.

Now that all the excitement was over, I felt rather dreary myself, especially as I observed the depressing struggle of some scrubby vegetation to survive on acre upon acre of waste tips; but some water flashes caused by flooded workings glinted and caught the eye and I thought that the place might improve with time.

The Leigh Branch is, for me, one of those links which sometimes have to be sailed, although on this particular occasion we were pleased to ply its waters to Leigh and find a safe mooring alongside a landing stage where a house, next to an old warehouse, sheltered a friendly helpful woman who promised to keep an eye on *Maori* until the following Saturday, when we would sail her to Lymm.

All that remained outstanding was a 'phone call to Stan, who dropped whatever he was doing to fetch us to fetch our car (still recovering at Bingley). Then, a fast transition back to the real world, where a week's dirty washing still lay concealed in the Ali Baba basket and where work, in the shape of eager, expectant piano students, awaited me at the 'Poly' next morning!

CHAPTER TEN

'The play's the thing
Wherein I'll catch the conscience of the king.'
William Shakespeare

D id I say work? Teaching the piano, work? Not when I reflect
upon the extraordinary life and times of Gordon Coupland, a
lengthsman on the Calder and Hebble Navigation. His association
with the waterways began when he was launched from the safety of
his mother's protecting love into the less sheltering hands of a hard,
domineering father. Their living was earned by the poor, unfortunate
horses that trudged towpaths hauling heavy loads, sometimes until
overwork dropped the wretched underfed creatures dead in their
tracks. He was a tyrannical task master, albeit not a very intelligent
one (for dead horses had to be replaced) which necessitated a tight-
fisted individual parting with his money. Consequently, Gordon
often had to stand in and become a human bow-hauler to the barges.

When still at school, Gordon unfailingly rose at four in the
morning to feed his scrawny equine charges. Sometimes, during a
coal shortage, (when in dire need of a warm drink to soften the
harshness of his dark awakening) he had to clamber up on a chair,
to hold a pan of water above a gas mantle which managed to sibilate
adequate light but very little heat.

At fifteen years of age he also started working at the 'pit', and after
a nine-hour stint (which began at six a.m.) he would slog away for
his avaricious, unfeeling dad. So it was small wonder that he often

dozed on a horse's back or, if he managed to stay awake long enough, slept on a bed of hay in the stable. Perhaps in an adjoining stall stood the abject, forlorn creature which (according to Gordon) was never allowed to lie down because of its suspected inability to be able to rise again!

The remuneration for these long, arduous hours was hardly inflationary — a twelve-hour haul of a sixty-ton laden barge paid the princely sum of twenty-six shillings. Of this, fivepence in the shilling went to Gordon and sevenpence to the horse's owner. Should the barge be empty — shortening the time to seven hours — twelve shillings was divided again in Papa's favour!

Man and beast often had to trudge many miles to their starting point and even a long rough trek (say from Brighouse to Barnsley) earned the boy nothing until the actual hauling began. During one more lucrative period, Gordon considered himself to be really well-off earning three pounds six shillings a week for toiling sometimes twenty-two hours a day. This was, of course, seized by the head of the household who then reluctantly sorted out two sixpence pocket money for his son — unless HE was short hat week, in which case Gordon remained unpaid.

Not surprisingly, at the age of twenty-one he rebelled and ran away from home taking neither money nor food — but with freedom in his heart, after years of slave labour. And he survived to marry Lilian Kershaw whose father Sam skippered the first boat belonging to Sugden's Flour Mill at Brighouse and who herself, at only six months old, was a water-baby rocked to sleep by the gentle movement of narrow boat *Brenda*, as it traded between Hull and Wakefield.

One of her earliest childhood memories is of a fatal accident in Goole, when a woman was knocked off a barge by a large swinging tiller, made lethal in the strong surging tide. She saw, through a child's frightened wondering eyes, a dripping body hauled from the depths, later to be shrouded in a sheet, lowered into a cog-boat and rowed off into the enveloping night. No doubt eerie mists were rising and reflecting lights distorted as the oars splashed a rhythmic funereal beat all the way to its destination — Leeds. A strange ruling at the time decreed that a body could be transported anywhere by water, whereas on land, restrictions had to be observed and overcome. Another, equally strange unwritten law, applied to doctors' visits — the boat people insisting that he accept two pounds before even stepping aboard.

So two 'intrepid boat people', Gordon and Lilian, possessing just one pound between them, were married at a registry office and began their difficult and extremely frugal life together.

Eventually Gordon was employed by British Waterways and allocated a small primitive cottage, which boasted a tap without a sink. This anomaly was balanced out later when they moved to another which sported a useful sink — but no tap! To Gordon, after years among the horses and the hay, this was sheer luxury and he was delighted to pay three shillings weekly for shelter, which adequately protected them from the elements — especially the vital one, water!

Being short of money was the story of their lives, and sometimes, when things became desperate, he would dredge the River Calder's sandy bottom with a pan attached to a long pole; his reward for hours of difficult, unlawful, muscle-straining work — five shillings a ton! Although a non-swimmer, those same arms achieved several rescues during the course of his patrols. One poignant incident occurred when a small girl, happily picking flowers on a warm canal bank, ventured too near to an insecure edge and suddenly slipped out of a sunlit day down into dark, frightening depths. When Gordon pulled her out, weeping and badly shocked, she still clutched her also tearful, sodden bunch of bluebells.

Three times at least he has put himself in some danger when trying to recover some unfortunate involuntary bather, but he still survived, still could not swim and still remained a little aggrieved at a few 'perishing people' who did not even thank him after their rescue.

Gordon was a great leg-puller and his bright blue eyes absolutely twinkled mischief when he was in one of his waggish moods. 'Things' often appeared in Evelyn's and Arthur's garden; for when they were away from home, Gordon would, without their knowledge, seize the opportunity to plant a few seed potatoes, cabbages or lettuces. They were very grateful to him when a small apple tree 'appeared', but utterly amazed a short time after, to see one spindly branch weighed down by a large rosy apple which Gordon — needless to say — had tied on!

Throughout all that hard oppressive childhood he was, and remained, a prankster, which makes one think that we are what we are and cannot always blame our upbringing and environment. The waterways are rich with interesting characters, past and present, and they give us food for thought when we compare their placid life style with the materialistic shallowness of our fast-moving present day society. Is there any wonder that people crave an escape to a more basic way of life? The canals act as an outlet for some of these searching souls and provide a different dimension for lives ordered by routine and domestic monotony — a state which rules many, because of the need to earn their daily bread. Still I sometimes wonder if this restraint is self imposed, because people lack the desire, or more often the courage, to initiate a change.

Our annual change, which you may submit was no change at all, began on a sultry summer's evening at Lymm in Cheshire where an extremely hospitable boating club hosted us for a few weeks until our holiday began. Dave, driving my ailing Fiat, transported us from home to a *Maori* lying shyly quiet between two strange boats some distance from the car park. A wheel-barrow (thoughtfully provided) carried our victuals, suitcases and bedding, trip by bumping squeaking trip, past hedgerows comely with entwining cornbine and promising to future blackberry gatherers.

Our temporary mooring lay deep in the countryside alongside flowing waves of sunburnt barley. Deep shadows sailed across in swift succession to keep up with their flying counterparts voyaging across the sky. Later, when a calm evening made the canal surface oily-grey and deep looking, we walked past the motionless barley

field and further along a turfy towpath. Then past a great beast of a
bull whose belligerent eyes followed our progress towards a local
public house, with the strange name of 'Ye Old Number 3'.

Here, mussels and whelks slid down with martinis and whiskies
to launch the holiday off to a good, but as far as I was concerned,
slightly bilious start! Clutching a bag of mushrooms (bought from
the 'whelks' man) we departed poorer by abut three pounds and, as
we wished the bull's dark outline 'goodnight', bright stars from
millions of light-years away morse-coded thousands of 'goodnights'
to us. As I lay in that blissful suspension between drowsiness
and total oblivion, I wondered about the pub's funny name, tried
to recall the whereabouts of numbers 1 and 2, but then, as my
thoughts stretched out to a long, inviting holiday and anticipated the
ripening barley field which would greet us in the morning, I sighed
contentedly and passed out!

By next morning, some of the previous day's racing clouds had
returned to take up residence and provide a now green canal for
Maori, to sail the short distance to Agden Marina for diesel. A
handsome, converted steel lifeboat had priority and as it satisfied a
seemingly endless thirst, we heard from two young owners about an
enormous engine which drank petrol at the cost of two pounds an
hour, thus limiting their annual cruise to only one week. We thanked
God for our not so handsome, but economical *Maori*, allowed her
to drink her fill and then moved lazily along followed by a soft,
flowing, virescent train which bowed flexible branches and reeds as
we passed. Delicate grasses rich in variety adorned the banks and
seemed to quiver with delight at our presence. Hustling willow herb
pushed up colourful purple spikes to join the waving cow parsley,
head and shoulders above a wild throng of wide-eyed moon-daisies,
aggressive, pointing thistles, beaming dandelions, heavily-scented
clover, open-mouthed groups of foxgloves and great plate-like leaves
which huddled together protectively as *Maori* chug, chug, chugged
on her way.

At Runcorn Junction we were taken aback to come upon several
craft belonging to Yorkshire Dales Cruisers of Banknewton and

Pennine Boats of Silsden which, like us had escaped the drought affected Leeds–Liverpool canal.

Garbled fishy conversations came to us on the air when we passed an unusual competition, where gay anoraks, multi-coloured trews and bright, fluttering head scarves indicated a wholly female scene, quite different from the sombre, all-male events. Varying ages, shapes and sizes became uniform in their obvious enthusiasm and concentration and I wondered why I should be so surprised to come across a women's fishing competition. Is it because men have always fished — man the hunter, right from prehistoric days? 'If that is the case, we have a hell of a lot of idle hours to make up for!' I thought aggrievedly. 'If only we could be born into a world which didn't feed us preconceived ideas and concepts,' I reasoned. 'What freedom of thought could be ours perhaps, to find a completely different society and a new philosophy about our values and relationships one with another!'

A group of philosophical Jersey cows appeared to nod in agreement. A second later, my fickle thoughts had travelled over continents and oceans to New Zealand, where, they were taken R.D. (rural delivery) to The Pines, Merv and Joan Fernyhough's dairy farm at Kaihere, which nestles cosily in the hills around the eye-stretching Hauraki Plains. Here, in my tender 'teens', I had spent endless, sun-soaked, balmy days as a gum-booted cow-cocky feeding calves, spreading manure and of course, stripping Jersey cows. Installed in Merv's cowshed was a loud, crackly radio which poured out distorted musical offerings all through milking. Merv seriously maintained that his cows liked music and therefore, gave more milk. They also gave more 'cow-cacky' which I had to swill and sweep away!

Kaihere boasted one all-purpose store and one all-purpose hall, the latter becoming a primitive cinema showing ancient and somewhat serialised films one night a week. On these occasions the local kids, both Maori and Pakeha, always occupied the front seats and when a reel was being changed, (which was often) or when it broke down, (which was very often) they would use their sweet bags to make paper aeroplanes and fire them all over the hall. Alternatively, some would jump up and down in Haka fashion to project funny, distorted, shadowy shapes onto the screen while others clapped and stamped until the movie continued. On this important evening of the week the store would remain open and during the interval the entire audience, glad to lift their sore bums off the wooden benches, trooped out to buy hot pies and peas.

Once a month, this hall was also used for an eagerly anticipated dance which, in order to allow this far-flung farming community time to finish milking, feed itself and get scrubbed-up for the fray, began at ten o'clock.

All the unattended sheilas would sit talking on one side of the hall and surreptitiously eye the speculative jokers standing in groups opposite. Then, when a dance was announced, an almighty rush of males crossed the intervening space towards the partners of their choice.

I attended several of these 'hops' with Vic Wilkins (a farmer who was rather keen on me at the time) and my friends Joan and Merv would tell us (as we departed) 'to behave ourselves, to have a good time, and not to be late back!' One evening Vic and I, when returning from Patetonga, paused along the way to study the Southern Cross and various stars (from inside the car!) and arrived back at two-thirty a.m. Fearful, in case Vic's car had woken up my temporary guardians, I crept up to the house, removed my shoes, silently opened the back door and made for the light switch on the other side of the room. I tiptoed into a minefield of incredibly resonant tin cans which banged and crashed my arrival to the whole of Kaihere.

'Hello Cappa, had a good time?' called a giggling, muffled voice from the next room.

'You're late!' accused Merv as I bashed on towards my bedroom, where the flick of a switch revealed tightly-knotted pyjamas hanging from the light above my tangled heap of a bed — and triggered off more uncontrolled tittering from my 'friends'.

'Goodnight Cappa,' they guffawed and yawned as I wobbled and over-balanced in a determined attempt to free my sleeping attire.

'Goodnight you rotters,' I called good-naturedly to disguise my already vengeful thoughts.

Half an hour later, intent on retribution, I successfully re-crossed the minefield to where Merv's gum-boots were ready waiting for the morning. Gleefully I poured half a pint of water into each, smiled to myself, and withdrew.

This, was a stratagem I was to regret, for no sooner had I slipped into the realms of sweet unconsciousness, than an eruption threw me out of bed, unceremoniously lifted me over Merv's knee and belted the daylights out of me!

Joan's parents, the Westlakes, also had a farm in Kaihere and they employed an English 'Johnny' called Bill who would sometimes go out of his way to tease us young, sensitive sheilas. One week, when we had had more than our fair share of leg-pulling from this bloomin' Pommie, we decided to get our own back. Once again the monthly frolic was featured when, on the day of the dance, Jerry, Joan's sister, collaborated and removed all the bolts from Bill's bed and then carefully remade it to appear as normal. The brilliant idea was that Bill, retiring positively whacked at some ungodly hour of the morning, would collapse onto his bed and cause the bed in turn, to collapse onto the floor.

It must have been a special hop because we all wore evening dresses and tottery shoes. When the dance was over, round about two a.m., innocents in the know crept around the outside of the large, wooden farmhouse and unashamedly watched Bill getting undressed. The night was gorgeously warm, full of special New Zealand farm-smells and the hypnotic sound of cicadas singing their sultry summer song. Hands stifled our hysterical convulsions as Bill slowly disrobed. Impatiently we waited until, at last, attired in striped pyjamas, he got into bed. It disintegrated with a satisfying crash, causing an earthquake to shudder through the whole house and Bill in particular!

We stumbled away tittering and falling about, quite drunk with uncontrollable laughter. Back at The Pines, two miles away over a rough loose-metal road, teetering on high heels and tripping over long frocks we arrived completely exhausted to recount our misdeeds to an interested Joan and Merv, amazingly wide awake, sitting up in bed.

Bill, (according to Jerry) gave her some funny looks next day and we gave Bill some funny looks next time we met — but nothing was said!

By the time my thoughts had returned from Jersey cows down-under to Jersey cows in England, they were a long way astern and a pleasant pub at Broken Cross was inviting us to moor for the night.

Our subsequent departure next day at the respectable hour of ten o'clock, found us gliding along under square black and white bridges on a brown canal. At the spacious lagoons, Alec went only slightly off the main channel to put us nicely aground on some soft boat-sucking mud, which, despite all known freeing tactics, held *Maori* fast. A fortnight stranded in a sleepy lagoon did not attract us and the incongruous boat-skeletons already abandoned on the far side caused us some concern, so when narrow-boat *Iris* chanced along we were grateful for the line which pulled us free.

The day was one which a photographer might describe as cloudy-bright, but a chap, sometimes striding purposefully, sometimes running by the side of his narrow boat, his family remaining on board, struck me as being not so bright. This extremely unfit Captain Bligh commanded his long-suffering crew from the shore, bellowing like a bull if they went too fast for him to keep up. His puffing, panting, red-faced progress exhausted me and I had to retire to the cabin for a quiet kip.

When we arrived at Middlewich, a piercing whistle emitted by Alec did not have the desired effect of waking me and he was left to bring *Maori* alongside, switch-off and make us secure. Then he observed that, as he had done everything else he might as well 'mash' the tea. I could hear him mumbling and filling the kettle and in a belated attempt to redeem myself, called out that it was already full.

Alec, by then in the toilet, made an apt reply, which raised my eyebrows but not my comfortable, recumbent body. I decided to exercise a silent discretion (if nothing else) and wait humbly and thankfully for a restoring man-made cuppa!

Later, as we affectionately linked up with the Middlewich Arm yet again, I took my overdue stint at the wheel. At Minshull Lock, after we had risen easily in company with another boat, I was pleasantly surprised when the owner praised my handling of *Maori* and suggested that I might join his crew. My more than adequate chest swelled to Jane Russell proportions, especially when he endorsed his remarks to Alec, who was quite taken aback at this commendation of woman-kind issuing from a member of his own sex.

Later that evening, however, there was no such commendation forthcoming when we tried to moor in a particularly shallow stretch of canal. This time Alec was up forward peering into the murky depths and sounding with the long pole. Several times I allowed *Maori* to sidle towards a likely spot and each time, a prodding anxious Alec suddenly gesticulated for me to change direction. For some reason I was held personally responsible for the shallowness of the canal and after several abortive attempts and one or two heated exchanges, we really got our hair off!

During one of the brief calmer moments I tentatively suggested that we moor close to a bridge where the water should be deeper, but this idea was rejected as too dangerous, creating a hazard to other boats. Much much later, after some tense non-speaking miles, as we approached a large stone bridge, Alec broke silence and suggested that we moor there because the canal was wider and deeper! MEN!!

That night, before zipping up my sleeping bag, I looked out of the window at a mysterious moon floating behind a black lace mantilla of cloud, coolly aloof above a world turned grey, ebony and silver, where a dark, full-blooded *Maori* rested lazily on an inky black canal.

Next morning the Middlewich Arm let us go and we joined the friendly 'Shroppie' once more, rather anxious to arrive at Nantwich Basin and rid ourselves of a nasty assortment of rubbish which was forcing up the lid of our bin and giving off a particularly obnoxious pong. Arrayed in my mucky boating clobber, grubby, dishevelled, tired, clutching the offensive plastic bag in one hand and a bucketful of partly washed milk bottles in the other, I went ashore. A well-disguised disposal place was elusive and as I sought to discard my unbecoming accessories, I noticed a spruce middle-aged man making a sprightly approach. Attired in immaculate blue trousers, matching shirt, impeccable navy-blue blazer nonchalantly fastened with bright brass buttons, a casual 'Noel Coward' paisley cravat and a jaunty yachting cap, he sailed towards me. I, for my part, felt at one with the garbage I was carrying and wished that I could scuttle myself out of existence. But it soon became obvious that 'luxury yacht' and 'effluent barge' were going to meet, and when he was close on my starboard bow, I assumed a ridiculously affected accent to ask him the whereabouts of the rubbish disposal. He was as gentlemanly as his appearance, smiled charmingly, chatted about this and that, corrected my course and saluted smartly when we parted. Overcome by this flattering encounter, I returned to *Maori* and consulted the mirror hoping that a miracle had transformed me — but I looked just the same!

Sometime later a deodorised *Maori* and crew continued a sweetened sail through fresh undulating countryside past many cows, some of which had made muddy water-holes at the canal's edge. An especially belligerent individual, wallowing up to her knees stretched her neck, showed us the whites of her eyes and bellowed as we drew near. Alec, away in the bows, bellowed back at her and then at me — 'It wants its teeth washing!'

As the loss of two front teeth had recently caused him some annoyance, I facetiously shouted, 'You want yours replacing!'

'Not teeth, you daft bugger!' he counter-bellowed. 'I said TEATS! TEATS!'

'BLOODY WOMEN!' he called to some other female bovine spectators chewing things over, higher up the field.

They flicked their tails in meaningful reply!

At Audlem we started up the long flight of locks in company with

Andantino, which in musical terms means fairly slowly. It was the same in boating terms. When we sailed, bird-like and free out of the top-lock, a windy sunny afternoon carried us to *Maori*'s birthplace, Market Drayton. There, later on we consumed chops in savoury sauce, lots of cheap draught white wine, and some liquefying Audlem ice-cream. Slightly whoozy we collapsed onto the bunks on either side of the table.

Next morning *Maori*'s engine was due for some attention from Harry Machin and, as depressed clouds wept unceasing dejection to the earth, we were very pleased to stay put. *Maori*'s notoriously leaky windows (stuffed at all corners with toilet paper) were allowing tiny rivulets to run down inside the boat, and Alec, acting on Harry's advice, was out searching for a special filler used for sealing fish-tanks.

While he was unselfishly dripping around Market Drayton hunting for an appropriate shop, I was comfortably reclining, knees up, reading a book. A rather strong rocking movement did not really disturb my self-indulgence, but a booming feminine voice soon had me kneeling to peer through a dribbling, misty window at a large narrow boat coming in to moor on the opposite bank. Erect at the tiller was a veritable Amazon captaining a crew of damp twittering schoolgirls. Upon her thunderous command, a harassed bedraggled junior mistress leapt ashore with a line onto a steep gravely bank, tried to heave the boat in, and slid down to the bottom where her legs entered the water and she let go of her rope. More bombastic blasting from the bridge ensued and eventually the unfortunate mistress caught and held a wet, muddy line as if her life depended on it; then, encouraged by her commander, she pulled enthusiastically and as the stern came in, so the massive steel bow swung across the canal towards a small inoffensive fibre-glass cruiser.

'Stand by with the pole,' shouted the busty skipper.

'STAND BY WITH THE POLE GIRLS!' she bellowed several decibels louder, when her wide-eyed crew did not react.

'FEND OFF FORWARD!'

About seven shrieking members of the now panic-stricken crew dived to obey, fell all over each other and missed the pole completely. Captain Amazon acted, left her place of command, grabbed the pole, and in the nick of time — averted disaster!

On such a dismal day, I was very grateful for this amusing interlude and, when St Trinians afloat finally managed to tie-up, regretted that the entertainment was over. Once secure, all the younger crew members deserted the ship and a group of chattering, giggling, multi-coloured oilskins and anoraks scrambled and slipped up the bank and disappeared to create havoc at the Ladyline Centre. The 'voice' however, had remained on duty and I could hear her reverberating from the depths as she dressed down her erring junior officer.

When a thoroughly rain-washed Alec returned from a disappointing tour of the local shops, he changed his clothes and I changed the now sodden toilet paper in the windows, hoping for a further change — in the weather.

A slight improvement had us casting off after lunch and a startled Alec missed the boat by slipping on the wet towpath and sitting in a deep mud-puddle, with one outstretched leg in the canal. Intent on my steering I went on without him, until angry shouts turned my eyes to a trailing rope and a beached spouse, whose expressive waving gave me the impression that it was my duty to stop. As he grumbled on board, I pleaded urgent need of the toilet and handed over the wheel. Once inside the cabin, I was able to allow my scarcely-contained hysterical giggles to burst forth; but less happy sounds from outside had me hastily wiping away mirthful tears as I noisily pumped an unused toilet and soberly returned to the wheel.

Mixed weather could not detract from the uninterrupted beauty of the canal's passage to Autherly Junction where our eager exploration of the Staffordshire and Worcester Canal began. At the end of this navigation lay Stourport where, if conditions would allow us to, we'd lock out onto the River Severn's wide flowing waters.

As a cautious *Maori* gently nosed along the canal's upper reaches, my first impressions were of quiet remoteness and an intimacy with nature. Sweet-smelling hawthorn hedges are made heady by delicate wild roses; an untamed profusion also allows the clinging clematis free expression and tall Himalayan Balsam rises and splashes pink, purple and white, topping an extrovert population of uninhibited plants and flowers. Even on the lock walls, tiny, dainty ferns have found a sheltering niche in which to survive and grow. Bees and other insects made a mellifluent hum as they explored the beauty of their wild habitat and brilliant butterflies flickered their fragile ways from plant to plant. The birds seemed to enjoy their aerial view of this near-paradise and sang their appreciation to all. There was a feeling of the past, of little change, as we took in our delightful surroundings and breathed the pure air.

Most of the locks were old and quaint, some almost miniature and nearly all were positioned in quiet places. The small circular weirs, which most locks seemed to parent, were fascinating to watch as the water smoothly curved and then tumbled down the hole in the middle to disappear underground. Another type of lock which I rather fancied, had a steel plate over a central inlet hole which, when the paddles were opened, allowed water to squirt out on each side like a bristly, military moustache. Bratch Locks, which boast a marvellous eighteenth century octagonal toll-house, presented an intriguing layout of secret culverts and side-pounds which connected to the extremely short main pounds. Somebody had been enthusiastically slip-slapping with a white-wash brush and the bridges, parapets and toll-house shone dazzlingly white in the afternoon sunshine.

We were trying to puzzle out the best method of ascent, when the lock-keeper made a timely appearance, told us to treat them as individual locks and kindly put us through.

A waterway of great diversity then wound us under tall sand-stone cliffs and past cave-like places caused by faults, which had been found during the canal's construction. Miners were engaged to remove these from the rock — hence the resulting caves, which in the past were used for legitimate storage, but are now sadly misused for rubbish disposal.

As the cliffs on our port-side cast cooling shadows over a

smoothly moving *Maori*, I gazed mesmerised at a magnificent sunlit garden to our starboard, where the flamboyant Himalayan Balsam was living up to its name by rising to great heights. A low-flying heron skimmed their tops in an appreciative reconnaissance flight and then a movement in the undergrowth had me crying out in excitement as a grass-snake slithered into view. By the time Alec appeared, it had gone; and he was hard to convince — but I did not imagine it — the only snake out of captivity that I have ever seen!

We were on our way to the hill-nestling village of Kinver, where, if you are prepared to toil upwards out of the valley onto a high ridge, you will be rewarded by extensive views of the Cotswold and Malvern Hills. I toiled as far as the local hairdresser's, arrived at a time reserved for old-aged pensioners, prematurely fitted the bill and had a hair-do for fifty pence! An extensive shopping expedition followed which re-victualled *Maori* and avoided any further delay in our progress towards the River Severn.

Our sail transferred us from Staffordshire into Worcestershire along a canal sometimes made twisty by unyielding rock faces, themselves eroded and misshapen by time and the elements. As we neared Kidderminster, a large deserted-looking church on our left waited patiently for Sunday and looked down upon a *Maori* impatient for Saturday, when she hoped to lock out onto the, as yet, unknown river. Farther on a statue of Richard Baxter, a famous thinker of the seventeenth century, stood aloft — and thought; and I in turn thought that Kidderminser Lock was going to drop us straight into the centre of a busy main road alive and noisy with shoppers and traffic. But we slipped unnoticed under a tunnel into a secluded cut, shut off by old factories, warehouses and high screening walls.

At Caldwell and Falling Sands locks we previewed the interesting split iron bridges prevalent along the Stratford Canal, which have an inch gap between spans to allow bow-hauled boats passage without disconnecting their horse-power. Falling Sands was well named after some insecure, perpendicular red-stone faces rising dramatically straight out of the canal, which a hovering River Stour tried to join at Pratt's Wharf. But the river couldn't find a way through the overgrown disused lock and after sniffing a nearby sewage works, it moved away.

We were surprised that the canal maintained its quiet character even within the outskirts of Stourport, and a relaxed *Maori* and crew eventually crept, completely unobserved, into a grassy mooring close to York Street lock.

Stourport owes its existence solely to the canal and to the fact that James Brindley met with strong opposition from the residents of Bewdley when he planned to join his navigation onto the Severn at that point. Just as we oppose the advent of undesirable motorways, they objected to a canal arriving uninvited on their doorsteps and when they won the day, he had to think again. This time he chose to copy the little River Stour which already entered the larger river at Lower Mitton and so a port was born. As enthusiastic boaters we greatly admired the spacious unsymmetrical connecting basins, the reflecting wavering shapes of many craft, the unusual mixture of broad and narrow locks and some interesting bridges and old warehouses. A charming clock-tower accurately timed our stroll by two Georgian inns, one of which, the Tontine, was built way back in 1788.

The golden glow of early evening lit the remains of a former golden age with a lustrous unreality and we were momentarily held within its stillness — taken back in time. Then, the intrusive present had us strolling by a gentle, harmless-looking River Severn and up the welcoming gangway of SS *VIC 99*, a Rossythe vessel, sadly out of character in the role of a floating club and restaurant. We soon signed on as members, ordered some drinks and crisps and chatted to the barman about — what else — boats!

Later, as we wandered along unfamiliar ways, warm and unhurried on a sultry summer's evening, we were drawn back into our childhood by the bright lights of a fair-ground. We rode, smoothly rising and falling, on a timeless merry-go-round, and then glued up our non-timeless faces with ever-sugary, ever-pink candy floss. It was one of those special moments when time should have left us alone — but we had yet to telephone Huddersfield to check whether Emily and Penny were alright — and time won! When we received the unexpected news that somebody wanted to buy *William Hennell*, problems relating to the present claimed us with a vengeance, for in spite of the many difficulties experienced during our short relationship, in our heart of hearts we didn't want to let her go.

Back on board *Maori*, as we once more weighed up the pros and cons, a sad inevitability about our discussion was evident — a putting off of what was already a foregone conclusion. And after Alec had contacted Stan, asking him to negotiate the sale, two downcast beings commiserated together into the joyless small hours, their pending sail down the Severn suddenly unimportant and lacking in attraction.

Next morning, however, when I had rubbed restorative sleep out of my eyes and looked out on the beginnings of a perfect day, I rose revitalised to prepare for our sail to Worcester. All our previous apprehension melted away when, at eight o'clock, in company with the narrow boat, *Superior*, we locked into a tranquil, sun-warmed river. As *Maori's* busy propellor fizzed us forward, two white tongues of spray fanned out from her bows and, in turn, two newly-exposed white bodies were fanned by the early morning air.

Superior soon lived up to her name and drew ahead leading us past some optimistic fishermen who had themselves risen early to catch early-rising fish. Because of *Maori's* small propellor, we were worried about our lack of power, but when, with the current assisting, she plied along at a great rate of about six knots, we relaxed and plied ourselves — with suntan oil. Lovely rural scenery marked our way and clusters of moored boats, tied up to pretty weekend chalets, bobbed about as we passed. Huge, wide weirs dared us to shoot their rapids, but we preferred the big electric locks, where handy chains hanging down the walls assisted a gentle drop.

The spectacular part of our sail came at Worcester, where, as we passed beneath an impressive, five-arch stone bridge, our eyes (and our thoughts) were drawn heavenward by the cathedral's superb, soaring tower. Having stood in awe within its impressive interior on a previous trip (by car), now, from the other side of the river, we saw this supreme architectural triumph to its best possible advantage. Though defaced by ravages of time on the soft local stone, it sat regally upright like an ancient king on his throne; suffering from age but still handsome and beautifully proportioned under its magnificent, pointed crown.

On the water, rowing eights were out in force and as foreigner *Maori* intruded into a traditional English river scene of potent high summer, visible heat covered everything in a shimmering haze. Buildings, boats, birds, trees, water, air and even people were caught in the sparkle of that bewitching morning.

Meanwhile, Alec standing stiffly upright (like the cathedral pinnacles) was intent on controlling *Maori* ready for a swing to port to enter Diglis Locks and the Worcester and Birmingham Navigation. He, recalling my abortive attempt on the Trent, looked anxious but he swung her around in masterly fashion and executed a perfect entry. I sighed with relief and took my usual physical and emotional easement in the toilet!

After negotiating a few locks we tied up, left *Maori* to take her ease and plunged into a Saturday afternoon shopping melée in and around The Shambles in Worcester. After our peaceful trip down the river, the jammed, over-populated streets held no joy for us — endless traffic noise was deafening and we were relieved to escape along some characterless back-streets to our floating refuge. On this canal there are fifty-eight locks — only fifty-four to go!

At the seventh lock diplomatic relations between fishers and boaters became somewhat strained. Upon our approach Alec and I were very put out to see two fishermen, with accompanying tackle, completely obstructing the bollards provided for boats to secure to before entering the locks. Deploring their lack of consideration, we nevertheless pulled in further back so as not to disturb their fishing and put ourselves hard and fast aground. Alec strained our long pole to near-breaking point but the two immobile figures concentrating with abnormal intensity on two tiny, orange floats, completely ignored our plight. Alec then filled the lock and, hoping to flush away any lurking fish and refloat mud-bound *Maori*, opened all the paddles; but she still stayed put — and so did the fossilised fishermen! However, another lock-full of surging water had *Maori* rising on the flood and, as I pointed her towards the lock, Alec, armed with our stout fending-off pole, marched purposefully along the towpath. He directed a few choice words at the fishermen, whom, I hoped would be accidentally shoved into the cut to catch their fish first hand. When we moved out of the lock and along the next pound, an irate fisherwoman was waiting to tell us off for using so much water and lowering the level of the canal! Needless to say, we soon put HER straight and she, bearing the brunt of our frustration, was left in no doubt as to our current opinion of the local fishing fraternity.

Without further hindrance or aggravation we pressed on to Tibberton, a quiet canal-side village which, in the late afternoon, and after a toil of sixteen locks, seemed ideal for a peaceful night. A fine, tranquil evening had a calming effect on spirits which had been somewhat ruffled by the afternoon's events, but when a telephone call informed us that *William Hennell* had been sold, two dispirited souls sought and found a pub called 'Speed the Plough', where alcoholic intake first of all deepened but then dimmed their despondency. They returned to *Maori*, morose and tired, desiring only to slip into that engulfing chasm of oblivion — sleep!

BANG! BANG! 'Hello Bill.' 'Hello Arthur.' SCREECH! BANG! 'Rotten morning, Sid.' 'It is that Arthur.' SCREECH. SCREECH. BANG! BANG! 'Wet Stan.' 'It's bloody peeing, Arthur!'

Suddenly wide-eyed within the cosy gloom of my sleeping bag I listened unbelievingly to an incredible racket of grinding tyres, slamming doors and shouted conversations about the weather.

'Alec, wake up! Can you hear what I can hear? What's happening?'

Alec stirred, and knowing that he was awake gave my still-weary body the courage to sit up and blink through a tiny chink in the curtains at a rain-drenched, grey non-dawn, and straight into the eyes of my 'favourite' human being of the moment — a fisherman!

The now quagmire of an area next to our boat was covered with cars, fishing tackle and congregating men who were going to tackle the fish! Predictable dialogue continued to be bawled against further tyre-balding skids and aggressive slams; consequently, the peaceful rural scene was changed within minutes to one of complete bedlam by an incredibly noisy prelude to a fishing competition. It must have included a special prize for the one who could make the most row and frighten away all the fish.

Having considerably cut short the usually prolonged Sunday slumbers of the whole village, they then moved off to their allotted stations further along the canal where, if my fervent prayers were answered, the rain would pour very hard on them but not on anybody else.

This it did, (and on us as well) as we spent a listless yawning morning gazing through cascading windows at hundreds of plopping miniature fountains which dispelled into thousands of rings and fascinating bursting bubbles on the canal's grey surface. Thoughts of cold, miserable fishermen, sitting soaked to the skin by a canal completely devoid of fish were my only consolation as we read and re-read the papers, listened to the weather forecast (which told us it was dry and warm) and consumed coffee by the gallon.

A firm decision to weigh anchor after lunch (no matter what the weather) was smartly deferred when someone above energetically pulled the chain and flushed torrential rain upon us. My former pleas to the Almighty were soon superseded by a single request for the fulfilment of the radio's forecast — but He was reluctant to humour me a second time and a drizzly two-thirty saw us kitting up to face the elements. Identities tend to vanish when boats become crewed by engulfing anoraks, oilskins, hoods and Wellington boots, and on this occasion an unseasonable drop in temperature had half-hose being pulled over full-hose and jumper sleeves stretched to cover frozen 'fish-fingers'. This is an effective way to lengthen slightly shrunken sleeves or, as in this case, spoil a good, well-fitting sweater. As I shivered silently at the wheel, only my teeth chattering, I could hardly believe that sun-tops and shorts had been our dress of the previous day. However, visions of a dark, swollen, rain-swept Severn offset my discomfort, and I was glad not to be on it.

Anoraked, hooded, I stood gazing ahead like a horse in blinkers — neck stiff and sore from having to hold my head straight. A change in position to observe anything to port or starboard necessitated turning all the upper part of my body, for a turn of the head only had me gazing into the dark interior of my anorak hood.

Just as I was contemplating the fortune I might make by inventing a swivel-necked anorak, we came upon the fishermen. My prayers had been answered in full! Silent as the grave they sat, their faces drooping beneath dripping, round-shouldered umbrellas, while protruding, muddy feet imprinted foot-shaped puddles among those already surrounding them. Quickening, *Maori* effectively disturbed any fish that might have been considering their bait and we surged along happy in the knowledge that justice had been done.

Because of unlimited showering from above into ample water beneath, and more water in the form of coffee flowing into the inner regions, my calls to the toilet were abnormally frequent. As you already know, at best this compartment presents a tight squeeze, and with head fixed within my hood, I had to fumble with layers of clothing — waterproofs, trousers, roll-ons, tights and pants. An icy-cold, wet anorak dropped a shock-inducing poultice onto my back and just when I had managed to get organised, a lock would generally appear. Alec then shouted a summons which I could not quickly obey and testily (and somewhat predictably) inquired (as I emerged) as to what the hell I'd been doing! Sometimes I told him!!

Bladder troubles not assisting, we still moved along our watery way under wide, brick bridges and in due course through Dunhampstead tunnel where conditions were even damper inside than out. The thought of Tardebigge Locks, thirty in number, plus the unabating dreary drizzle, made us seek anxiously for somewhere congenial to moor and relax before the long haul of our ascent next day. So, when a 'Queen's Head' looked graciously down on two of her subjects and invited us to stay, we tied up near to some willows, (which were actually weeping) found our identities again, had a meal and accepted her hospitality. A warm, friendly atmosphere buzzing with conversation thawed us out and we soon forgot that *William Hennell* had been sold, forgot about the flaming awful weather, forgot that thirty locks had to be climbed in the morning and enjoyed a good night.

As we were sleeping deeply and contentedly, a change came over the land. Seeking to freshen other pastures, the clouds had headed away, and the sun, thankful for their departure was silently stealing away millions of diamond droplets which still hung on everything — even upon the most delicate tips of grass. It soon became evident that this was to be a memorable climb — what did it matter how long we took on this unbelievable bespangled morning? Our gentle dreamlike uprising carried me along the silky, virgin waters of some other world, where a sensitive wondering *Maori* nosed past newly-created gleaming fields and bejewelled flowers.

At the half-way mark I emerged from this trance-like state to take a picture of a practical pink-legged Alec, now changed back into shorts. We had unwittingly devised a smooth, unhurried system which allowed me to remain on board (and dream!) while Alec did all the work! It went something like this.

Alec, having enclosed *Maori* and me in a lock chamber, opened the paddles and, leaving us to rise, plodded on to prepare the next one. Once we had ascended, I condescended to drop the cloughs and opened the lock gate, which Alec (now returned) closed after me as I sailed on (still dreaming) towards the next lock. He then trudged the length of towpath between locks for the third time and it all began again. Distances varied of course, but even short ones were made lengthy when multiplied by three. Consequently, when we moored by a wharf at the top of the flight and I suggested that we should walk to Tardebigge village for a change, he called me a cheeky sod and told me to go by myself.

As I climbed up and away from the tranquillity of the canal, my emergence onto a busy thundering main road took me by surprise. Somehow I managed to knock the local vicar off his bike but he seemed quite pleased to cease his exertions in order to direct me to the nearest store. Upon my laden return, Alec was delighted to learn that a long walk had made me very tired and after we had lunched on the fruits of my labours, he allowed no time for rest as we pressed on towards the entrance of the Stratford Canal. King's Norton Tunnel, two thousand seven hundred and twenty-six yards long, devoured us for what seemed an eternity and I felt certain that we had parted from Earth and sunlight forever. No pin-point of light appeared to indicate an end to the gloomiest and drippiest of all tunnels, but ghostly figures on two shadowy boats passing from the opposite direction, spoke to us in eerie echoing voices of liberation ahead. When a minute glow became visible our relief was great and then *Maori*, a creature of warmth and light, strained eagerly towards it. Although I cannot write from first hand knowledge of either place, our deliverance was, I imagined, comparable to a departure from Hell into Paradise, but unfortunately Paradise soon became a canal full of rubbish and we were back on Earth once more.

Romantic thoughts about William Shakespeare and all that, heightened the excitement of our entry into the Stratford-Upon-Avon Canal, where a guillotine stop-lock consisting of wooden gates mounted in iron frames, seemed permanently and ominously raised above our heads. Not wishing to suffer a fate similar to some of his famous characters, we passed under quickly and along a suburban canal made shady for a while by trees and bushes bordering pleasant secluded gardens.

To sail to a performance of a play by 'Will' made for a poetic voyage and was quite a change from our occasional night out at the A.B.C. Cinema in Huddersfield. When we came to Brandwood Tunnel, the Bard himself (decapitated onto a stone plaque) welcomed us and as we were slurping coffee at the time, we gallantly raised green and red tin mugs in homage to his image. Total absorption with our surroundings caused us to forget the hours passing, until we entered one shadowy, tree-lined stretch, which made the day hasten towards night and the canal, now wispy with rising mists, suddenly dark and chilly. Once again we had trouble finding a suitably deep mooring, but eventually two men in a boat advised us that we would be alright at Bridge 27 — and so we were.

I have often sung of an enchanted evening, but never, as yet, of an enchanted morning. We woke to one, and as the slight nip of early rising was counteracted by a pulsating orb in the sky, the cold mists of dawn dissolved in light and warmth. Everything glinted — the canal glinted, trees glinted, even our morning cup of tea glinted, and, after an application of sun-oil, WE glinted! After a lingering breakfast, we sailed gently through delightful wooded ways, our passage interrupted only for Alec to swing aloft on a lift bridge. At last I understood fully the fisherman's simple philosophy as I 'just enjoyed being there'.

Our tempo was slow and relaxed. Sometimes I had a long wait before making a contented descent to cook in the hot lock-ovens. At one, I kept company with a long, flaccid snail, which, considering itself 'done', was making an almost imperceptible climb over the great stones of the lock wall. As *Maori* gradually dropped, I stroked his slimy back in passing, but he was far too relaxed to register any alarm or to move any faster.

At Lock 21 we had a break and explored a shop full of canalia purchasing a license which allowed us to cruise further along this delightful waterway. But on restarting, even our unhurried progress soon became unbearable and at Lock 27 we came to a halt for the remainder of the afternoon. Here, we further relaxed by carrying our chairs, cushions, cups of tea and sun-tan oils to the lock-side, where our complete immobility was enhanced by watching other people work. Even this proved to be tiring and I dropped asleep.

When my eyes clicked open Alec was missing but as I glanced to where *Maori* lay lazing, my unbelieving eyes focussed on his familiar figure paddling in the canal. No! not just paddling — actually immersed! Before he could emerge, I raced back to *Maori* at the speed of light, grabbed a camera and recorded the event. After this we sat laughing and chatting on the canal-side, dangling and swishing relieved feet in the water like a couple of overgrown kids. As the also relaxing sun waned towards the west, we began to feel more energetic and decided to paint *Maori's* roof. Alec washed her with canal water while I mixed the paint, and then we were both out on top, slapping vigorously and parrying the verbal thrusts of passing boaters who told us that it was (as we already knew) 'Nice to watch other people work!' and that 'Theirs needed doing when we'd finished.' We gave as good as we received and the exchanges remained as repetitive and unoriginal as the mushroom coloured paint we were applying to *Maori*.

Because we had promised to contact some friends, Peggy and John, who lived in Kenilworth, and our canal booklet indicated a public telephone at Lowsonford, I suggested, as a fitting end to a perfect day, a pleasant evening stroll in that direction. On paper it looked short; on foot, a long trek soon had Alec complaining that it was a damn silly idea anyway, especially as we were sailing in that direction next day. To take his mind off his protesting legs I put full blame on a 'completely misleading map' and then attempted to draw his attention to our idyllic surroundings.

'It's just like another world,' I enthused.

'And just as bloody far!' he countered, refusing to be side-tracked from his grumpy mood.

During an interminable return journey, I also confessed to having sore and tired legs.

'I'm walking on my bloody thighs,' whined Alec. 'Never mind legs!'

A sympathetic woman, leaning on the tiller of a passing boat (going our way) stirred things up by asking if we'd walked a long way, and a boatman (going the other way) who'd seen us working earlier, called out to enquire if we had tired of painting.

'She's got me walking instead!' exclaimed Alec, completely ignoring the fact that the friends we'd been anxious to 'phone were HIS long before they became MINE!

Time passed as each curve of the towpath revealed yet another one ahead without *Maori*; the greyness before the darkness gathered around us and the grass rubbed its dewy dampness against our sagging legs. This revived them, eventually enabling us to reach *Maori*, where we simultaneously groaned onto opposing bunks and waited for each other to make a pot of tea.

Next morning, a shortage of sugar at breakfast became a national shortage on the news and we wished that we had replenished our supplies. Owing to a shortage of water (in the canal), progress was slow, and an acute shortage of shops left us, by mid-day, short of milk, bread, sugar and (because it had run out at coffee break) calor gas! Even the bridge-holes were short on room and, with overhanging hawthorn reaching out to scratch the unwary helmsman, *Maori* needed careful aiming.

A useful boatyard (as we thought) seemed the answer to all of our problems; but it didn't sell gas, a tiny shop didn't offer provisions, and although a large tank contained diesel oil, (which we also needed) they didn't sell that! However, the yard did boast a rubbish disposal and we felt that our stop had not been a complete waste of time when we were able to let them have a large, whiffy, plastic bag of THAT!

As we proceeded towards the wharf at Wilmcote, conditions worsened. The canal became muddier and muddier and seemingly farther and farther from civilisation. Our reasons for wanting to get there were three-fold: firstly, gas was available at the Wharf — at least, according to the canal book; secondly, provisions were available at Wilmcote; and thirdly, the canal went that way, so we had no choice. As we drew near, our way was completely barred by two narrow boats which, as they had optimistically attempted to pass each other, had become mud-bound under a bridge. One minute later, two immobile boats became three — as we joined them.

Boats need water! Without it they lose their easy graceful charm and become awkward wallowing things, difficult to manage, truculent and often immovable. Boat hooks and long wooden poles stirred the whole canal into a gorgeous, syrupy gunge, and gently assisting with an occasional whirl of the propellor, I philosophically supped my milkless, sugarless tea, and waited for the alligators to slide into view. When the other two craft had sucked themselves free, we managed to ooze *Maori*'s nose up to a small, rickety jetty and lean our gangplank onto it. Then Alec fetched the gas, and clutching a large, heavy cylinder to his breast, balanced precariously along an insecure plank, (which he could not see) wavered, wobbled, nearly joined the alligators and fell swearing on board! He declined to struggle an extra thirty feet along a six-inch-wide deck to the other end of *Maori* and dumped his load unceremoniously onto her bows.

Although we were more moored than moving, within the canal's slimy hold, we sloshed on towards the next lock where, we had been assured, we might actually find some water.

This information proved to be correct, but we also found ourselves a long way from the shops and a glance at a positive clock-face set at five-twenty-five, had me tearing along an uneven towpath for fear they would be closed. In my usual state of disarray, mud-splattered and breathless, I fell into the one shop which was open. Finding a sympathetic shop-keeper, I got carried away, filled my bag to overflowing, and then staggered lop-sided and disgruntled back to *Maori*.

As darkness fell, so did the water level, changing the whole pound into an enormous, chaotic mud-pool into which late arriving boats slithered, manned by tired confused crews, quite unable to cope in the quickly gathering gloom. We peered out at the shadowy but very audible figures and their struggling ghostly craft, until they finally ceased their floundering and flinging of ropes. Then, having decided that hairdressers were non-existent in that part of the world, I made an effort to boost my sagging morale by setting my equally sagging locks.

'What for?' inquired Alec.

'Just to give it a bit of body,' I explained.

'You've got body enough, without any more!' came his truthful but unnecessary comment . . .

Later on, when all the boats had settled their hulls down for the night, and only chinks of light escaped from curtained cabins, I sat unbecomingly in my rollers relishing some hot chocolate and anticipating the restful, enfolding arms of sleep. Then the lock-keeper's generator started up!

How can I describe the remainder of our improbably journey? I could sing 'Mud, mud, glorious mud,' and you would get the picture;

I could tell you of pounds so low that we were resting on lock-bottoms trying to level up; I could tell you of a see-sawing *Maori* jammed amidships on a sill; of boats slewed at crazy angles, of frustrated boaters jumping up and down on boats, rocking boats, shoving boats and cursing boats; of rushing, excited crews indiscriminately opening and shutting paddles; of two hire-craft which reluctantly admitted defeat and turned back, their disappointed crews vowing to reach Stratford by bus or train. But I will tell you instead of an intrepid *Maori* warrior whose perseverance received its just reward when conditions miraculously improved and allowed us to enjoy a bright, windy, unimpeded sail to our meeting with Peggy and John. They were immediately pressed into service and initiated into the art of working locks and heaving muddy ropes.

Before long, a funny back-alley of a canal caused us to stoop under a very low bridge and then, in sudden contrast, we experienced the incomparable thrill of emerging into the wide gleaming basin of Stratford. Spacious parkland surrounded us as we entered a habitat for silently dipping swans, noisy 'Donald' ducks, bread-crumb-seeking birds, ice-cream sellers, ice-cream lickers, tourists, boaters, babies, dogs and their walkers and theatre-goers. We could see the Royal Shakespeare Theatre away on our starboard bow as we pulled into a romantic mooring beneath a magnificent spreading weeping willow. A statue of Will, half turned towards us — until something more interesting held his gaze, while Hamlet, completely unaware of our existence, had eyes only for Yorick. Peggy and John were thrilled to have their tea aboard a boat and later in the evening, when we went to Kenilworth, I was thrilled to be in a house where unlimited hot water prompted me to wash my hair. Next morning a 'fuzzy wuzzy' looked back at me from the mirror and I had to make a quick reconnoitre of Stratford's hairdressing salons to find someone who could work a miracle on the disaster.

We were looking forward to a visit from Rodney and Chris, who, having increased their family since our last meeting, were bringing a fairly new baby all the way from Wales. When they arrived we spent a contented afternoon taking photographs of the baby, feeding the baby, talking at the baby, admiring the baby, holding the baby, discussing the baby, changing the baby and sunning ourselves — and the BABY! When, after tea and many farewells to the BABY, they finally departed, Alec and I changed into our glad rags ready for the long-awaited visit to the theatre.

Alec, by now nicely tanned, looked extremely handsome (I thought) and smart in a new jacket, and when I had draped myself (carefully because of my special hair-do) in a black and silver kaftan, we bore absolutely no resemblance to the fly-blown scruffy crew of the previous day. Yards and yards of softly flowing material made climbing out of *Maori* difficult until Alec assisted me to an undignified landing by a forceful shove up the behind! He leapt to join me, smoothed his hair, straightened his tie, and then we strolled arm in arm over the soft, green, litter-strewn lawns — two characters about to make an entrance.

Because we were very early, our entry caused no stir at all and we sat upright in solitary state in our box. We read our programmes from end to end, watched with interest other people's entrances and waited for the play to begin. I reminisced to Alec about my initiation, at the impressionable age of fifteen, to a performance of a Shakespeare play. This happened in New Zealand when, as a pupil at the Auckland Girls' Grammar School, I was forced to join an organised visit to His Majesty's Theatre to see 'one of those dead-boring plays by that English joker, William Shakespeare.' I have never forgotten it! King Lear, portrayed by that amazing actor Donald Wolfit, was a complete revelation to me as the real poetry and meaning of Shakespeare's language entered into my consciousness for the first time. When he staggered on-stage to answer many curtain calls, I was not surprised at his exhaustion, for he had actually become the King, had actually suffered the terrible tribulations of his life — and I with him.

King John was no match King Lear (although it had its moments) and Alec became somewhat restive during its slightly slow passage. The play's climax came during the final scene but heralded an anti-climax for us as we crowded out among the chattering, departing audience (all declaring with too much conviction that they had enjoyed it). Then back over the now dark and damp, still littered grass to drop onto the stern of *Maori* and finish off our slightly disappointing appointment with royalty, shoes off, feet up, drinking mugs of instant coffee! Regrettably, the curtain was about to fall for us, and next day, a newly formed company, directed by Dave, would take over *Maori* and begin a short season of one-night stands at various pubs back along the canal. So, for us it was 'Farewell — weeping willow. Farewell — swans,' as

> 'The poor soul sat sighing by a sycamore tree.
>   Sing all a green willow
> Her hand on her bosom, her head on her knee.
>   Sing willow, willow, willow.
>
> The fresh streams ran by her, and murmured her moans;
>   Sing willow, willow, willow.
> Her salt tears fell from her, and softened the stones.
>   Sing willow, willow, willow . . .'

'Farewell Will!'

CHAPTER ELEVEN

My soul is an enchanted boat
Which, like a sleeping swan doth float
Upon the silver waves of thy sweet singing.

Shelley

Nineteen seventy five was the year of the heatwave, the year of the drought, the year of my separation from Alec, the year of the flat and being alone, the year of heartache and soul-searching — and the year that Penny went to university in London.

It held a summer so perfect, that we could have made that idyllic cruise about which all boaters dream, but each clear bright day was (for me) over-shadowed by the parting to come. I was incapable of any enjoyment — nothing held any permanency — all things became unreal, intangible — all beauty transient and endued with an inescapable element of sadness; and for the second time in my life, uncertainty covered all!

Dave, accompanied by some friends was first to holiday on *Maori*. An absolutely disastrous week (during which a crew member was taken ill) recorded winter temperatures, low depressing skies, unabating rain, strong winds and occasional stinging hail-storms to torment their passage from Banknewton to Parbold — and gave no hint of the uninterrupted heat to come.

On Saturday, July the 26th, *Maori*'s young and totally cheesed-off crew changed to a rather sombre, mature one — and the weather changed too.

After we had listened sympathetically to their tales of woe, all was activity as they transferred their belongings from boat to car, and we transferred ours to an ever-rocking *Maori*. Only after a great deal of to-ing and fro-ing did we slam them in tightly — hardly able even to wave farewell. They left us in peace under an increasingly warmer sun, which sought us in the shade of an old brick windmill.

Later in the evening, I took my thoughts for a long walk down the towpath and added my own reflectiveness to the clearly defined, brightly-coloured images in the canal. Much later, Alec and I took our combined thoughts to a packed-out pub called (predictably) The Windmill, but we thought it was too smoky and noisy — and left after one drink.

Next morning, some only slightly submerged, disturbing thoughts surfaced and woke me early. Leaving Alec fast asleep, I walked in absolute solitude, opened my arms to a heavenly morning and felt the warmth of an embrace returned — but found no comfort. I did, however, find some fresh milk and the Sunday papers which I returned along with myself to *Maori*.

Our original holiday plans to rendezvous with Dave at Worsley and then make for the Shropshire Union Canal, had to be changed at the last minute by the unforeseen closure of the Barton Aqueduct. This amazing swinging tank of water would have taken us over the top of the Manchester Ship Canal. Now, we were planning to invade the little-known Rufford Branch which lies off the Leeds–Liverpool Canal. So, late on that perfect Sunday morning we pointed *Maori* towards Liverpool and enjoyed a smooth easy sail until an air-vent discarded (at long last) some black tape, which was more or less holding it together. *Maori* was soon overcome by the heat. We moored, and created havoc in our over-loaded tool locker, but couldn't find anything to do the repair. After lunch, we were luckily found by a psychic dog whose master was a mechanic. He insisted on driving a fair distance to his home, returned with some tape, helped us to administer first-aid to a sun-stroked native and wouldn't accept any payment. He did, however, accept a cuppa and then we were on our way again seeking a large, arched bridge dated 1816, which, according to the canal book, would give us entry to the Rufford Branch. There, windlasses would have to be immediately at the ready to negotiate some locks.

Our invasion of this slightly gone-to-seed canal coincided with an invasion of weeds and flies, the former causing much aggravation to a hot and bothered Alec who was continually dripping perspiration down the weed hatch as he bent to clear the prop. Aided by the continuing hot sticky conditions, the fly population had reached plague proportions and they inundated the boat, causing us to moor hurriedly and lay about us with folded whip-cracking newspapers. This ploy effectively covered *Maori*'s interior with dead or whirring, leg-waving fly-bodies. Sweaty and uncomfortable from our exertions we dived deeply into our suitcases, came up with some swimsuits, donned them, lowered ourselves gently into the cooling canal, swished about amongst the weeds and then returned to a boat once more alive with buzzing flies!

Having put fly-killer high on our mental shopping list, we pressed on through a waterway which was also alive with darting, flashing fish — a phenomenon easily explained by a towpath completely devoid of anglers. We seemed to be the only travellers savouring the neglected charm of this waterway, until we reached the grounds of medieval Rufford Old Hall. There we moored under shielding trees, astern of a familiar craft *Joanne*, flying a yellow Airedale Boat Club pennant.

Next day, an energetic sun was up at the crack of dawn and shone and shone and SHONE! It woke up hosts of equally energetic flies and we sweated, swotted and swam during a heat-saturated sail to Tarleton, where the canal locks out into the River Douglas. This tidal navigation, having temporarily reduced to a narrow semi-liquid channel, oozing between soft banks of mud on its way to the Ribble, was unnavigable when we arrived. A splendid three-masted yacht *Helen* gazed down rather haughtily at *Maori* as we came alongside, but its more sociable owner invited us on board. He told us of adventures during the evacuation of Dunkirk and impressed us with his own journeyings and sailing expertise at the age of seventy three.

He escorted us around an immaculate craft, and gave us an excellent sherry in well-cut glasses. We returned rather disconsolately to our own fly-blown *Maori*, for an equally fly-blown cup of Co-op '99' tea.

Shorts were dress-of-the-day as we made a brief clammy sail back to Town End Swing Bridge where (we had been told) there were some good shops 'just up the road'. Lethargic, blushing legs slowly placed one foot after the other as we sweated towards them. At last a friendly-looking blue and white Co-operative store welcomed us and we thankfully inspected its rather sparsely stocked shelves, trying to remember our needs. A staff of two waited as we shadowed a rather dissatisfied customer who, having already asked in vain for five items, suddenly gave way to his exasperation and inquired of a rather surprised assistant, 'Well, what HAVE you got?' As we arrived at the check-out, he dumped his meagre purchases on the counter and presented a five pound note for payment. Short of goods — the 'caring, sharing Co-op' was also short of cash. However, in spite of a despairing customer, arms raised, crying 'God in Heaven help us!' a pleasant, middle-aged lady at the till kept her cool, asked us to pay for our goods and smilingly gave him his change. We had fared better than he and we staggered back to *Maori* with bulging hand-scoring plastic bags which housed, amongst other things, fast liquefying New Zealand butter and some Co-op fly-killer.

While I sunbathed on deck and chatted up two workmen leaning actively on a fence, Alec shut himself up with the flies in a hotly protesting boat, which rocked and tugged at its restraining ropes as he charged violently to and fro aiming his deadly aerosol. Just as the workmen had casually observed that Alec might possibly do himself in, the doors flew open and he staggered out choking, coughing and gasping for air. Our re-entry found an abundance of fly-bodies lying in a toxic boat, which prompted me to suggest (rather unwisely at the time) that newspapers were, perhaps, less dangerous and equally as effective. On the menu at teatime was ham salad, yoghurt and mousse all flavoured with fly-killer. Very nice!

When we returned to Parbold, we were surprised to learn that the smoky Windmill pub had burst into flames during the previous night and was badly damaged. This sent us up another road, to find a smoky, but not yet ignited pub called The Station.

Day followed sun-soaked day as we climbed laboriously up the Wigan Flight and then along the Leeds–Liverpool canal towards Banknewton where our swimming, swotting, sweltering, sailing holiday was to end. At Roddlesworth Aqueduct, *Maori* rubbed gratefully against a refreshing grassy bank where we moored. We wandered only a few steps away from her into a lovely natural wood which, as it dropped away down a steep embankment, drew us into its deep, inviting shadows. Many paths offered exploration but we chose a mysterious way and joined a little stream which shyly crept with us through the undergrowth. Curious as to its source we re-tracked upstream and came upon a sizeable pond, fed by the River Roddlesworth which, having been adopted by a nearby paper mill, emerged at this point through a large pipe. Its eagerness to re-enter a more natural habitat was held up temporarily by an effective child-made dam. A friendly young man and one or two small anglers were lazily swishing nets, in contrast to some boisterous dam-busters who preferred leaping from rock to rock and splashing anyone within hand-cupped range. We were initiated into the art of finding 'bull-heads' and carefully lifted several rocks to test our newly found knowledge. We also heard tell of trout which 'came down with the rain', for when it poured hard enough a local trout farm sometimes overflowed and (according to our informant) down came the trout! We then wandered back alongside the gurgling stream, lifting stones as children would, shouting with delight if we disturbed a bull-head; a fully-clothed Adam and Eve savouring the solitude of this deep beautiful gully. Eventually face to face with the embankment, we had to climb out of our innocent reverie and get back on board *Maori* once more.

That night, as sunburnt flesh exuded relaxing warmth within a heat-retaining bag, I lay listening to a programme about the Maoris and their desperate clashes with the invading Pakehas (white men) during the early days of New Zealand's colonisation. I thought about their first great voyages, made in open canoes across wide unpredictable oceans, to find the Land of the Long White Cloud. Then obliterating sleep took over.

As each succeeding heat-charged day seemed hotter than the last, I could say that Thursday, August 7th, was the hottest; and when we slid out of Barrowford Top Lock to find Elsie doing a brisk trade in pop and icecream, we moored quickly in case she should run out. Here we took our ease and next day walked into the pretty village of Barrowford where in Rushworths an elderly gentleman made carving meat look like a work of art. In another shop, a butcher, who had visited New Zealand during the War, melted time away and also an icecream which Alec had bought for me during his separate perambulations.

For once the chilly dampness of Foulridge Tunnel was welcome as we nosed into its depths and at the first air vent I noted that the fish were still circumnavigating the spotlight, seemingly unable to break the confining pattern of their instinct. *Maori* disturbed it for a brief moment as she passed through and eventually out of her confinement to become part of the gentle Lancashire countryside. My scanning eyes found a herd of statuesque domino-cows splashed black and white against the green of a distant hill and sheep, like soft balls of wool, lay bleaching in the sun.

Alongside the canals there are many public houses called The Anchor, and as we curved under the shadow of hump bridge number 151, (number one being Caroline Street Changeline Bridge in Liverpool) we pulled in at one for a welcome drink and lunch. Here we had an interesting conversation with a couple of boating enthusiasts who had been canalling for sixteen years. They were in a car!

When they departed, so did we towards Greenberfield, where we would meet up with that inimitable character, Jim, and two other characters, singer and actress Rita McKerrow and her endearing dog, Muzzlie. His quizzical likeness, listening to an old-fashioned gramophone, has rotated all over the world on His Master's Voice records. Muzzlie listened patiently for hours to his mistress's voice when she was teaching — until she executed one particular highly pitched exercise and then he would sit up, stretch his neck and howl an effective portamento scale.

If on some peaceful relaxing day a resonant top 'A' caused you to start in surprise or inadvertently slip overboard, it was probably Rita, for boats, cars, towpaths, footpaths, public toilets (and private ones) were all the same to her when she felt a 'note' coming on!

As she was coming to join us the following morning, I spent the latter part of the forenoon-watch sitting on a sunny grassy bank by the side of the main Barnoldswick Road. Then when Rita's sailor-blue (would you believe it?) Ford van hove into view, I flagged it down and piloted her and an excited Muzzlie to the top of Jim's locks.

When *Maori* had tipped them aboard we cast off for a trip to Barrowford and our passage back through the tunnel was fraught with anxiety when a succession of Rita's top notes threatened to bring the roof and the sizeable hill above it, down on us all. Further on, a fluorescent Kingfisher, perched on a flexible branch by the water's edge, evoked a wave of excitement amongst the crew of a suddenly listing *Maori*.

On the return journey we passed through a large shoal of clearly visible fish which were tantalising a lone, frustrated fisherman who had baited them all day. We moored a little further on and when Alec strolled back to commiserate with the forlorn-looking figure, Rita, rejoicing in the ever-present heat, decided to take a plunge. The fact that she hadn't a swimsuit was no deterrent and when she jumped from *Maori* attired in a suitably coloured, but rather loose pair of aquamarine pants (once her mother's) and a 'bra' having difficulty containing her very ample bosoms, her twelve stone landing on the towpath was something to see. I glanced along at Alec still held in conversation with his ruminating friend, and felt that even Rita and me prancing in the nude would not have drawn the fisherman's gaze away from his elusive shoal of fish. However, one or two of the fish were interested and swam our way to inspect the unusual wallowing mammal (Rita) which floated, splashed and swished and swirled, with uninhibited pleasure.

This merry mermaid, although doubtless well developed by the process of evolution, had great difficulty making the transition from water to dry land. However, it persevered and eventually clawed its way up a steep canal bank and fell drippingly spread-eagled onto the towpath. By the time Alec returned the creature was dry, human and fully dressed again. Once we were back at Greenberfield Rita and Muzzlie left us and headed homewards towards some thunder which was grumbling away in the far distance.

The following day we sailed my favourite sail, high on the hillsides to a nostalgically beautiful Banknewton and our last holiday together was at an end.

CHAPTER TWELVE

'Navigare necesse est vivere non est necesse.'

For a whole year looking back was far too painful for me, so you will now find yourself in 1977 with Alec and me remaining apart but owning a confused *Maori* jointly. Penny is still in London, and Dave, having spent some fruitful years in Cambridge, has become a Doctor of Philosophy, while I am living in a Waterway's cottage trying to work out my own sorely tried philosophy. It happened like this...

Having survived (but only just) one of the most traumatic periods of my life, I had adapted to living indefinitely in a very comfortable flat which occupied part of an old house in Huddersfield; but fate extended a guiding hand one day when Rita, Muzzlie and I called on Evelyn and Arthur Crisp to be told about an empty cottage close to the canal at Shepley Bridge. A quick drive soon had us brushing aside long wet grass and peering through cheerless, dribbling windows at neglect, peeling paper, dirt and damp. Cold, wet and uncomfortable we wandered around, but our spirits were less dampened by the rain as we agreed (supreme optimists both) that the place had possibilities!

As Alec and I had registered seven years previously for a canal property and had renewed our request each year, I felt justified in contacting British Waterways in Leeds.

I acquired Calder House in June 1976 and moved in four months later exhausted from scything, digging, painting, scraping, scrubbing, worrying, waiting, deciding, packing, sorting and eventually moving. Most decisions were made in consultation with Alec Schweidler, a Hungarian builder and philosopher who spoke pidgin-Yorkshire, and even though we frequently downed tools to slurp coffee and philosophise to each other, towards October the conversion I had planned steadily neared completion. However, the financial pressure of paying two rents added to other indescribable pressures, necessitated my occupying Calder House before it was finished.

Problems arose. At one stage of the proceedings, when I was waiting for the Water Authority to connect a fresh supply, the only water available was a tiny, fluctuating trickle from a pipe in the depths of the cellar. This meant that all my needs for washing, cooking and flushing the toilet had to be, first of all, caught in slow-filling containers and then humped up two steep flights of steps. Things came to a head one memorable morning when my source dried up completely and I couldn't even use the 'loo'. Although I had a key for the Waterway's toilet, (a trek away down by the canal) nature and time would not allow me to get there, so for the first time in my life I used a bucket.

'Habit dies hard,' I thought as I carried it into the bathroom. Seconds later, a thunderous, banging at the door told me that Mr Schweidler had arrived early. The now offensive bucket (with a Yorkshire Post lid) had to repose in my bedroom all day until he made an unusually late departure. Then I stole, watched only by full-faced moon, across a damp field, along the edge of a yawning dry dock, to the toilets — where I emptied its spoils.

My Steinway piano stood on its side in a damp, draughty passage for a fortnight, (which did it no good) my Hillman Imp sat in a field for a month (which did IT no good), and wouldn't start most mornings, (which did ME no good!).

After wintering in my new 'old' abode, I felt sufficiently rested and fit enough to think about holidaying on *Maori*. Casting around among my most energetic friends, it occurred to me that enthusiastic walkers Mary, Margaret and Harold Newman must also be fairly fit, so I asked them to join me.

Mary (smilingly round) is a soprano and the conductor of Outlane Methodist Church Choir; her husband, Harold (smoothly white haired) a tenor, conducted Salendine Nook Church Choir; their vivacious daughter Margaret (also a soprano) had trouble conducting her lively Sunday School class, and we all came together every Friday night to be conducted by the chorus master at the Huddersfield Choral Society's weekly rehearsal.

Having arranged to begin our holiday on August 7th, (a Sunday when the church choirs would have to conduct themselves) our plans unexpectedly suffered a 'slight' hitch!

Dave, accompanied by his girl-friend Cheryl was once again sailing *Maori* and my musical crew was to take over at Autherley Junction. Because of my Imp's limited capacity, Penny and Carol Poppleton (whose job was to return my car home) had arranged to go with Alec in his car on Saturday (along with our suitcases and bedding) when he fetched Dave and Cheryl. Then on Sunday the Imp, would endeavour to conduct a squashed in semi-chorus to *Maori*.

The first chilling hint of a major crisis in the offing came when Penny and I accepted an invitation out to tea. On a warm relaxing Friday evening we picked up the Newmans' luggage and went straight on to a meal being made by Penny's newly-married friend, Susan Sykes. Thorough, but delaying preparations had us supping gins and waiting for a nine o'clock supper of casseroled mutton, rice pudding and coffee, which we ravenous beasts devoured and partially digested before Penny rang Alec to make final arrangements. An extremely agitated Alec, who had been trying to reach us all evening, answered, and a worried daughter had my scarcely settled meal turning over as she declared that 'something was up with the boat.' Alec related the story to me — as an anxious Dave had done to him — earlier in the evening.

Finding himself with time to spare, Dave had explored the Trent and Mersey Canal for a spell and during his return to Autherley Junction had struck a submerged object. A loud 'clunk' under her hull had startled but not unduly worried her crew — not until later that is, when somebody casually observed that water was oozing out of the floor. Dave acted! and all the lethargic, sunbathing bodies reacted. Boards (all tightly screwed down) rose in panic-motivated hands which then grabbed anything that held water and baled frantically to prevent *Maori* from sinking. When a small leak was located they showed great presence of mind by stuffing it with an oily rag and a thwarted canal was held temporarily at bay.

Alec was upset — I was upset — we rushed over to tell the Newmans who, despite plans made suddenly uncertain, pretended not to be upset. We called to see Carol (who was more likely to giggle than be upset) and found her to be out.

Alec decided to go to Autherley Junction next day to find out if *Maori* could be repaired and a sleepless night had me listening to Saturday's dawn chorus and wondering what the day would bring. It brought a heavy headed coffee-soaked morning of anxious waiting. Finally the 'phone jangled a death knell to our holiday with the news that *Maori* could not be welded until the following week. The work would take three days and cost in the region of one hundred pounds. Dave came onto the line to suggest that we take a chance and sail with an oily rag between us and disaster — but because I was trying, in difficult circumstances, to remain reasonably sound in mind, (not to mention body) this interesting idea was rejected.

Acute disappointment was my first reaction — not so much for myself, (although I felt that too) but for my friends who had for weeks been borrowing canal books and maps from Huddersfield's Public Library, who had made and purchased nautical clothing, baked special cakes, and bought some extra large bottles of vino for the sail.

As I disconnected Dave's troubled voice from my ear, Penny, in an Imp still full of Newmans' luggage, arrived with a newspaper full of fish and chips. But the day had turned as sour as the vinegar she had liberally sprinkled on them — and I could not eat.

My second reaction was to try and find an alternative holiday — the seaside — the Lakes — a towpath walk — or even another boat! Aided by the magazine *Waterways World* I rang (within fifteen minutes) a hire firm on the Peak Forest Canal, Valeswood Boats at Shrewsbury, Wrixall Marina on the Llangollen Canal, Harold

Newman at Huddersfield, Alec at Autherley Junction and Bradford Boat Services about our insurance. In between the outgoing calls our red-hot-line received ones from a giggling Carol Poppleton, a sympathetic Mary Newman and Alec Schweidler who, with incredibly bad timing, had decided this was the moment to collect a large sum of money which was owing to him. I could hardly defer payment to cover all the expenses which were mounting literally minute by minute, so arranged for him to call.

The surprising outcome of all my frantic telephoning was the offer of a boat for a week by Wrixall Marina for one hundred pounds and all at once our holiday was on again, in a different county — on a different canal — in a different boat!

By now you will be assuming that at least some of our problems were solved and that on Sunday, four substantial people would overload a badly-shocked Imp (now sporting a hastily-borrowed roof-rack) and, given reasonable luck, should be afloat on the beautiful Llangollen Canal by evening. Not so! Come Sunday, in fact we were all floating in a sea of bemused thoughts on board *Maori* on the Shropshire Union Canal!

As I collapsed around a double Martini prepared by an attentive Harold at the end of what was at first a frustrating, then a triumphant day, I found the events leading to this swift transition difficult to believe.

As soon as I had confirmed (on Saturday afternoon) our booking with the obliging manager of Wrixall Marina, Alec rang through with the news that an equally enterprising firm called simply 'Gregory's' had arranged to survey *Maori* on Sunday morning and would, if possible, effect an immediate repair.

Having been deprived of my lunch by an uncomfortable nausea, (the result of worrying over *Maori's* critical state and the initial shock of a much-needed holiday up the spout) by tea-time I had achieved a choice of two holidays on two boats! With hammers beating inside my head and a stomach churning like a fast-filling lock, I reeled weakly away from the telephone and, experiencing a stunned feeling of inevitability, reached first for the 'Settlers' and then automatically for the phone to ring Wrixall Marina.

'I'm sorry to muck you about,' I apologised in a strange, unrecognisable little voice, 'But the circumstances are rather unusual.'

Unusual?? They were bloody unique!

Sensing my embarrassment and genuine concern, an unbelievably sympathetic man, having been involved in our problems for two hours, offered to hold his boat at our disposal pending a decision on *Maori*.

On Sunday morning an ill-balanced quartet wedged indivisible in a badly listing Imp, set forth for Autherley Junction and, against all odds, arrived safely at half past eleven to find a non-plussed Alec waiting for 'Gregorys' to arrive at ten o'clock. Half an hour and ten calls later, we were still waiting. Great perseverance ringing a number displayed on the office door brought no response — mainly due to the fact (we found out later) that the number WAS the office and it was (as we very well knew) empty!

Returning again and again to a telephone kiosk devoid of directories accounted for a long frustrating period during which we had frequently to allow access to more successful callers. I nurtured dark, sinister thoughts about one girl who kept us standing fifteen minutes while she fed in piles of coins and, judging from her demeanour, endless sweet nothings to a receptive male.

Hunger at last joined desperation and we decided to prepare our overdue lunch while Alec went off yet again — this time to contact Harry Machin at Market Drayton. As soon as his dust-cloud had settled, Mr Gregory threw up another and arrived with his survey party — a young man and a very young boy — and while we were busy talking and viewing the oily rag (miraculously intact in the hole) Alec, having arranged for *Maori* to be dry docked and welded at Norbury Junction, returned. A somewhat (until then) indecisive Mr Gregory thought this was an excellent idea, seemed relieved to be rid of the responsibility and settled down to have a comfortable chat — about boats! While I was organising a meal they continued talking boats and when lunch was on the table they were still at it. Harassed and famished, I was wondering how I could tactfully request Mr Gregory to 'bugger off' and allow us to eat — when he suddenly read my inhospitable thoughts and did.

Post lunch found us strengthened and able to tackle the eighteen mile sail to Norbury — but not until we had contacted Wrixall Marina and Dave and Cheryl who had gone to Huddersfield to collect some belongings. As a precaution against my Imp having to be welded along with *Maori*, they were also collecting the remainder of our luggage and we had arranged a rendezvous along the canal halfway to Norbury. We also arranged — should we actually MEET — for them to return me to the Imp, which I would then drive to *Maori*'s destination and await her arrival. If all went well she would be repaired on Monday and then off we would go on a jolly boating holiday, just in time to avert a nervous breakdown and permanent brain damage!

Unbelievably, (with our luck) the weather was kind and an indelicately stuffed *Maori* behaved beautifully during a soul-restoring sail. However, I was somewhat taken aback when locking through at Wheaton Aston to see a daughter, who was supposedly many miles away in Huddersfield, materialise onto the towpath — followed, of course, by Dave and Cheryl, with whom she'd cadged a ride. In no time at all I was motorised and heading back to where we had just come from!

This saga must come to an end, so I will simply state that we all arrived safely (if unsoundly) at Norbury and then Alec and Penny headed towards Huddersfield — a wise Dave and Cheryl having already returned to London.

Small wonder that I was grateful for Harold's brain-numbing Martini and then later, even more grateful to collapse onto a bunk, where visions of oily rags and boats that sink in the night deprived me of sleep for the second night running.

Next morning, the responsibility of having to manoeuvre *Maori* into the dry dock made me forget my fatigue, and there we left her, shyly awaiting the tender attention of Seamus the welder.

Now we had time to kill, and clutching our lunchtime butties we enviously watched boats coming and going. After a short country walk, we visited the Shropshire Cruiser's shop, made friends with a likeable donkey, and then went to the Junction Inn. Eventually we sat, a fed-up quartet stroking icecreams with our tongues, on a bench overlooking this active, colourful basin. With little else to do we tuned into other people's conversations and in particular to two men chatting nearby. When one enquired of the other if he knew the definition of a blunderbuss, we all pricked up our portside ears and waited for his reply. 'A coachload of bastards!'

Relaxed holiday makers moving on and off their boats looked startled when four people, who had been huddled quietly and gloomily together, suddenly began shrieking with hysterical laughter; an outlet, no doubt, for the tensions of the previous days.

When a boat hirer, who had moored to empty his toilet, complained to an unsympathetic crew that he kept passing canal-side pubs but never actually got inside one, Harold observed that at least he didn't suffer from alcoholic constipation like the chap who couldn't pass a pub! And more rocking rolling merriment from the seat had the thirsty boatman casting apprehensive looks, untying quickly and shoving off.

As rain, which had always been threatening, began in earnest, we drooped away from the useful bench and grouped wistfully under a draughty hump bridge to eat our squashed and dented sandwiches; and then the Junction Inn and its nice clean loos enjoyed our patronage until the moody skies cleared.

By the time we emerged, Seamus had gone and *Maori* was ready to do some enthusiastic mud churning as she moved astern down the short arm which had led us to the dock. After some questionable seamanship I brought *Maori*, with her sharp end pointing in the right direction, alongside a grassy bank where we refilled with water, topped up ourselves with a cup of tea and prepared to begin our holiday.

Maori gave an eager response as Mary astern and Harold forward untied her restraining ropes and we were away at last! I automatically glanced to check the engine cooling water, which should spurt out of a hole in her side and wet any unwary feet standing on the towpath — but it was non-existent. We tied up again.

While Harold went off to fetch a mechanic, I ruminated on the prospect of an entire holiday spent at Norbury Junction. I brightened at the news that help would arrive in a minute, became submerged in a poetic sea of despondency after a twenty minute wait, hopefully surfaced when an overalled body appeared, but then fell back into the depths when he couldn't locate the fault and disappeared to tend a hire craft requiring assistance some miles away.

However, he had (after learning from me that it was probably an air lock) diagnosed — an air lock! So I decided to motor on and hope that it would clear itself. Forty-five minutes later, it hadn't and a worried boat-load pulled into The Anchor at Bridge 42 near High Offley. My plan (which seemed rather brilliant at the time) was to contact Harry Machin and ask his advice.

High Offley is so named because it sits on a hillside. Its telephone box is situated next to the church which stands, as befits a place used for worship of the most high, at the top. Mary and I climbed and sweated along the ever-steepening country lane which led the local inhabitants to prayer and us to ask for help from a surprised, then helpful, Harry. At my breathless request for aid he barked out some instructions which my struggling, overheated brain tried to assimilate. As we weakly leaned the door of the kiosk open, I continuously recited Harry's orders and paused for a moment to look around. According to the canal book there were some good views to be had, but footsore and tired, the only view Mary and I took was a dim one.

Nevertheless, heartened with hope and helped by the downward slope, we set off at a cracking pace to return to *Maori*. There Harold, with an array of tools at the ready, stood waiting to obey instructions which I was chokingly incapable of issuing because of lack of breath. I recovered, and Harold doubled up over the engine well where he disconnected the water hose, got cramp, allowed the canal to bubble alarmingly into the boat, and quickly stopped it. He primed the hose startling Margaret (who had her thumb stuck in the outlet hole) as a beautiful, curving arc of light-reflecting H2O rainbowed over to the towpath.

After all our recent exertions and anxieties, success was doubly sweet and we cheered and waved like uninhibited children. Harold now fancied himself as an engineroom artificer and I fancied a forty-eight hour kip.

Instead we sailed on into one of the calmest of evenings, the deepening night-clouds interspersed with brilliant blue flashes of sky while the low setting sun became a succulent blood-red orange framed by the hump bridges as we moved serenely along. The countryside was mellow, green, gold and beautiful and magnificent herbaceous borders on either side had Margaret, equipped with a wild flower book, identifying scabious, willow herb, vetch and storksbill.

Because all our boating plans are flexible, not to say unpre-dictable, I was not surprised (having decided to stop at Bridge 45) to be searching for a mooring at Bridge 55 by Wharf Tavern near Cheswadine. A hungry horizon had long since devoured the orange and we had been pipped to all the best moorings. So we had to sail enviously past boats occupying a neat concrete edge into nettles, where insufficient depth necessitated use of a gangplank.

Only Mary and I crossed it to visit a very lively Tavern and make a reassuring call to Alec about *Maori*; and after we had taken our time over a sherry and a brandy, we hastily made our bumpy way along a boat-lined towpath, where we nettled our legs, then walked the plank — and went to bed.

When I surfaced, the morning had not yet wiped the mistiness from its eyes and heat hung visibly poised to envelope us. This it did as a wide-awake day became gloriously sunny and evoked a genuinely, carefree holiday mood at last. We sun-worshipped in varying creations of unattire, sailed, sipped Italian wine, passed the time of day with other basking water travellers and gratefully soaked up some pleasure-giving hours of boating at its best.

The Newmans were enthralled as we passed through the deep rock cutting of Woodseaves. Densely wooded, hung about with long drooping vines — within this unruly exotic jungle, we became intrepid adventurers and explorers. Margaret, the ornithologist of the party, searching diligently for new species of bird-life; Mary, the biologist, observed and identified its rich natural foliage; consultant Harold, confirmed or questioned their claims and Doris (coxswain and linguist) emitted a voice-straining Tarzan-call to invite Johnny Weismuller to swing in-board on a vine!

But he did not respond, so we moved on to the ever-appealing Tyrley Locks where we decided to stay and do ourselves to a turn, in the uninterrupted heat of a perfect summer's afternoon. A man with time to spare unhurriedly tended a smoky garden fire, ripples played and danced with the sun's beams as boats plied lazily back and forth and we lay stretched out, soft and hazy with warmth and wine.

'Put that bloody fire out!' shouted a house with all its windows open — causing many recumbent bodies on many boats to shoot up simultaneously and look around; but the voice was bodiless, and when the man tending the offending fire carried on as if nothing had happened, our interest waned — and we all lay down again.

'What day is it?' called a contented boatman.

'1977,' I answered facetiously.

Margaret and I favoured continuous inactivity, but walkers, Mary and Harold, elected to go ashore for a stroll. Much later they returned in true naval tradition assuming a rolling, inebriated gait along the towpath.

'Obviously a case of alcoholic constipation,' I commented as they sniggered and staggered aboard, pleased with what was only a partial deception because they had in fact, called for one (or two) at the Four Alls public house some way from the canal. Here, on a sign (they told us) a King declared, 'I rule over all,' a soldier, 'I fight for all,' a bishop, 'I pray for all,' and an ordinary man, (as ever) 'I pay for all!'

I suggested black coffee for all — with biscuits, which mightily pleased a friendly golden Labrador who had followed my friends zigzag course and hopped on board. As he paddled all over me and tentatively licked off some suntan oil, I recognised that our quiet time was over and reluctantly sat up. And it certainly was when Sandy (in true canal-dog fashion) introduced us to his equally friendly and talkative owner from the boat *Dewsbury*. They had once lived near me, (not far from the town of Dewsbury, after which the boat was named).

We sailed and locked in company along the short stretch to Market Drayton where *Dewsbury* reached the end of their holiday and we moored for the night. As we were making *Maori* fast, a bum-boat sailed past — at least, we christened it such because the chap standing on its stern had the tiller stuck up his bum and was steering by that means. Quite oblivious to some tittering females falling about on *Maori*, he went serenely by, making all necessary adjustments to port and starboard without once using his hands, while my unabashed laughter and anticipation of his agony, should a vulnerable tiller suddenly swing — brought tears to my eyes!

After a somewhat clammy night within our clinging sleeping bags and before exploring and shopping in Market Drayton, we all trooped, well-greased and sun-topped to call on Harry Machin.

'It's a lovely morning,' I called cheerfully, as he slammed his arrival at the boatyard.

'Not if you're here!' he replied, taking me aback until I realised his reference to *Maori*'s recent water troubles. When I assured him that, as a result of his lucid instructions, the water pump was working perfectly, he warmed enough to ask me how I was. When I praised the work of Seamus the welder and bought some of his canalia, he warmed some more — but wouldn't supply us with diesel for *Maori*, whose tank needed replenishing.

Having expounded on one absolutely perfect day, how does one describe another which seemed even more perfect? For on this truly heaven-sent day, Sun and Earth, enjoying an uninterrupted view of each other, communicated to our advantage, and a blue, blue sky, once it had glimpsed its azure image in a mirroring canal, admired itself all day.

Even the numerous locks of Audlem made a leisurely pace more so as we waited for boats to rise and pass, or for leading boats to descend. At one point, when we were moored waiting our turn for a lock, some wolf whistles from a bank high above us made Margaret and me sit up. These seemed to come from a large wooden shed partially screened by bushes, and in holiday mood we blew a blast on *Maori*'s horn in reply. Workmen often used this shed and very soon a gay horn and whistle duet helped pass the time as we waited. When we moved forward into the opening arms of the lock, I took a backward glance at the now completely visible shed and was amazed to see a door on which was scrawled the illuminating word — GENTS!

Head turning neither to left nor right, with ears deaf to all subsequent whistles, I was glad to disappear down several locks before mooring just below a well-known canal-side pub called the Shroppie Fly. Earlier that afternoon Mary had emulated a Shroppie fly when she jumped hastily onto a moving boat, just made it and landed on one end of a seat which tipped her with a bang, flat-footed into the well of the boat. Her noisy, airborne landing caused me, standing dreamily at the wheel, to momentarily lose control, had Mary wide-eyed with shock and evoked merriment among us all.

When engines have done their work and boaters have done the same — then boats can, for an hour or two, add their shapely images to enhance a lovely scene — these are the rewarding times — the precious times in between.

During this evening's magical 'in between' Harold, lying flat on his stomach, fished a ladybird out of the canal to 'save it from drowning', a grazing mare and foal in a nearby field drew a few appreciative 'oo's and ah's', and a reddening ball hung in the sky once more before it dipped downwards to be caught in the silhouette of tall black-leafed trees as they allowed it to slip slowly through their branches and disappear.

Later an over-indulged beagle from a boat moored astern waddled up to make our acquaintance but he was obviously a newcomer on the canals and did not follow the protocol of introducing us to his owners. This was just as well for we were sipping our pre-dinner drinks, after which Shroppie fly (Mary), followed by her companions, went off to another Shroppie Fly and settled there for the remainder of the evening.

Thursday followed Wednesday — (as usual) and the sun shone and shone — as usual! At last, an almost forgotten promise which I had made to myself was kept when I accompanied the Newman trio around Audlem, where we inhaled tempting smells of freshly baked bread mixed with heady scents from a delightful garden. Stocks, zinnias, larkspur, marigolds, roses, little dorrit, lobelia, petunias and phlox all combined in a dazzling display which had droves of bees a-humming and cameras a-clicking.

A visit to the icecream shop had us a-licking and it was late morning when our expedition straggled back along the towpath, Margaret ahead — a hip-swaying native-bearer, with *Maori's* new red bucket poised on top of her head. When all was stowed away, we left this pretty village behind and sailed, sun a-shining all the way, to Hack Green Locks where we stayed for lunch. Here, on the 'Canal D'azur' we lounged — some red and sore — others bronzed, on our luxury yacht. We ordered drinks from our perfect English waiter, (Harold) — martinis or Italian wine. These complemented a special Audlem pizza served with freshly-cooked beetroot and delicious cooling salad, which was followed by succulent chopped peaches in homemade icecream, topped with liberal helpings of whipped cream. As we over-stuffed ourselves with coffee, cheese and biscuits, I was reminded that *Maori's* tank had yet to be topped up and I resolved to remedy this as soon as possible.

But a further fruitless call for fuel at Nantwich Basin left us no alternative but to press on and hope for the best. As we approached Hurleston Junction, where the Llangollen Canal joins the Shropshire Union, a man silhouetted on a bridge some distance ahead began waving vigorously.

'What's up with that silly devil?' I asked anybody who was listening.

No one knew; but as we crept closer to a figure gradually increasing in size and clarity, the 'silly devil' became clearly identifiably as wine-maker and boater, Rodney Bass. He and Eileen (in *Dragonfly*) had left Brighouse about three weeks before and by the most amazing coincidence we had both arrived at the junction simultaneously. Now we all waved madly and I turned *Maori*'s wheel to come alongside and moor. For the first time during the trip Mary was up in the bows, so I shouted to her to take a rope ashore. As *Maori* neared the towpath our own Shroppie fly took off and actually landed, but in her haste failed to allow enough rope and was immediately pulled backwards into the canal betwixt boat and bank! By the time that Eileen and Rodney had negotiated their last lock and arrived to join us, Mary was back in the water looking for her glasses which had fallen off in the melée and Margaret and I, having hastily donned our swimsuits, had joined her.

As a somewhat puzzled Eileen (looking askance at a groping Mary fully-dressed in the canal) walked up, she remarked on our quick change from boating party to bathing party, while Hans (their boisterous boxer) came bounding up to a sudden stop, head quizzically on one side — peering at me — obviously disappointed that he was unable to greet me in his usual affectionate fashion — by knocking me flat on the floor!

The canal bottom, as we felt about with sensitive feet, was very rocky and slimy and three 'Rhine Maidens', who drew many queer glances from passing boaters, were also fair game for the wits amongst them. Harold, wishing to do his bit, thoughtfully fetched warming or cooling drinks, (according to whether you were in our out of the canal) and from then on we spent a jolly time chatting and drinking — those still immersed refusing to give up the search for Mary's specs.

About half an hour later a chilled Mary went to dry-off and change, and as soon as she had disappeared into *Maori*, Margaret, having hooked the lost glasses with her big toe, raised a triumphant shout which was echoed lustily by all hands as she waved her lucky find aloft.

Pleased to vacate a cold, murky canal, I eagerly rushed over to *Maori* to bear the good news to Mary. I peered in through the door to behold a scene of absolute chaos. Within a gloomy, curtained cabin a partially clad, ghostly figure stood rubbing its bedraggled hair amidst great pools of water, heaps of dripping clothes and damp towels, all thickly coated with highly scented talcum powder — which she had inadvertently dropped. As I gawped in astonishment and added my own drips Mary, overcome at last by recent events, began to giggle. Very soon I joined in and then two hysterical, overgrown schoolgirls laughed, cried and rolled about until their sides ached and until complete exhaustion persuaded their uncontrollable mirth to subside.

Moored close together for the first time, *Dragonfly* and *Maori* entered into a close relationship and arranged to keep company as far as Chester. To celebrate their mutual joy at meeting, a towpath barbecue was hastily organised to take place that night. Along the way, at Calveley, a roadside garage was also a canal-side one and a notice advertising diesel had *Maori* gratefully grazing her side on its landing stage and filling up.

All fears regarding fuel now allayed, we were able to appreciate a carefree sail to a lovely spot by Tilstone Lock where we ceased our puttering noises and became as one with the peaceful leafy surroundings. Having completely recovered from the farcical events of the afternoon, we now looked forward to our pooled meal of rump steak for four, (cut to feed six) lamb chops for two, new potatoes, mixed salad and rich red wine. 'Afters' were to consist of peaches from *Maori*, apricots from *Dragonfly* and appropriately, because of our proximity to where it is produced, Cheshire cheese — with biscuits and freshly-ground coffee to finish.

By sunset on a balmy evening, preparations for the feast were well under way. Easily collected and ignited, dry twigs merrily crackled and warmed the black dead-looking charcoal which, encouraged by explosive doses of 'meths', soon came alive and glowing with darting, erratic flames. Eventually, the desired white-hot coals awaited our fare and cooking began. Hans, jowls dripping saliva, his nose creasing and uncreasing, edged slowly, crouched on all fours, ever closer and closer to the spitting, smoking steak. But Rodney sharply ordered him off, and he slunk reluctantly away casting aggrieved, reproachful looks at his master.

'After all,' his downcast expression seemed to say, 'It is a party!'

Next time I looked he was edging back again; and, eventually as a reward for his persistence he was allowed a dog's fair share.

After every morsel had disappeared from every last plate, Hans voluntarily moved away and contented bodies then grouped lethargically around the still warm embers and discussed the day. Margaret and I effectively screened off any heat from the others by holding our still damp swimsuits out to dry, and then Rodney, remembering some rubbish that needed burning, carried away the last dying coals to light *Dragonfly*'s stove — and smoked the whole boat out! Helped by good food and amiable company, a great sense of camaraderie existed on the towpath that evening and many stories were swapped and much laughter ensued. Hans, wishing to show his appreciation, desperately wanted to join *Maori*'s crew for the night, but as he is a very large dog and we were very crowded, we persuaded him to return to his own smoky craft.

By the time we had washed up, raised *Maori*'s canopy, sorted out sleeping bags, blankets, pillows and pyjamas, made the beds, had washes, taken pills, put on hair nets, face creams and made final visits to the 'loo', it was extremely late.

'Yes,' I thought snug in a sleeping bag full of me full of food, 'Definitely a night to remember!'

Nobody seemed anxious to rise next morning and it wasn't until we had completed an unhurried visit to *Dragonfly* for 'elevenses' that we pulled out our mooring pins and moved towards Chester.

Two interesting locks, one stone — one iron, dropped us into a scene of incredible beauty. High summer's colourful guests had congregated together, in high-fashion colours of purple, yellow and white on each side of a deep blue aisle, down which we slowly processed, caught in the fragrant, languorous atmosphere. An absorbed *Dragonfly* was leading slightly ahead, but the spell was broken when a check on their finances had Rodney and Eileen urgently needing to arrive in Chester and find a bank. Having arranged a later meeting they motored quickly away and then we also sought a canal bank — where-at to moor and have our lunch. But a shallow canal tantalised and hungered us and would not let us moor. Deeply-keeled *Maori* moved along uncomfortably, irritated by her scraping, chafing progress and made several brave attempts to come alongside — but to no avail. As anxiety added its sweaty uneasiness to the day, the heat became oppressive. Eventually we came to a marina at Eggbridge where fatigue and a sinking emptiness had me hailing a brown muscular stranger and eagerly asking for a mooring.

'There's plenty of water here,' he cried as his willing hands caught and pulled at our rope with a mighty, muscle-rippling tug.

'That's funny,' he said, as *Maori*'s keel ground her to a halt three feet from the shore.

'It should be deep enough,' he gasped, as another heave left her firmly unrockable.

'Can't understand it,' he observed, as one more try had us beached and immovable.

Determined that we should enjoy his hospitality, he then tied *Maori* securely to the shore, satisfied himself as to her complete immobility, and went back to his interrupted work, leaving us, at past three o'clock on a hot and bothered Friday, to prepare our much-needed lunch.

Endless cups of tea and corned beef sandwiches did wonders for our flagging spirits and after the gangplank had connected us to dry land, we visited some nearby shops and then we were ready for the shallows once again. Harold, on shore, (with little thought as to how he would re-board) levered *Maori*'s stern with her long stout pole while Margaret, Mary and I distributed our combined weights in the bows — without success. Our newly made friend came along with an even longer pole, rocked us alarmingly and her stern floated off. Encouraged, I tried going gently astern, but we were still stuck amidships. Our 'friend' then appeared with a massive piece of scaffolding (the sight of which made *Maori* and me wince) and tried to up-end us as we moved out yet further — almost into the middle of the canal 'but unbelievably still aground! Nothing daunted, our 'resolute friend' (worried because he could not now even reach us) disappeared again and returned with a very long ladder, and then *Maori* — after another shove — gave in. We shouted relieved thanks to our panting, smiling, ladder-waving friend and sailed uneasily away.

But — as it happened — not so far away, because it soon became blatantly obvious, as *Maori* juddered and thrashed about, that something was affecting her propulsion. Having just passed a lone Waterway's man rhythmically scything on the towpath, we interrupted his slow, swishing sweeps with a call for assistance to guide *Maori's* nose into the reeds.

Harold, having only heard second-hand of the difficulties involved in clearing the prop, now stripped for first hand knowledge. After achieving the major operation of getting down into the well, he struggled determinedly — but, prone to cramp, short armed and (in his words) cursed with 'funny' knees, he could only just reach the top of the propellor blades — and after ten minutes grovelling and grunting — gave up.

Now I stripped for action — but modestly donned my swimsuit for the second time during that holiday. However, don't run away with the idea that I intended an under-water survey of our problem — my swimsuit is not for swimming! It is for groping about on canal bottoms and for leaning over oil-distributing engines and deep, unfathomable propellor blades!

After trying about six positions, (all equally uncomfortable) I actually managed to touch the blades which were tightly entwined with wire and weeds. Then followed several back-breaking minutes which made no impression at all and necessitated my coming up for a breather — soon to return below armed with our serrated bread knife. This was better. Great patches of weed came floating to the top and, although I was by now covered with red weals caused by unyielding bits of engine which had deposited oil on my face, arms, legs, shoulders, bosoms and swimsuit, I lunged again and again to attack the unknown enemy.

A temporary victory had the propellor turning only slightly until a large piece of rough cloth came into my searching hands. Then I wrestled with the foe, pulling, twisting, grunting and (unusual for me in the Newmans' presence) swearing — but we had reached an impasse. Harold offered reinforcements, but the matter had become a personal one and, after a brief withdrawal, I grasped the knife (now lashed to a boat hook) and sent rapier thrusts into the heart of my opponent.

Capitulation followed, and I triumphantly dragged a hateful towelling jacket which had been the culprit, into the boat. Harold dashed for his camera to record the moment for posterity and as I was far too exhausted to argue, I posed — oily, tired, dishevelled, saw-knife and jacket aloft, wearing a past-caring expression which just wouldn't say 'cheese', for a snap which (thankfully) didn't come out!

Our erstwhile friend had told us of some deep water lapping up to Ye Old Trooper Inn which lay a short journey along the canal, but by the time I had de-oiled myself and had a reviving cup of tea, the few miles from Eggbridge to Chrisleton had accounted for two whole hours. Although we nurtured grave doubts as to 'friend's' ability to define a deep mooring, these were dispelled (but only just) after several attempts had us secured in the only thirty-foot length which would allow *Maori* to remain afloat and us to reach shore.

Almost before *Maori*'s engine had sighed to a stop, I fell gratefully onto a cushioned bunk, while Harold disappeared like a shot into the Trooper — to watch the cricket! Off and on, between crises, we had been following the Test Match and a crackling radio informed us that Boycott, well into his second century, was slowly grinding the Australians down. Feeling somewhat ground-down myself made me sympathetically inclined towards my fellow Antipodeans, but I lay back to rest my aching limbs hoping that England would win the Test and that if WE had any more tests — we would win them too!

Next day we caught a bus into the centre of Chester to look for Rodney and Eileen to explain our non-arrival at the rendezvous. Mission accomplished, we then explored this very interesting and attractive city; its ancient walls, its shops, its restaurants — its further shops, its lively, popular river — its other shops, its red stone cathedral and, some additional shops! After a fantastically expensive pot of tea and three cakes, which cost two pounds (all but a miserable penny) we decided to return to *Maori* as soon as possible. Being fleeced within the shadow of the cathedral had left a nasty taste of over-priced cake in our mouths, and appetites temporarily spoilt. This delayed our meal of cheese omelettes and salad on board until nine o'clock.

A lively discussion followed during which we sought to put the whole world to rights — found we couldn't — and played Scrabble instead!

Slightly dispirited, because of Margaret's impending departure by train next day, we listlessly made our routine preparations for bed. But fickle moods changed abruptly when a toothless Harold (in pyjamas) suddenly made his entrance from the galley pulling an incredibly distorted funny face — the spitting image of Popeye — so his surprised and delighted audience declared.

That night the ship's company was continually disturbed by cars crossing a nearby hump bridge where notices (one at each end) extended a friendly invitation to all motorists to sound their horns!

Two unsettled nights at this convenient but noisy mooring had us anticipating a more restful period deep in the countryside at Wharton Lock; and that is where we arrived, sadly minus one crew member, late on Sunday afternoon. But we were happy to hammer home our mooring pins in this delightful spot and rest upon a *Maori*, moist and warmly still with the evening. From her stern our eyes covered the considerable distance to the ruins of thirteenth century Beeston Castle, on its commanding position high above the Cheshire Plain.

On Monday we were accompanied up most of the locks by a couple with two boys who, on a borrowed boat, were experiencing a canal holiday for the first time. In a tiny fibre-glass cruiser inside which one could not comfortably swing a caterpillar — let alone a cat — they had, in appalling weather conditions, set out from Stoke. Negotiation of Chester's Locks soon had them soiled and soaked to the skin, and one of the boys, a delicate hole-in-the-heart case, had fallen into a lock. By the time we teamed up they were having great trouble with a freshening wind and also some controversy on board, mainly because the woman felt miserable in the unfamiliar conditions and was fed-up to the teeth. However, for our benefit she put on a brave face, and later when the sun shone and tempered the effects of the wind, the day and relationships both improved.

During the afternoon, as their craft, dressed over-all with flapping drying garments, bounced astern of us, I spent a really energetic hour lying in the sun and browsing through the Practical Information (cruising) section of the canal book. For some reason I began adding asinine comments in the margins. For instance . . .

'There is no better way of finding out the joys of the canals than by getting afloat.' (That figures.)

'When you meet another boat, the rule of the road is to keep to the right, slow down and aim to miss the approaching boat by a couple of yards.' (Seems sensible.)

'If you meet a boat being towed from the bank, pass it on the outside rather than intercept the towing line.' (Or incur four faults?)

'On running aground. If all else fails, lighten your load, make all the crew leave the boat except the helmsman.' (Especially good idea if stuck in the middle of the canal!)

'All boats carry metal stakes and a mallet. These are used for mooring.' (Not for hitting husbands on the head?)

'Never stretch your mooring lines tight across the towpath, you may trip someone up.' (Eight faults!!)

'A lock is a simple device.' (No comment.)

'When going down a lock a boat should never be tied up or it will be left high and dry.' (The mind boggles!)

'The best way to tackle bridge holes is to slow down well in advance and aim to go straight through.' (What — no wind?)

'Before operating any moveable bridges make sure that any road traffic approaching is aware of your intention to open the bridge.' (What — no road?)

'Lift bridges which are moved vertically are raised by pulling down on a balance beam. The heaviest member of the crew (not me) should swing on the chain. (Definitely not me!) Serious damage could be caused to the boat and to the helmsman (could be me) if the bridge were allowed to fall.' (HELP!)

'If you see another boat in the tunnel coming towards you it is best to wait until it is out before entering.' (Especially if it's a one way tunnel.)

'Respect should be shown to the engine.' ('Excuse me — can I mess about with your parts?')

'*Fuel.* Running out is inconvenient.' (Flaming disastrous to a diesel engine!)

'So long as you are sensible and keep to the rules, mooring can be a pleasant gesture of individuality.' (No rude gestures, please!)

Well we moored — at Calverley. I don't know whether we achieved individuality, for we just bunged in a couple of pins and tied up!

At the beginning of our second week the holiday was already running itself down, for soon at Middlewich Harold would depart for Huddersfield to resume his normal job as a shoe salesman. During the holiday he had worked hard — leaping on, leaping off, winding up, winding down, washing up, washing down, screwing up, screwing down, pushing open, pushing closed and bashing in and pulling out — to mention but a few. On Thursday, back at work, he would be fitting on and pulling off for a change!

The strongish wind of Monday was really only an out-rider to the gales which arrived to harass us on Tuesday and when I slowed down well in advance and, (as instructed in the canal book) aimed *Maori* at the centre of a bridge-hole leading into the Middlewich Arm, a downright cock-up was the result. However, Harold was able to do some more strenuous shoving-off and eventual tying-up so that we could relax and enjoy an interesting lunch-time entertainment as we watched other boat owners having difficulty with their steering.

We joined in the excitement of their near-misses and direct hits, and marvelled at some colourful and — as Jim would put it — expressive language.

One of the most vigorous winds I have ever pressed against had billowing white balloons sailing at high speeds across the arc of a blindingly-bright blue sky. *Maori*, as she bravely squared up to this aggressive sparring partner, pushed stubbornly and almost sideways along a chopped up plip-plopping canal. Having to fight every inch of the way made us more than relieved to pull into one of the most delightful moorings of the whole trip, where a springy grassy path bordered a wood. Mature posturing trees gazed down at the winding, aptly named River Weaver, and then away in widening perspective to the gentle rise and fall of shadowed and sunlit pastures.

The sun, when its ardour wasn't repelled by a cool, self-occupied, energetic companion, was really hot. Mary and I, prostrate in a sheltered spot on *Maori*'s stern, turned, basted and roasted ourselves slowly all afternoon — at least until a voice out of nowhere called 'Are you from New Zealand?' This had me sitting up sharply and glancing firstly at a bare towpath and then along an empty canal. Two, temporarily hidden, bobbing canoeists, rubbing up against *Maori*'s hull, supplied tangibility and I, an affirmative answer to their question.

These intrepid Kiwi paddlers, having launched their canoes in Manchester, had already navigated the Bridgewater and Trent and Mersey canals to Middlewich and the Middlewich Arm to us. Further ambitious plans were taking them along the 'Shroppie' to Chester where they could lock out into the River Dee and seek access to the open sea. Then they would follow the coast of North Wales to their destination, Rhyl.

Not surprisingly, a long glass of lemonade each, supplied by us disappeared in one extended gulp and just as I was going to offer a refill they left abruptly to sail in company with a passing boat to, and through the next lock. This we understood, because somewhere among their outstretched legs, was stored food, clothing and camping equipment — a heavy burden (even minus the legs) to carry from one level of the canal to another. As we waved them a hasty farewell and shouted 'Good luck', we greatly admired their youthful enterprise and energy. Then we succumbed contentedly back to our lack of both and resumed exhausting inactivity once more.

Thought processes lay dormant in the deepening warmth of the lengthening day — until I began to wonder about *Dragonfly* and its whereabouts. Mary, reading my thoughts, remarked that Eileen and Rodney should soon be due — and sure enough, about an hour later a distinctive air-borne mating call had *Maori* all eager and animated again.

Assisted by barking lookout, Hans, (who had apparently recognised us from afar) a lively exchange between highly individual air-horns had the desired effect. Some accurate throwing and strenuous heaving, (because of the still strong wind) had *Dragonfly* and *Maori* re-united. Hans, handicapped by an inexpressive two-inch tail, tried to push me backwards into the cut, but was foiled when a pouncing Rodney carried him aloft back to *Dragonfly*. Our arrangement to join together later that evening did little to appease him or alter the soulful glances of despair at our separation, so soon after meeting.

Back on board *Maori*, Mary and I were also aware of our pending separation from Harold the following day — especially when he declared his intention to walk two miles to Church Minshull to find out about trains and buses. Mary decided to join him whereas I, having given the impression that I must sadly stay aboard and work, waved them around a concealing curve of the towpath, paid a private visit to the loo, and then got my head down! *Maori's* soft rocking movement soon had me dozing in the quietness of the shadowy cabin, until I was rudely aroused by Eileen shouting about a lost bow-rope. Acting swiftly in a crisis, I fell off the bunk, ran out shoeless and jumped onto the towpath. Eileen, (just as quick off the mark) jumped onto the boat and completed an absolute reversal of our positions which now had her drifting out in an untied boat and me high and dry on the bank. Some quick rope throwing soon put matters right and had *Maori* secured to two pins forward to counteract a tugging headwind and the occasional bank-wave from an inconsiderate, passing boat.

Just as I had rearranged all the cushions and enveloped myself in the soft folds of a comforting rug, more voices prevented me from doing nothing and necessitated a strategic move to a better eaves-dropping position.

A passing boater, labouring under the misapprehension that a few boats moored together automatically indicated a pub, had hopefully pulled in and was chatting to Eileen. Thinking to myself that alcoholic constipation was certainly rife on the canal system, and also that I might be missing something, I adjourned to *Dragonfly*.

A VERY experienced boater was well launched into the narrative of his current holiday. Inexperienced canallers were his favourite topic as he proceeded to enlighten us about the excruciatingly funny things they do. Recalling some of the 'funny' things I was still capable of doing after seven years boating made me feel somewhat hypocritical as I nodded agreement to his intolerant observations.

After relating his impressions of a particularly hilarious episode, he then singled out one 'very nice chap who was an absolute menace on a boat, not practical at all, who should never go near a canal and who must have been a book-learning type, or a teacher or something like that!' As all of us present were music teachers I averted my eyes from Eileen's, stifled a rising surge of maniacal laughter, and pretended to go and look for Mary and Harold who had not yet returned. They were nowhere to be seen; but shortly after, when Eileen dropped bouncing coffee granules into *Dragonfly*'s oft-filled beakers, they bounced and dropped on board.

Harold soon got into the swing of things and took the floor with a few stories of his own. These had nothing to do with boating and one concerned a friend whose work with the Electricity Board entailed calling at houses and meeting the public at large. A long journey to an outlying suburb of Huddersfield and to one house in particular, had him waiting a long time for an indistinct, lurking figure to peep suspiciously around the door. After identifying himself satisfactorily to the elderly male inhabitant and being asked to 'Cum in lad,' he apprehensively crossed an uninviting threshold and entered the dark interior of the room. As his eyes adjusted to the flickering light of a blazing fire, he was surprised to note that the whole seat of his host's trousers had been patched with a flat cap. He was even more surprised to see one end of a huge railway sleeper actually burning in the fire — the other end, resting on a stool, waiting to be pushed up!

When more potent beverages followed our instant coffee, story after tall story was recounted with increasing alacrity and all hands agreed that truth was both stranger and funnier than fiction. Then Eileen's visitor, remembering a wife and two passengers abandoned on his boat, made a hasty retreat and our last evening together was virtually over. And upon our arrival at Middlewich next day, the holiday itself was virtually over as all three of us waited, huddled like martyred fishermen, beneath a dripping inadequate umbrella, for the bus which would take Harold on the first leg of his journey home. Soon it hove into view, and as we semaphored it to a leg-spraying stop, Harold hopped smartly aboard, paid his passage and was gone. One by one *Maori's* crew members were deserting and we were now only two. Tomorrow, when the Imp would carry us away — there would be none.

We whiled away our last damp afternoon reading, writing and inhaling the aroma of steak and onions braising in *Maori's* oven; then a generator started up at the engineering works on the opposite bank, soon to be joined by the excruciating row of an excavator driven by a learner-driver. He practised for hours with an unabating enthusiasm which, had it been so directed, could have excavated the whole of Middlewich. Then, at six o'clock on the dot, having completely demolished our peace and rest, he ground to a halt and left.

After tea, when the evening had brightened, Mary and I wandered by a broad, freshly-silvered Trent and Mersey Canal, allowing the wind to blow away the claustrophobic effects of a cabined afternoon. Eventually we succumbed to melancholia and alcoholic constipation within the comfort of a 'Kings Arms'. A bright sky become brilliant, enabled Mary to photograph the famous

Middlewich Canal signpost and made us reluctant to call it a day and return to *Maori*.

So we wended our nostalgic way back along the Middlewich Arm where the exotic crimson of a setting sun had the sky bursting with fire and flak and the canal a stream of glowing molten lava through a darkened lifeless land. A frighteningly beautiful vision had me rapt but apprehensive for all our futures — until my over-charged imagination returned to normal. Then, as one particular day in my life reached its final brilliant climax, the perfection of the countryside and the lights and colours moving and varying before me, seemed to sum up all that I love about canals. It set a seal upon a holiday which, in spite of all anxieties and some unsettling, awakened memories, had retained the magic which would entice me back again and again.

Next day Mary, identity shrouded in an enveloping anorak helped Penny and me, in waterproofs and yachting caps, to load the Imp in the pouring rain — and the magic temporarily disappeared.

I was quite content to return to my small Waterways house, where I could pause at a window to admire boats gliding in and out of Greenwood Flood Lock, or sometimes part the bedroom curtains to a moonlit canal and the visiting lights of a craft moored for the night. In the deep mid-Winter I could crunch along a deep towpath covered with minute diamante and follow gull-arrows to the locks. There I could see the snow covered tops of the slag heaps pointing their miniature mountain peaks into an arctic-blue sky unable to reflect into a sugar-coated, frozen canal — which lies still — but with hidden, moving depths. And where I could sit on a lock-arm, close to sounds of moving water and make the roar of a distant road unobtrusive or obtrusive at will or allow a rattling train to travel only fleetingly through my thoughts — which always return to the whiteness and the water — and the woe! And the weir which catches at the changing light and dances with it, rushes, froths it, bubbles, breaks and foams it, while the placid water beyond smooths and mirrors it blindingly back. A weightless gull with wings fully extended, turns, dips and glides — a noiseless passenger on the air currents. High, high above, in the clear atmosphere, a trailing jet draws a white vapour line across the crystal ice-sky and is made, through distance, noiseless too.

Colin, the lock-keeper knows in advance of my approach as his cackling geese strain ever-stretching, aggressive necks to squawk a warning, soon to be joined by the wolf howls of an Alsatian named Lancelot and by the staccato yapping of a smaller dog. Their owner, usually toiling on his barge conversion, sometimes waves and invites my envious inspection of what *William Hennell* might have been!

Sometimes a goat, moored on the towpath, bars my way and tries — as I tentatively stroke him and make polite conversation — to blink coded messages in reply. Further on, pad marks enlarged in the snow make me wonder fancifully what my reaction would be if a lolloping lion (stalking my white, bearded friend) should suddenly appear!

Then I am startled by the flapping of disturbed wings as I pass beneath the shadowy cave of a large river bridge and along a hoary towpath to watch an approaching Waterways' barge tearing into the thin sheet-ice and cracking thicker ice into big jigsaw patterns. The perfectly interlocking pieces then separate forever and float away.

With warmer weather and melting snow, they find their way to the River Calder which swells alarmingly and sometimes floods the popular Ship Inn, where an old mariners chart bears these words, 'Navigare necesse est vivere non est necesse.' Roughly translated, this suggests that it is more necessary to sail than it is to live! 'The Swan', also close by, on higher ground, perhaps prefers to live and not to sail, but is a friendly port of call.

Another very friendly port was a lockside cottage belonging to Les and Nora Oliver. They gave helpful advice to passing boaters when they were confused by the two large, adjoining locks, one with its gates securely chained open to prevent use. On one well-remembered day Nora, alone, minding her own business inside her flower-bedecked cottage, was interrupted from outside by a great commotion.

'Get a bloody hammer and bash 'em off,' bellowed a belligerent boat-bound voice — referring apparently to the restricting chains.

Somewhat taken aback but wishing to be helpful, Nora left her cottage to advise them (a man and two lads) that they would save much time and effort by not using the first lock.

'Christ!' ejaculated an unbelieving, male chauvinistic voice, 'It's bloody women lock-keepers now!' at which Nora went back inside — leaving the door ajar.

When, after much fuss and kerfuffle, they ascended the correct lock, the voice began blasting again.

'Christ, Armitage, look what you're doing with that bloody toilet, you're spilling shit all over my feet!'

Armitage, a seemingly docile character but thoroughly browned-off with being constantly ordered about, at last replied.

'Well,' he droned in a dull, toneless voice, 'Most of it is your shit!'

When they proceeded to dump refuse onto the lock side, Nora emerged again and directed them, in no uncertain terms, to the rubbish disposal where she undoubtedly thought they belonged!

So that is what it is all about — this canal business; humour is caught up with sadness, beauty with ugliness, fear with fulfilment — and Nature with humankind. Complicated restless beings, we are always searching — sometimes without even knowing why or what for. Perhaps freedom is our ultimate and greatest desire — freedom of thought, freedom to wander and freedom to be individuals unfettered by convention.

On the canals I seem to achieve, to some extent, that essential sense of freedom and that is why they hold such magic for me.

So, if you are searching for some faraway indistinct star, it might — just might — come within your grasp one sultry summer's evening, when the heavens curve low over a shimmering English canal. Who knows?

GLOSSARY

Balance beams   Long extended wooden or metal arms for operating lock gates.

Bridge hole   Space beneath a bridge on a waterway.

Butty   A boat without an engine which requires towing by another with an engine.

Cut   Another name for canal.

Fender   Something which hangs over or protects the side of a boat. Usually plastic or rubber.

Gongoozler   People just standing around watching.

Legging   How boats were taken through tunnels with no towpaths. Crew laid out sideways and 'walked' the tunnel wall or top.

Lock   A chamber holding water which takes a boat up or down from one level of a canal or river, to another.

Mooring pin   A metal spike to hammer into the towpath and use for tying up.

Narrow boat   Usually 6ft 10ins wide in order to fit 7ft wide locks on narrow canals.

Paddles   Openings in locks which open and shut to let water in or out. Gate paddles in the lock gates and ground paddles under water near the bottom of the lock.

Pound   Stretch of water between locks.

Sill   A solid ledge (usually concrete) against which the bottom gates of a lock, wedge.

Staircase	A series of locks close together, one lock leading directly into the next.
Summit	The highest point of a canal.
Tiller	An arm attached to the rudder for steering.
Tom Puddings	A 'train' of oblong iron boxes pulled by a tug. These could be lifted out of the water to empty their load of coal.
Towpath	A path alongside canals or rivers, once used (mainly by horses) for towing boats.
Winding hole	Part of the canal made wide enough for boats to turn.
Windlass	A bent handle used for operating paddle gear at locks.